TWO COMEDIES
BY
THOMAS D'URFEY

Thomas D'Urfey, reproduced from *Portraits of the British Poets* (1824)

TWO COMEDIES
BY
THOMAS D'URFEY

*Madam Fickle; or,
the Witty False One*

*A Fond Husband; or,
the Plotting Sisters*

*Edited with Introductions and Notes
by*
Jack A. Vaughn

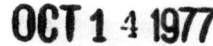

Rutherford • Madison • Teaneck
Fairleigh Dickinson University Press
London: Associated University Presses

© 1976 by Associated University Presses, Inc.

Associated University Presses, Inc.
Cranbury, New Jersey 08512

Associated University Presses
108 New Bond Street
London W1Y OQX, England

Library of Congress Cataloging in Publication Data

D'Urfey, Thomas, 1653-1723.
   Two comedies.

   "Chronological listing of D'Urfey's dramatic works": p.
   Bibliography: p.
   CONTENTS: Madam Fickle; or The witty false one.—A fond husband; or, The plotting sisters.
   I. Vaughn, Jack A., 1935-   II. D'Urfey, Thomas, 1653-1723. A fond husband. 1975. PR3431.D3M27 1975   822'.4   73-21191
ISBN 0-8386-1478-7

PR
3431
.D3
M27
1976

PRINTED IN THE UNITED STATES OF AMERICA

To
KAWIKA
(at last!)

CONTENTS

Preface	9
Introduction	13
MADAM FICKLE; OR, THE WITTY FALSE ONE	33
Introduction	35
Text	41
Notes to *Madam Fickle*	135
A FOND HUSBAND; OR, THE PLOTTING SISTERS	145
Introduction	147
Text	154
Notes to *A Fond Husband*	251
TEXTUAL NOTES	261
Madam Fickle	263
A Fond Husband	276
APPENDIXES	
A. Bibliographical Description of Texts	287
B. Chronological Listing of D'Urfey's Dramatic Works	296
Bibliography	299

PREFACE

Readers of English drama tend to think of the Restoration period as one that produced only stylish and witty social comedies, as exemplified by the major works of its five leading dramatists: Congreve, Etherege, Wycherley, Vanbrugh, and Farquhar. Yet those works represent only a small percentage of the total output of some 180 practicing playwrights of the period. Despite attempts in recent years to resurrect the forgotten works of some of these lesser dramatists (e.g., Montague Summers's monumental editions of the complete works of Thomas Shadwell and of Mrs. Aphra Behn), many successful and prolific playwrights of the Restoration years have been ignored by modern scholars. Among these one finds Thomas D'Urfey, whose career as a dramatist spanned a period of nearly fifty years, from 1676 to 1721, and who gave to the London stage no less than thirty-three dramatic works.

D'Urfey was a popular figure in the literary coterie of Restoration London. He produced more works for the English theater than any other dramatist of his time, and many of them were well received and highly acclaimed, both by the general public and by royalty, through five successive reigns. He earned the dubious distinction of being singled out as a prime target in the Reverend Jeremy Collier's indictment of the London stage in 1698, and as late as 1713 we find such men of letters as Addison and Steele lauding his efforts and pleading for public support of a benefit for the aging dramatist. Finally, in addition to being a popular playwright, D'Urfey was a successful writer of ballads and satiric songs, and in this capacity he won even greater renown and admiration, especially from King Charles II and his court.

In view of such success and recognition in his own time, it is unfortunate that the name of Thomas D'Urfey is all but unknown to modern readers and that not one of his dramatic works has appeared in print with editorial treatment since the eighteenth century. One reason for this neglect is that the critics have not always been kind to D'Urfey. In the last century, especially, with its prevailing Victorian attitudes, D'Urfey's plots of sexual intrigue and racy dialogue found little credit with writers who dismissed him as "a scurrilous and witless buffoon" or identified him as "the literary nadir of Restoration comedy."

From a more modern, enlightened viewpoint, however, Thomas D'Urfey well deserves attention by serious students of the Restoration period. His comedies (more properly, farces) display an inventiveness and an inextinguishable gaiety that are in the best tradition of farce. They reveal the tastes of Restoration and early eighteenth-century audiences. The sprightliness of both their dialogue and their situations kept them current on the London stage, well past the time when sexual intrigue had given way to sentiment. Moreover, his works are representative of the mainstream of Restoration drama, and through their topicality they offer valuable insights into the social and political concerns of Restoration London.

The only significant modern criticism on D'Urfey is that of Cyrus L. Day, whose dissertation on the poet's life and nondramatic works, together with his published volume of some of the songs, may be considered the most extensive treatment of D'Urfey's career as a lyric poet. A study of D'Urfey's plays was offered by Robert Stanley Forsythe in 1916, but much of it is factually and critically inaccurate. Its chief virtue lies in its inclusion of a reprint of one comedy, *A Fool's Preferment* (1688). Another reprint, *Wonders in the Sun* (1706), appeared in 1964 under the auspices of the Augustan Reprint Society, and in 1972 Benjamin Blom reprinted a volume of D'Urfey's operas and poems. Some of his dramas have been edited in dissertations in recent years, but apart from these few works, little scholarship has been devoted to D'Urfey's plays, and the interested reader has had to turn to microfilm or to original quartos.

The present volume includes two of D'Urfey's earliest comedies, *Madam Fickle* (1676) and *A Fond Husband* (1677), both of which were well received by their original audiences and the court of King Charles. The latter work especially experienced a comparatively long and successful stage career and may well be D'Urfey's finest comedy. The present editions are based substantially on the first quarto of each text, with some modification in punctuation and capitalization in the interest of readability. Careful attention has been given to textual variants in a section at the back of the volume, and Appendix A offers bibliographical descriptions of the texts used. Explanatory notes are provided with the intention of clarifying historical allusions and unfamiliar terms, and an introduction to each comedy offers theatrical data and some critical evaluation.

The editor is indebted to the staff of the William Andrews Clark, Jr., Memorial Library of UCLA for their assistance in providing materials for the study, as well as to those of the many libraries in England and America who also cooperated in this project. Special acknowledgment must be made of the encouragement offered by Dr. Abraham Grossman of the University of Denver, and of the assistance of the late Cyrus L. Day of the University of Delaware, who, like the editor, felt that there was something worth preserving in the works of Thomas D'Urfey.

INTRODUCTION

The dramatic works of Thomas D'Urfey, the most prolific of Restoration dramatists, have suffered two centuries of critical neglect. Consequently, little is known either of the plays or of the playwright himself. What information is available concerning the poet's life has only recently been gathered together by D'Urfey's sole biographer, Cyrus L. Day, whose detailed study of the poet's nondramatic works includes the most complete account of his life.[1]

The exact date of D'Urfey's birth is not known, though 1653 is generally accepted as the year. Charles Dickens, in a complimentary essay on the writer, noted the year as 1649, possibly relying on Baker's article in the *Biographia Dramatica*,[2] but the *Dictionary of National Biography* gives 1653 and Day has substantiated that year. The place of birth is commonly stated as Exeter, England.

There is some question as to whether his family were

---

1. "The Life and Non-dramatic Works of Thomas D'Urfey" (dissertation, Harvard University, 1930); and *The Songs of Thomas D'Urfey* (Cambridge, Mass., 1933).
2. (London, 1782), 1: 142-44.

of English stock or were descended, on his father's side, from the Frenchman D'Urfé, a Huguenot who reportedly fled France in 1628. Further uncertainty exists as to whether the poet Honoré d'Urfé was D'Urfey's grandfather, great grand-uncle, or, indeed, any relation at all.[3] Though D'Urfey's exact birthdate and paternal ancestry are uncertain, it is known that his mother was the daughter of one of the Marmions of Huntingdonshire, an established English family.

The *Biographia Dramatica* states that Thomas D'Urfey was "bred to the law," a claim substantiated in other sources, but Day has suggested that the legal training may have been little more than a four-shilling-a-week post as scrivener at Lincoln's Inn. It is unlikely that he ever attended a university, and his contempt for formal education is evident in many of his comedies, including the present texts.

As for the man himself, D'Urfey was physically most unattractive, a fact that may account for his never having married, as well as for his sensitivity in the face of any criticism, either personal or literary. From the extant portraits of him, one of which serves as frontispiece to this volume, it can be seen that the most dominant feature of his face was a large hooked nose, not unlike the beak of a bird, framed by small, deep-set eyes, a protruding jaw, and a high, flat forehead. He was further handicapped by habitual stuttering, an impediment that rendered him the butt of many lampoons, including the vicious anonymous satire, *Wit for Money; Or, Poet Stutter*, which appeared in 1691.[4] According to his

---

3. In 1683, D'Urfey discarded the Anglicized spelling of "Durfey," evidently in order to associate himself with Gallic forebears. The apostrophe first appeared in his name on the title page to *A New Collection of Songs and Poems* (1683). The first dramatic work to include the new spelling was *A Commonwealth of Women* (1686).
4. London, 1691.

own admission, his difficulty in speaking left him frequently ill at ease in the company of the nobility.⁵

The few indications of D'Urfey's personality that have come down to us from his contemporaries give us contradictory portraits of the man—now a sincere, well-intentioned gentleman, and again a pompous fool; a talented poet much admired by his fellows, and a hack writer who survived at Court only by playing the sycophant. There is probably no way of reconciling these opposing pictures, but we can be sure that Tom D'Urfey was a man of considerable reputation and a controversial figure who frequently drew criticism.

Among D'Urfey's detractors, in addition to the vitriolic writer of *Wit for Money*, were such literary figures as Alexander Pope and Jonathan Swift. Pope's few comments on the poet are couched in a tongue-in-cheek style that leaves us uncertain of the degree of irony intended. Writing in 1710 to Oliver Cromwell, Pope declared that he had recently "learned without book a Song of Mr. Tho: Durfey's, who is your only Poet of tolerable Reputation in this country," and there is veiled sarcasm in his testimonial to D'Urfey's catches: "In the same Manner as was said of Homer, to his Detractors; What? dares any man speak against Him who has given so many Men to Eat? . . . So may't be said of Mr. Durfey, to his Detractors; Dares any one despise Him, who has made so many men Drink?"⁶ Less subtle is the contempt evident in Pope's "Prologue Designed for Mr. D'Urfey's Last Play," written for D'Urfey's benefit in 1713. The Prologue begins:

> Grown old in rhyme, 't were barb'rous to discard
> Your persevering, unexhausted Bard:

5. See *Madam Fickle*, Dedication, 11. 30-36.
6. *The Correspondence of Alexander Pope*, ed. George Sherburn (Oxford, 1956), 1: 81.

Damnation follows death in other men,
But your damn'd poet lives and writes again.[7]

Pope also penned, at roughly the same time, a delightfully satiric poem on D'Urfey's pretensions: "Verses Occasion'd by an &c. at the End of Mr. D'Urfy's [sic] Name in the Title to one of his Plays."

Jonathan Swift's comments on D'Urfey are found in *Tale of a Tub,* whose dedication refers with heavy sarcasm to "Tom Durfey, a Poet of a vast Comprehension, an Universal Genius, and most profound Learning." Later in the same work, Swift labels the D'Urfey canon "Excrement."[8]

Chief among D'Urfey's champions were Joseph Addison and Richard Steele, who frequently wrote in personal support of the man, though they were not always enthusiastic about his work. Steele, evidently a close friend in D'Urfey's later years, made complimentary references to the poet in some of his essays, speaking of him as "my honoured friend" and "my ingenious friend." He seems to have had no great opinion of D'Urfey as lyric poet, however, and was apt to temper his praise with some amount of irony. Writing in *The Tatler* in support of the appearance of a new D'Urfey comedy, *The Modern Prophets* (1709), Steele comments: "Besides his great abilities in the dramatic, [he] has a peculiar talent in the lyric way of writing, and that with a manner wholly new and unknown to the antient Greeks and Romans, wherein he is but faintly imitated in the translations of the modern Italian Operas."[9] And, in a later essay, writing of D'Urfey the dramatist: "Mr. Dur-

7. *The Poetical Works of Alexander Pope,* ed. A. W. Ward (London, 1924), pp. 469-70.
8. Ed. Guthkelch and Smith (Oxford, 1958), pp. 36-37, 207.
9. No. 1 (April 12, 1709).

fey generally writes state-plays, and is wonderfully useful to the world in such representations. This method is the same that was used by old Athenians, to laugh out of countenance, or promote, opinions among the people."[10] The reader may decide for himself the extent of Steele's irony.

Addison wrote of D'Urfey in *The Guardian,* calling him a "diverting companion" and a "cheerful, honest, and good natured man."[11] He speaks of the dramatist as being "the delight of the most polite companies and conversations, from the beginning of king Charles the Second's reign to our present times," and notes that "many an honest gentleman has got a reputation in his country, by pretending to have been in company with Tom D'Urfey." Addison continues: "I myself remember king Charles the Second leaning on Tom D'Urfey's shoulder more than once, and humming over a song with him." Perhaps Addison's recollection of this chummy scene should be taken lightly, however, for he was no more than thirteen years of age at the time of Charles's death.

It is remarkable that, in spite of physical handicaps and constant criticism, Tom D'Urfey managed to become one of the leading figures in the courts of four reigning monarchs, as well as a constant and favored companion to them. His success may have been partly attributable to his talent for changing his politics to agree with those of the party in power, but certainly his skill in entertaining royalty cannot be overlooked. His satiric court songs, some highly royalist and anti-papist, appealed strongly to Charles and his companions; subsequently, he secured as well the patronage of James II, King William, and

10. *The Tatler,* no. 11 (May 5, 1709).
11. No. 67 (May 28, 1713).

Queen Anne, together with the personal esteem of Queen Mary, Prince George, and a number of other noble patrons.

In addition to his success as a writer of songs and catches and as a popular playwright, D'Urfey was noted and admired for his skill in performing his own songs, in the theaters and even at Court. The title page to *Wit and Mirth,* the major collection of his songs, states that many of his congratulatory verses were "spoken by himself on the Stage,"[12] and Addison notes that he "accompanies his works with his own voice."[13] In the dedication to *Wit and Mirth,* D'Urfey records his own success as a performer: "And when I have perform'd some of my own Things before their Majesties King CHARLES the IId, King JAMES, King WILLIAM, Queen MARY, Queen ANNE, and Prince GEORGE, I never went off without happy and commendable Approbation." So skilled was D'Urfey in entertaining royalty that even the conservative and sober William was known to have been moved to hearty laughter by the poet's songs.

Tom D'Urfey lived his entire life on an income consisting only of the receipts from infrequent benefits, pittances from the sale of his plays and songs, and gratuities offered by his many patrons, chief among whom were the Dukes of Richmond, Albemarle, Ormonde, Bedford, and Argyll. In his many epistles dedicatory to these men, D'Urfey seems almost desperate for their continuing support, as evidenced by his effusive flattery. Especially notable in this respect is the dedication to *Madam Fickle* (lines 30-42 in the present edition). Such laudatory epistles were, of course, standard Resto-

---

12. *Wit and Mirth; Or, Pills to Purge Melancholy* (London, 1719-20), title page.
13. *The Guardian.*

ration practice, but our poet was especially adept at flattery.

As early as 1713, D'Urfey's influence with royalty and the nobility had begun to decline. His debts had mounted, and he was reduced to dependency on the income from theater benefits. Addison and Steele, in *The Guardian,* pleaded for public support of a benefit of *A Fond Husband,* to be presented June 15, 1713.[14] Addison urged attendance at the performance, claiming: "I . . . heartily recommend to all the young ladies, my disciples, the case of my old friend, who has often made their grandmothers merry. . . . I hope they will make him easy." He also allied the impoverished poet with Pindar, as "two who have excelled in lyrics" and noted that D'Urfey had, in his time, written "more odes than Horace, and about four times as many comedies as Terence." Regardless of such touching testimonials, benefit performances hardly provided an adequate income, and D'Urfey lived in debt until his death.

According to his memorial marker, Tom D'Urfey died on February 26, 1723. The stone may be found today inside St. James, Piccadilly, where he is buried. Because of an annexation to the church building, the marker now adorns a wall above the sink in a custodian's closet, a poor memorial to this poet and playwright. He was literarily active almost to the end. His final three plays were published in 1721, nearly fulfilling Addison's prediction that "our British swan will sing to the last."

D'Urfey's dramatic works number thirty-three, of which twenty-three are comedies, five are tragedies, four are operas, and one is a tragi-comedy. Another work, *The English Stage Italianiz'd,* a satiric scenario, was earlier

14. *Ibid.*

attributed to D'Urfey but has been proven spurious.[15]

Many of D'Urfey's plots are drawn from earlier works by other writers and some are outright adaptations, a standard feature, of course, of much Restoration drama. Gerard Langbaine, a contemporary of D'Urfey, singled him out in this regard as one dramatist especially guilty of plagiarism, noting that his wit was always borrowed from others and that he, "like the *Cuckow,* makes it his business to suck other Birds Eggs."[16] D'Urfey's admitted adaptations are *Trick for Trick* (1678), a highly altered version of Fletcher's *Monsieur Thomas; The Injured Princess* (1682), a reworking of Shakespeare's *Cymbeline; A Commonwealth of Women* (1685), from Fletcher's *Sea Voyage; A Fool's Preferment* 1688), from Fletcher's *Noble Gentleman; Bussy D'Ambois* (1691), after Chapman's tragedy of the same title; and the three parts of *The Comical History of Don Quixote* (1694-95), after Cervantes's novel.

Three of D'Urfey's works—*The Two Queens of Brentford, The Grecian Heroine,* and *Ariadne*—were probably never acted; the texts appeared together in a single volume in 1721.[17] Another play, *A Wife for Any Man,* was apparently acted sometime in 1696 or 1697 but is lost.[18] The remainder of D'Urfey's plays received at least one representation on the London stage, and many of them were performed repeatedly as late as 1785.[19]

---

15. See Robert Stanley Forsythe, *A Study of the Plays of Thomas D'Urfey* (Vol. I, no. 2, of *Western Reserve Studies.* Cleveland, 1916), pp. 175-80.

16. *An Account of the English Dramatick Poets* (Oxford, 1691), pp. 179-85.

17. *New Opera's, with Comical Stories, and Poems, on Several Occasions* (London, 1721). Reprinted as *Operas and Poems* (Benjamin Blom, 1972).

18. See Day, "A Lost Play by D'Urfey," *Modern Language Notes* 49 (May 1934): 332-34.

19. See Day, "Dates and Performances of Thomas D'Urfey's Plays" (Charlottesville, Va.: Bibliographical Society of the University of Virginia, 1950). Mimeographed.

D'Urfey's output was prodigious, but not all of his plays merit study by modern readers. His chief accomplishment was as a writer of comedies, especially of the sexual-intrigue variety. Certainly his five tragedies and four operas may be cursorily dismissed, as most critics have readily agreed. Essentially, the tragedies suffer from excess of incident, sensationalism, and inferior verse. *The Siege of Memphis* (1676), D'Urfey's first play and an obvious copy of Dryden and Howard's *Indian Queen* (1663/4), is a heroic tragedy replete with rhyming couplets and sententious epithets. According to his own admission in the Dedication, the work represented "the first fruits of an Infant Muse" and earned "little credit with the World."[20] His next tragedy, the adaptation of Chapman's *Bussy D'Ambois*, is somewhat more palatable and closely follows the original, though D'Urfey, who claims in the Preface to have eliminated Chapman's "obsolete Phrases and intollerable Fustian," has merely replaced the impressive verse of the original with doggerel.[21] The two parts of *The Famous History of the Rise and Fall of Massaniello* (1699) are D'Urfey's most bombastic tragedies; in sensational dialogue and bloody scenic effects they out-Seneca Seneca. His final tragedy, the unacted *Grecian Heroine*, bears all the defects of *The Siege of Memphis*, less the heroic couplets.

The four operas are similarly lacking in merit. *Cinthia and Endimion* is a masque-like potpourri of classical myths and deities, originally intended for Court presentation in 1694 but withheld on the death of Queen Mary and subsequently given at the Drury Lane in 1696. It is slow moving and poorly constructed. *Wonders in the Sun*

20. *The Siege of Memphis; Or, The Ambitious Queen* (London, 1676), dedication.
21. *Bussy D'Ambois; Or, The Husbands Revenge* (London, 1691), preface.

(1706), a satiric opera, is loosely related to the *Birds* of Aristophanes. It is quite lengthy, involves dozens of characters, and requires elaborate staging and costuming. Downes notes in *Roscius Anglicanus* that this piece "lasted only Six Days, not answering half the Expences of it."[22] The final two operas, *The Two Queens of Brentford* and *Ariadne*, were never performed. The former is a dull and awkward sequel to Villiers's *Rehearsal*, and the latter is yet another unsuccessful attempt at classic mythology set to music.

It is as a comic writer only that D'Urfey made a contribution to the theater that we can appreciate today. His comedies well deserve attention by serious students of Restoration drama, for they are entirely representative of the mainstream of Restoration comedy. They reveal, more accurately than the highly polished works of the well-known dramatists, the tastes and preferences of the Restoration audience. The great popularity of these comedies cannot be overlooked. Moreover, because of their highly topical nature, many of D'Urfey's comedies serve to illuminate the social and political concerns that confronted Londoners during the Restoration years. Finally, many of these works are theatrically viable and must have been highly entertaining to their original audiences. They make up in spirit and action for what they may lack in excellence of dramatic construction.

Most of D'Urfey's comedies properly should be called farces. They rely heavily upon frankly contrived situations into which the characters—standard types of the period (the bully, the fop, the jilt, etc.)—are skillfully fitted for maximum comic effect. The humor is often de-

---

22. Ed. Montague Summers (London, 1928), p. 50. *Wonders in the Sun* was reprinted in 1964 by the Augustan Reprint Society (Los Angeles), pub. no. 104.

pendent upon visual appeal: beatings, physical defects, and outlandish costuming. All the plays are complexly plotted, some having as many as three different plot lines. Such standard devices of the intrigue comedy as disguise, mistaken identity, eavesdropping, and elaborate trickery are used repeatedly to good effect. Because of this emphasis upon the elements of low comedy, many of the plots begin to weaken in the fourth act and the resolutions, though lively, are clearly contrived. D'Urfey was master of the *deus ex machina*.

As was common in his time, D'Urfey frequently incorporated profanity and obscenity in his comedies, and he was one of the writers most vehemently attacked in Collier's *Short View of the Immorality and Profaneness of the English Stage*.[23] Though it is true that D'Urfey pulled no punches in displaying elements of sexual intrigue, his plays are no more licentious or indelicate, really, than many comedies by better-known Restoration writers, such as Wycherley, Mrs. Behn, or Shadwell. Still, Collier cites D'Urfey's three Don Quixote plays as particularly offensive, based upon three objections:

> I. *His Profaness [sic] with respect to Religion and the* Holy Scriptures.
> II. *His Abuse of the Clergy.*
> III. *His want of Modesty and Regard to the Audience.*

Collier then goes on to cite specific passages from the plays as illustrations of the offensive nature of the works, and he closes his attack with a note on D'Urfey's penchant for boastfulness and false modesty in his epistles dedicatory, noting that they "are to the full as divert-

---

23. (London, 1698), pp. 196-208.

ing as his *Comedies.*" All in all, Collier devotes thirteen pages of his treatise solely to D'Urfey.

The playwright was quick to retaliate in the form of a preface to the printing of his next play, *The Campaigners* (1698), the title page of which announces the inclusion of "A FAMILIAR PREFACE UPON *A Late Reformer of the STAGE.*"[24] D'Urfey begins his defense by answering Collier's charges, but he devotes an equal amount of space to attacking Collier personally, calling him "an angry malcontent . . . in the garb of an humble Churchman" and describing him as "raging and even foaming at the mouth." His defense is essentially a plea for poetic license. He asserts that the dramatist, in creating his characters, must accurately reproduce natural speech, even though it may include obscenity and profanity.

Collier's indictment at least elevated D'Urfey to the company of such men as Congreve and Vanbrugh, who also came under fire in the clergyman's attack. There is evidence, in fact, that as a result of the Collier essay the justices of Middlesex brought an indictment against D'Urfey and Congreve on May 12, 1698, on the grounds of their having written obscene material. No record exists, however, of either of them having been convicted or even brought to trial.[25]

In spite of his penchant for the obscene, D'Urfey was one of the earlier playwrights to successfully incorporate elements of sentimentality into Restoration comedy. As early as 1678, he displayed exaggerated sensibility in the

---

24. *The Campaigners; Or, The Pleasant Adventures at Brussels* (London, 1698). The Preface to *The Campaigners* was reprinted in 1948 by the Augustan Reprint Society (Los Angeles), pub. no. 12.

25. For a full discussion of D'Urfey's involvement with Collier, see Sr. Rose Anthony, *The Jeremy Collier Stage Controversy: 1698-1726* (New York, 1966), pp. 106-7.

character of Cellide in *Trick for Trick*. This virtuous heroine, contrary to good Restoration tradition, refuses to submit to the advances of her suitor before marriage. This was eighteen years prior to Cibber's notedly sentimental *Love's Last Shift*.

That D'Urfey was aware of this sentimental strain in his work is clear from a passage in his defense against Collier, where he cites, as evidence of his sound moral tone, five of his own comedies: *The Virtuous Wife* (1679), *The Royalist* 1682), *Love for Money* (1691), *The Marriage-Hater Matched* (1692), and *The Richmond Heiress* (1693), "all whose whole Plots and designs I dare affirm, tend to that principal instance, which he [Collier] proposes, and which we allow, *viz.* the depression of Vice and encouragement of Virtue."

Of these five titles, all of which contain strong elements of sentimentality, *Love for Money* is probably the best. Its hero, Will Merriton, is a "witty, modest wellbred Gentleman," in love with Mirtilla the orphan, "witty, modest, and virtuous." She is, unknowingly, an heiress, deprived of her inheritance by Sir Rowland Rakehell. Her kindly guardian, Old Merriton, is the only person who knows her true identity, but he keeps the secret in order to insure her humility. Though Mirtilla loves Will, she cannot confess her feelings for lack of a proper dowry. Will, of course, being a gentleman of honor, is loath to importune. In the final act, Old Merriton reveals the truth, Mirtilla accepts both the fortune and Will, the villains are punished, and all ends happily in the best tradition of sentiment.[26]

26. For further analyses of D'Urfey's sentimental writing, see Kathleen M. Lynch, "Thomas D'Urfey's Contribution to Sentimental Comedy," *Philological Quarterly* 9 (1930): 249-59; and Donald W. Sanville, "Thomas D'Urfey's *Love for Money*: an Edition" (dissertation, University of Pennsylvania, 1950).

The more typical D'Urfey comedy, however, relies mainly on sexual intrigue. Particularly dependent upon this theme, in addition to the present texts, are *Squire Oldsapp* (1678), *The Banditti* (1686), *The Intrigues at Versailles* (1697), *The Campaigners, The Bath* (1701), and *The Old Mode and the New* (1703). Both *Madam Fickle* and *A Fond Husband* are discussed below in separate introductions and amply illustrate D'Urfey's technique in the handling of elements of sexual intrigue.

Many of D'Urfey's comedies aim at social or political satire. Especially strong in political commentary are *Sir Barnaby Whigg* (1681) and *The Royalist*. Sir Barnaby, as a Whig, is a figure of ridicule. The first-act statement of his political inconsistency can be seen as ironic, since it might well have applied to D'Urfey himself: "In all turns of State, [he will] change his Opinion as easily as his Coat, and is over zealous in Voting for that party that is most Powerful." This comedy is also notable for its delightful character of Porpuss, an old sea captain, who emerges as one of D'Urfey's most effective *humours* characterizations. His lines are cast in sailors' jargon, and the scene in which he describes his fox-hunting adventure entirely in terms of a sea battle is especially amusing. D'Urfey's other major venture into the comedy of humours was *Squire Oldsapp*, in which Jonsonian gulling is central to the action. In the present texts, the characters of Sir Arthur Oldlove in *Madam Fickle* and Old Fumble in *A Fond Husband* serve to demonstrate D'Urfey's skill in creating *humours* characters.[27]

The other political play, *The Royalist*, is one of D'Urfey's few "period" pieces, set in the Commonwealth

---

27. For Jonson's influence on D'Urfey, see C. B. Graham, "The Jonsonian Tradition in the Comedies of Thomas D'Urfey," *Modern Language Quarterly* 8 (1947): 47-52.

years. The titular figure is Sir Charles Kinglove, a staunch royalist whose plain-dealing ways recall Wycherley's character of Manly in *The Plain Dealer*. The debt to Wycherley is further evidenced in D'Urfey's character of Phillipa, a young admirer of Kinglove, who, like Fidelia in the Wycherley comedy, follows her master about with doglike devotion.[28]

Those comedies particularly strong in social commentary are *The Fool Turned Critick* (1676), *A Fool's Preferment*, *The Marriage-Hater Matched*, and *The Modern Prophets*. By far the best is *A Fool's Preferment*, which is one of D'Urfey's most tightly constructed plays. The main plot, dealing with social climbing in the middle class and a current gambling rage, is clear and uncomplicated, as well as highly amusing. The roles of Cocklebrain the social climber, Toby the comic servant, and Phillida the buxom country wife are among D'Urfey's most consistent and amusing type characters. The several songs in the piece were set to music, the title page informs us, by Henry Purcell.[29]

Like several of his colleagues, D'Urfey felt compelled to try his hand at improving Shakespeare. *The Injured Princess* follows the plot of *Cymbeline* rather closely and is, on the whole, a far more successful Shakespeare adaptation than many of its contemporaries, for example those by Nahum Tate. The action is colorful and highly romantic, and its speeches are filled with chauvinistic sentiments affirming the nobility of the race of Britons. Evidently D'Urfey had no great opinion of his treatment of *Cymbeline*, however, admitting in his Prologue: "And every Artist knows that Copies fall, /

---

28. Wycherley's comedy first appeared at the Theatre Royal in December of 1676 and was probably much admired by D'Urfey.

29. *A Fool's Preferment* was reprinted in 1916 as a part of Forsythe's study.

For th' most part, short of their Original." At least one of D'Urfey's critics, the anonymous author of *Wit for Money*, agreed with this admission, protesting: "Witness his laying violent hands on Shakespeare and Fletcher, whose plays he hath altered so much for the worse, like the Persecutors of Old, killing their living beauties by joining them to his dead lameless [sic] Deformities."[30]

D'Urfey's reputation in his later years rested mainly on his final attempts at adaptation, the three *Don Quixote* plays that had so inflamed Collier. The first two parts, produced in 1694, proved to be D'Urfey's most successful and famous plays, as he notes in the Preface to Part II. There is evidence of these two comedies having been performed (possibly on a single bill) at least fifty-five times, as late as 1785. Montague Summers called them "excellently done," a "notable achievement," and the best of some fourteen plays in English based upon Cervantes's novel.[31] This success may be attributed to the playwright's fidelity to his source, which was popular with the English at the time, and, frankly, to Collier's attack, which kept the plays in the public attention. Part III of the series, produced in 1695, was a failure, as D'Urfey admits in its Preface. Though the incidents in these plays were popular with the Restoration audiences, the *Don Quixote* trilogy does not represent D'Urfey's best work as a dramatist.

Tom D'Urfey's dramatic output was great, in scope as well as bulk. His works range from heroic tragedy, through the comedy of manners, to sentimental romance and opera—a diversity uncommon in most dramatists. Diversity is evident, too, in the quality of his writing, which fluctuates from the excellence of his

---
30. P. 10.
31. "Thomas D'Urfey," *Bookman* 63 (1923): 273.

farces to his less successful attempts at opera and tragedy. No single D'Urfey play stands today as a great piece of dramatic literature, but the comedies as a group are important for their revelation of the tastes of the Restoration audience. Moreover, they frequently display a theatrical vitality, especially in dialogue and situation, which rendered them viable as stage vehicles in their time, and which could well serve to animate them in the theater today. As the present texts will indicate, the best of D'Urfey is well worth our attention.

The two plays chosen for this volume, *Madam Fickle* (1676) and *A Fond Husband* (1677), are two of D'Urfey's earliest comedies. They are among the most entertaining and sprightly of all his works, and they evidence a freshness of invention that is lost in some of the later comedies. Contrary to the usual pattern, our dramatist's skills did not necessarily improve as his career advanced, and these early works are fully representative of his comic talent. Their characters are delightful and, in some cases, warm with life; their dialogue is spirited and, often, genuinely witty. Whatever defects they bear should be viewed in the perspective of the period. These plays represent the early work of a young poet—shy and physically handicapped—attempting to make a place for himself in the cold, brilliant, leisure-class society of Restoration London and, eventually, in the Court of King Charles himself. In this attempt he was eminently successful.

TWO COMEDIES
BY
THOMAS D'URFEY

*Madam Fickle; or,
The Witty False One*

INTRODUCTION

Madam Fickle, D'Urfey's second play and first attempt at comedy, received its original production by the Duke's Company at the theater in Dorset Garden on November 4, 1676. It was subsequently licensed for printing on November 20 and appeared in the Term Catalogues for Hilary Term, 1676/7.[1]

D'Urfey notes in his epistle dedicatory that the play was well received by the Court and that "His Majesty, according to his accustomed Royal and Excellent Temper, was pleas'd to descend so far, as to give it a particular Applause." Its subsequent stage career was not outstanding, though positive evidence of at least three further performances may be found. The first of these was on July 24, 1704, at the old theater in Lincoln's Inn Fields, and according to Genest it was a benefit for the actors Short and Mrs. Willis.[2] The next known production was at the Drury Lane in 1711 and two performances have been recorded, on September 29 and October 1. The cast for these performances may be

1. Ed. Edward Arber (London, 1903), 1: 267.
2. *Some Account of the English Stage* (Bath, 1832), 2: 310.

found in Genest.[3] In addition, the comedy was probably revived in the seasons 1681-82 and 1690-91, since the text was reprinted in 1682 and 1691; however, no definite proof of performances in these years has been found.

Gerard Langbaine cited this comedy especially as one in which D'Urfey had been guilty of plagiarism in assembling his plot. Langbaine asserts, speaking of the Horatian epigraph on the title page, that "the Author did well to prefix that Verse of Horace before his Play, . . . plainly implying, that he could not write a Play without stealing."[4] *Madam Fickle* is, indeed, one of D'Urfey's most derivative comedies. The various incidents of the plot clearly show borrowings from at least four earlier plays: Thomas Jordan's *Walks of Islington and Hogsdon* (1641), Marston's *Parasitaster; Or, The Fawne* (1606), Shackerly Marmion's *Antiquary* (1635), and William Rowley's *Match at Midnight* (1622).

From the Jordan play D'Urfey took much of the farcical business of the tavern bush, which appears in Act V, Scene 2. In Jordan's *Walks,* Sir Reverence Lamard lowers himself on a rope from a window and conceals himself by hiding in a bush. Pimpwell then enters, drunk, with a torch, railing against constables, and threatens to set fire to the bush. The situation is duplicated almost exactly by D'Urfey with the characters of Zechiel and Tilbury, with the exception that in the original version Sir Reverence urinates on Pimpwell, whereas Zechiel throws orange peels at Tilbury.

D'Urfey's characters of Zechiel the swaggering bully and his country-bumpkin brother Toby owe much of their nature to two characters in Marston's *Parasitaster.*

---

3. *Ibid.,* 2: 487.
4. *An Account of the English Dramatick Poets* (Oxford, 1691), p. 182.

Zechiel is the counterpart of Herod Frappatore, a braggart whose brother is "Sir Amoroso Debile-Dosso, a sickly Knight." Frappatore, like Zechiel, tries to inspire his backward brother to deeds of bravery and amorousness. The parallel is obvious, and D'Urfey even goes so far as to duplicate a speech of Herod's almost verbatim. (See I, i, 425-32 in the present edition.)

Marmion's *Antiquary* served as the inspiration for the character and much of the business of Sir Arthur Oldlove in *Madam Fickle*. In Marmion's comedy, Veterano, like Oldlove, is a collector of antiquities and a scoffer at all that is modish and new. In the third act he shows off several of his prized antiques, among which are "the great silver box that *Nero* kept his beard in," and the breeches of Pompey the Great. D'Urfey incorporates both items among Oldlove's collection, as well as some direct dialogue from Veterano. (See III, i, 21-23, 72-73, and 154-56.)

Much of the general idea of the main plot of *Madam Fickle* is reminiscent of Rowley's *Match at Midnight*. In the latter, a widow leads her various lovers on, not knowing that her servant Jarvis is in reality her disguised husband. The final scene especially is similar to the unraveling of the Fickle-Dorrel complication in *Madam Fickle*. *Match at Midnight* also contains the characters of Bloodhound and his two sons, Alexander and Tim, a trio that clearly influenced D'Urfey's drawing of Tilbury, Zechiel, and Toby.

Notwithstanding these many borrowings, *Madam Fickle* emerges as a fairly entertaining and amusing comedy of sexual intrigue. Like most of D'Urfey's farces, the plot is carelessly constructed and its denouement is artificially contrived. This structural deficiency is further complicated by the subplot which, with its debauchery and horseplay, bears little relation to the main plot. Still, the characterizations and much of the dialogue are stageworthy and must have been highly entertaining for the Restoration audiences who delighted so in intrigues and amorous deception.

Probably the most serious defect in the comedy is the poor handling of the Dorrel-Friendlove disguise. Friendlove, Madam Fickle's husband, has, with little motivation, gotten himself up as Dorrel, a servant, in order that he may observe his wife unbeknown to her. What he observes in her behavior is the most flagrant promiscuity and double-dealing, yet he is perfectly willing, at the finale, to reveal himself, ask her pardon for his deception, and reclaim her as his wife. Even more disturbing, however, is that the audience is given no clue to Dorrel's true identity until the end of Act III, which takes the meaning and dramatic value out of his earlier actions and comments.

Madam Fickle's disguise in the fifth act also is poorly motivated and serves no purpose other than to afford the actress a "breeches" scene in which she can strut and swagger about the stage in imitation of a town bully. This scene, with its flamboyant speech at lines 149-62, is a *tour de force* for the actress and was probably received with much applause from the audience. The fact remains, however, that the disguise is unmotivated.

Most of the comedy's characters exemplify popular types of the period. Madam Fickle herself conforms to all the characteristics of the "jilt." She deceives a succession of lovers, working her intrigues to prevent each from finding out about the others, and her motivation is the conventional ploy of revenge for a past wrong done her by her unfaithful husband, Friendlove. Sir Arthur Oldlove, Captain Tilbury, and old Jollyman are excellent examples of D'Urfey's handling of *humours* characterization. Oldlove's controlling passion is his adoration of relics of the past and his contempt for all that is fashionable and new. Tilbury and Jollyman are chiefly lovers of wine, women, and song. Each of the three is highly entertaining in his own way, and Oldlove's obsession especially provides some excellent comic scenes. Tilbury's two sons, Zechiel and Toby, represent two standard types of the period, the "hect'ring" bully who wants nothing more than to be modish, catch wenches, and drink immoderately, and the country bumpkin —physically clumsy, inept in a love intrigue, and easily intimidated by the constable's watch.

One unusual feature of the dialogue is the occasional use of blank verse, especially in the amorous interviews that Fickle conducts with her various lovers. Most of these passages, however, show little reason for the text's verse lineation of what is obviously prosaic dialogue, and in the present edition some of these passages have been rendered as prose. In every case the emendation has been noted. The slang and cant expressions of the "nightwalking" crew enliven the dialogue of the subplot's figures—Zechiel, Toby, Flaile, and so on—though they pose problems in meaning for the modern reader. Such terms have been noted and explained wherever possible.

All in all, the play's language and dialogue are quite standard fare for a comedy of love intrigues. Some of the speech is self-consciously ornate and convoluted, much of it is truly witty (*e.g.*, II, ii), and all of it is surprisingly free from the obscenity and licentiousness that were to characterize much of D'Urfey's subsequent work. Perhaps by virtue of its being the dramatist's comic debut, *Madam Fickle* is D'Urfey's cleanest comedy. In any case, it provided him a successful entrée into the London theater, for which he was subsequently to provide well over a score of similar comic dramas.

MADAM FICKLE:

OR THE
Witty False One.

A
COMEDY.

As it is Acted at his Royal Highness the
DUKE's THEATRE.

Written by *Tho: Durfey* Gent.

HORAT.
Non cuivis homini contingit adire Corinthum.

Licensed *November* 20. 1676.
ROGER L'ESTRANGE.

LONDON,
Printed by T. N. for *James Magnes* and *Rich. Bentley*
in *Russel Street* in *Covent-garden* near the *Piazza's*.
M. DC. LXXVII.

TITLE PAGE OF THE FIRST EDITION OF *MADAM FICKLE*. The Duke's Theatre was the theater in Dorset Garden. The apostrophe did not appear in D'Urfey's name on the title pages of any of his plays until *A Commonwealth of Women* (1686). The Latin epigraph is from Horace's *Epistles* (Book I, no. XVIII) and is a Greek proverb meaning literally: "It is not every man's lot to get to Corinth." The proverbial sense is that not every man can gain the prize of virtue or excellence.

TO HIS GRACE
THE
Duke of Ormond,

Lord High Steward of His Majesties
Houshold, Knight of the Noble Order of
the Garter, and one of His Majesties most
Honourable Privy Council.

May it please your Grace,
Though the presumption I might have been guilty of in this Dedication, is somewhat excused in your Graces permission: yet the meanness of this trifle, infuses a secret shame into me, when I consider how ill a present I have made to a person of such eminent merit and grandeur, whose obliging, and not to be exampled clemency, induces him to patronize a piece that rather diminishes, than brings the least addition to his fame. Had it been an heroick poem, I might have open'd my eyes with greater assurance, and cherish'd my ambitious thoughts with the resolution of honouring some happy heroe with your Graces illustrious character, and so under pretence of a slender merit springing from the work, have insinuated my self into your favour. But whereas other authors are happy in this particular, how little have I to boast of, when all I can say in my defence is that its only good fortune was in being the subject of the Courts diversion, where their noble clemency and good nature were extremely requisite, in covering its defects from the too censorious; His Majesty, according to his accustomed royal and excellent

temper, was pleas'd to descend so far as to give it a particular applause, which was seconded by your Grace, little considering, my Lord, the pride a young author might be infected with, in seeing his play honour'd with so dignified an approbation. But when I had the honour to wait upon you, and saw shining in all your actions the glorious beams of humility, courtesie, true honour and virtue, perfections seldom seen in great men, 'tis impossible for me to decipher my thoughts, nor had I power to utter them; for my minds surprize added to the imperfection of my speech, though I had leisure to consider how despicable a thing is pride, when supprest by the pious inclinations of a generous virtue. Pardon me, my Lord, if the indefatigable zeal I owe your Grace makes me wander from the nicer rules of dedication; and I beseech you believe that as to admire you I never can enough, so to flatter you is far beyond my power, you being far above it. I have more reason to beg your pardon for this trespass than to incur your anger for another default: a buffoon, though he may be often stil'd the sport and diversion of princes, would very ill become the name of their companion. And so this play, though it had the fortune to please you as spectator, must needs blush at its insufficiency, being receiv'd as a bosome friend. Confession (my Lord) *makes an abatement of the crime, and to make it wholly pardonable, the rest must be impos'd upon your Graces clemency that authoriz'd my boldness; the clemency that drew me from a melancholy retirement, where Content and I were often quarrelling about a slender fortune, to visit the blissful habitation of virtue and grandeur. Birds sing most sweetly that sit in the sunbeams; and 'tis, I confess, the natural ambition of most poets, to shelter themselves under the wings of nobility, encouragement adding more sweetness to their pens, and more vivacity to their fancy: but to study to deserve the blessing of your favour, shall be ever the great and sole ambition of,*

MY LORD,
Your Graces most humble,
and most devoted Servant,
   Tho: Durfey.

DRAMATIS PERSONAE.

Lord *Bellamore*.	Mr. *Betterton*.
Manley, friend to *Bellamore*.	Mr. *Smith*.
Sir *Arthur Oldlove*, an Antiquary.	Mr. *Sandford*.
Captain *Tilbury*, an old fashion'd blunt fellow.	Mr. *Medbourn*.
Zechiel. } Sons to *Tilbury*.	Mr. *Anthony Leigh*.
Toby. }	Mr. *James Nokes*.
Old *Jollyman*.	Mr. *Underhill*.
Harry, Son to *Jollyman*.	Mr. [*Jevon.*]
Flaile, Servant to *Tilbury*.	Mr. *Richards*.
Dorrel, alias *Friendlove*.	Mr. *Norris*.

WOMEN.

Madam Fickle.	Mrs. *Mary Lee*.
Constantia, Daughter to Sir *Arthur*.	Mrs. [*Barry.*]
Arbella.	Mrs. *Gibbs*.
Silvia, Attendant to *Fickle*.	Mrs. *Napper*.
Three *Wenches*.	

*Constable, Watch, Footmen, Maskers,
Musitioners and Attendants.*
SCENE
Covent-Garden.

Prologue by Mr. *Smith*

Fancy and Sence, the glorious twins of Wit,
That us'd t'imbellish what a poet writ,
Are now as poor and despicable grown,
As an old wrinkled trader of the town, 5
With hollow eyes, no teeth, and tatter'd gown;
Like her they are neglected by you wits,
And forc'd to trade with country squires and cits,
Who with their eighteen-pence uphold the stage,
Which you would ruine with your critick rage, 10
By Heaven, Sirs, it is a cursed age.
Too late 'tis now for poets to get fame,
Their works are only fit for you to dam.
They toil, 'tis true, but gain, instead of praise,
Malignant censures; thorns, instead of bayes. 15
The great cabal so partial do appear,
An authors wit lies buried in his fear.
And as a painter in his skill grown nice,
Still mends and mends till he has spoil'd the piece;
So too much care in striving to essay 20
New scenes of wit, oft ruines a good play.
The Factious Club are merciless of late,
Carping, ill-natur'd, and degenerate;
Sifting so much to find each little fault,
They lose their best diversion in their thought. 25
And though facetious playes, and th' learned pit,
When colledges have fail'd, have taught them wit;
The stages ruine unconcern'd you see,
And dam th'original of gallantry.
Shou'd we leave off then, we should hear you say, 30
Dam 'em, what drones are these, why don't they play?
'Sblud, I shall never leave this wenching vein,
Jack, *my last swinging clap's broke out agen.*
And if we do play—then you censure raise,
And to encourage us, dam all our playes; 35
Nothing will please, I wonder what a Devil
Makes men of wit so formally uncivil.
But since 'tis so, and you thus cruel prove,
We must appeal t'our friends that sit above,
Whose wise indifferent censures grace a play, 40
As squibs and crackers do—a Lord Mayors Day.

MADAM FICKLE;
OR, The
Witty False One.

ACT I. Scene 1. [*A public place.*]

Enter Jollyman *and* Harry.
Jollyman. Sirrah! Not a penny: I say 'tis lost upon thee.
Harry. I say—— How, Sir!
Jollyman. How, Sir? I'le tell you, Sir. First thou art a melancholly fellow, a kind of hypocondriack, as I am told, and instead of making, spoilst good company.
Harry. Pish! Good Sir, believe it not.
Jollyman. Secondly: Sirrah, thou hast quite forgot to sing, a quality that was hereditary, a benefit that has grac'd our family for above these 20 years, and like a varlet thou hast neglected it.
Harry. Not I i'faith, Sir! You are mis-inform'd. I am not melancholly, nor any thing of that which you imagine. I can sing too, loudly, and for the benefit of company. 'Tis true, Sir, want of money——
Jollyman. Sirrah, Sirrah, a lye deserves a cudgel. Do not vex me. Udsbores, did I not see you yesterday at Sir *Arthur Oldlove*'s, holding your hands up thus, conning your lesson? What business can you have with Anti-

quaries, except it be to practice disobedience, or turn Precisian to disgrace thy family?

Harry. Why, Sir, I'le tell you what.

Jollyman. No, Sir, you need not; I know the trick already. Speed the plough, Sir. Alas! What shou'd you do with money? To you that neglect the world money's a torment. I have consider'd it and will not tempt you. Money was made for those that laugh, and drink with appetite, whose merry souls put padlocks on dull conscience, and live the life of sence *cum privilegio*.

Harry. I will excel in mirth, Sir. Every day shall give you proof, each hour variety; your house shall ring with shouts of joy and musick. I long have wish'd it so, but still the duty, the reserved reverence that I bore you, Sir, made me forbear. But since you'l have it otherwise, it meets my wishes fully.

Jollyman. And mine too, Sir. And a pox on reverence I say; an ounce of true *English* mirth is worth a pound on't. But this Antiquary—— What business had you there, Sir? Answer me that.

Harry. Sir, there is a rich widow lodges at his house, one to whom my private inclinations have been long devoted; and by feigning an austerity yesterday in Sir *Arthur*'s company, I got access to her.

Jollyman. Is she merry; can she sing?

Harry. To a miracle, Sir. She's extreamly musical: plays o' th' guittar, and tells a story with the best grace I ever saw.

Jollyman. 'Sbud, a fine woman, I warrant her. Hang pinching, *Harry,* thou shalt have her.

Harry. She's very reserv'd; but withall uses a modest freedom that's infinitely taking.

Jollyman. Udsbores! I like it well; a merry modesty, and an unstain'd integrity add much to feminine capacities. Let the world rub, *Harry*—— I say thou shalt have her. There, there's money for thee. Nay, if thou wer't there upon design, 'tis another matter, I must allow that. When I was a young man I was the best at a design. Ah, I could ha' gone through stitch, i'faith. But come, hang pinching——*Harry*, thou shalt have her.

SONG.

Away with the causes of riches and cares,
That poison our spirits, and shorten our years:
    No pleasure can be,
      In state or degree,
  But 'tis mingl'd with trouble and fears.
Then perish all fops by a sobriety dull'd,
Whilst he that is merry reigns Prince of the World.

The querks of the zealous of beauty or wit,
Tho' supported by power, at last must submit.
    For he that is sad
      Grows wretched or mad,
  Whilst mirth like a monarch does sit:
It cherishes life in the old and the young,
And makes every day be both happy and long.

Jollyman. By Heav'n a rare woman, a most divine creature. Sirrah, there's more money, and do but wheedle dexterously. Do but get this woman, and then hang pinching, let the world rub.

Harry. I'le warrant you, Sir. [*Aside.*] So, I have open'd his purse at last! How now, who's this?

              Enter Tilbury *and* Toby.

Jollyman. Hoh! My old friend and fellow-collegian Mr. *Tilbury*. I'faith, I am glad to see you. This was good luck to meet you here after so long absence. Pray, how fare all our old friends in *Salisbury?*

Tilbury. In health, Sir. Hard labour, plain diet, and hearts ease are still the best physicians. All well——All well——

Jollyman. Why let the world rub: I am glad on't i'faith. This is your son, I think, Mr. *Tilbury.*

Tilbury. One of 'em, Sir. *Toby,* your hat. T'other hand, Sirrah! Well, this boy will never learn breeding.

Jollyman. Oh I'le warrant you, Sir, here he'l soon learn that; a very hopeful youth indeed.

Tilbury. Ay, ay, God send him Grace, Sir, he may do well enough! What Mr. *Harry*! By Coxbodikins, I did not know you. You are grown a lusty stripling since I saw you last. Ah—— Lord, how time passes! I am heartily glad to see you, good Mr. *Harry*. 'Sbud, he sprouts up finely. I hope your mother's well, Mr. *Harry*.

Harry. Very well, Sir.

Tilbury. (*To* Toby.) Still twirling your hat, and squeezing your gloves. Sirrah, leave that trick, or by St. *Jago* I'le lame thee. I wonder when you see Mr. *Harry* in such a posture.

Jollyman. Oh give him a little time, Sir; he is not yet wean'd from the country.

Tilbury. No, no, my cudgel shall wean him. Good Sir, let me go. Sirrah! Sirrah—— Have I not told you of this?

Jollyman. He'l mend it quickly, Sir. Pray, have a little patience. And setting this apart, what business brought you to town, good Mr. *Tilbury*?

Tilbury. Why, Sir, I have a suit of law depending here ith' *Chancery,* which I am resolv'd to make an end of; and my next business is, I intend to marry both my sons to two fortunes, which are here provided for 'em.

Jollyman. Both! Why, have you another son?

Tilbury. Another! Yes, *Zechiel.* Did you never hear of *Zechiel*? H'as been a student in the *Temple* this three years, another-ghess fellow than this, I assure you, all air and spirit he. 'Sbodikins, I am told in the country there's not a true wit in all the fraternity but he.

Jollyman. Why then hang pinching; he's a brave fellow. Come, Sir, here's a glass of excellent old Hock here at *Longs.* I'le give you your wellcome to town.

Tilbury. Old Hock! What a Dickins is that? Sir, a dish of racy Canary if you please; I am for no Hocks! 'Sbodikins, wine was never good since it has been corrupted with such barbarous notions.

Jollyman. Well, Sir, I'le warrant you I'le please you.

Tilbury. [*To* Toby.] Sirrah, walk you yonder in the (what d'e call 'ems) the *Piazza's,* and if *Flaile* my man come, direct him hither. And d'e hear, leave that sneaking dog-look of yours, or by St. *Jago*—— Well, I say no more for this time. [Don't] provoke me.

(*Exeunt* Tilbury *and* Jollyman.)

Toby. What a peevish old fellow 'tis! Sure he has been stung with a wasp to day. He's so fretful—— But, Udshash, I'le not be controul'd so, and so I'le tell him when time serves.

Harry. Faith, Sir, he's a little too severe. Why, he uses you like a meer child.

Toby. Ay, like an infant—— Huh—— Because he's old, he thinks no body has breeding but himself. But, Udshash, in *Salisbury* I assure you I pass for the more accomplish'd person.

Harry. Without doubt, Sir, he were an arrant coxcomb that wou'd dispute that. Why, you have a good presence.

Toby. Yes; thank a good Nurse. I am pretty well fortified by Nature, and yet every thing I do, he forsooth mislikes, as if I were a fool, and knew not how to carry my self. Udshash, I wonder he has no more civility——

Harry. O Sir! Old men that have the prerogative of being fathers, think it but decent to use that liberty. But setting aside this discourse; Mr. *Toby,* may not my ambition desire the satisfaction of knowing the name of this excellent person you are to marry.

Toby. Why, Sir, to tell you the truth of the business, I don't know her name my self; for I never saw her yet. For the old fool my father carries matters so closely, that I can never know any thing. But by *Jeroboam* I'le fit him, for if I marry without good pre-meditation, I am the son of an *East India* bagpiper; and so, Udshash, I'le tell him.

Harry. Marry a stranger, and one you never saw? By Heaven, 'tis unreasonable.

Toby. Udshash! He's the most unreasonable cormudgeon you ever knew. I' th' winter he will not let me come near the fire for fear of catching chil-blanes.

Harry. Not warm your self——

Toby. No. Did you ever hear the like? But, Zooks, I fitted him once; for I burnt a whole stack of hay down to the ground on that occasion, and warm'd my self in spight of him.

Harry. Ha, ha, ha—— A witty invention, by my life. But Mr. *Toby,* I suppose you know what quality she that must be your wife is.

Toby. Yes, yes. She's of very good quality, and a widow, and very rich I am told.

Harry. A widow, Sir? [*Aside.*] 'Sdeath, if it should be my mistress——

Toby. As to her conditions. I am ignorant of 'em; but they had need be good; for I have miss'd many a wealthy match for her sake.

Harry. Certainly, Sir, I've the honour to know this lady; pray, where does she lodge?

Toby. D'e know her? I'm glad o' that, i'faith. You may do me a great kindness in telling me some of her conditions. Why, Sir, she lodges here in *Bridges-street* at the house of Sir *Arthur Oldlove,* the fam'd Antiquary.

Harry. [*Aside.*] The same, by Heaven. 'Sdeath, was ever

such luck? Sir, I was involv'd in a mistake. I thought she had been a lady of my acquaintance. But, good Sir, how came this match so forward, since you say she's a stranger to you?

Toby. Why, Sir, to tell you the truth of the business, I my fathers intimate friend, and this widow lodging at his house, he presently gave notice of it, telling him he doubted not but he could make her a match for me. But the main cause of his kindness is, because he designs my brother *Zechiel* to marry his daughter.

Harry. (*Aside.*) Very good! Now have I an itching mind to swinge this rascal, but 'tis so notorious a fool, that a beating is lost upon him. Then you'r resolv'd to marry——

Toby. Yes! Hang't, I will marry. I fancy there's a great deal of pleasure in't. First to command a family, and sit at the upper end of the table. Then to make my wife serve instead of a *vallet de chambre,* and never pay her no wages neither. Then to command her this way, that way, t'other way, and every way; for this thing, that thing, t'other thing, and every thing. Udshash 'tis very pretty——

Harry. But, Sir, you still miss the right end of marriage.

Toby. That's all one, Sir. Why, we must take our fortune. 'Tis as the Fates decree.

Harry. Gad, the Fates are very uncivil to meddle in a matter that so nearly concerns you. But Sir! There's one thing more; there's a certain ill fate attends marriage——horns, Sir. Are you not afraid of being a cuckold?

Toby. A cuckold! Ha, ha, ha—— [*Aside.*] I see he's a little foolish. A cuckold, Sir! Udshash, in *Salisbury* they know not what it means. 'Tis your *London* air that breeds cuckolds. Here's your horny forrest. But, Udshash, they say here a courtier can't walk the streets without being perpetually troubled in returning the complements to some of his cuckolds. Besides, they'r so general a society here, that no body minds 'em. But in *Salisbury,* if a man is suspected to be a cuckold, he presently gets into office, either of Constable or head Church warden, that his degree may recover his disgrace. Nay, for better security, some of 'em padlock their wives. And, Udshash, that is certainly the safest way; and I wonder the citizens here don't take it into consideration.

Harry. Get one of the Common Council to petition the King for an Act of Parliament to that purpose.

Toby. 'Tmay be necessary as things stand sometimes. But see, here comes *Flaile.* Udshash, my brother too. Now for a peale of wit.

Enter Zechiel *and* Flaile.

Zechiel. Hah, *Toby*—— Beangarson, touch flesh, touch flesh. Wellcome to town, i'faith. Upon honour, thou lookst well, only thy clothes a little disguise thee; but no matter. Where's my father, hah? *Bandog* and I have been seeking him this hour; prithee, where is he?

Toby. Gone to the tavern with an old friend of his.

Zechiel. Come! Let us go thither too. Upon honour, the tavern's a sweet place, and next to the play-house, the most becoming a gentleman of any thing. (*To* Harry.) Sir, I kiss your hand, and beg your pardon for neglect in salutation, but my eyes being serenely fix'd upon my brother, there happen'd an accedental eclipse between my imprison'd aspect, and, Sir, your person. But the luminaries of my soul being kindled by discretion, I have now liberty to acknowledge and amend my fault committed in point of demeanour.

Toby. What! What's all this? Udshash, *Zechiel*'s mad——

Harry. Sir! I am very unskilful in a repartee of this nature, and therefore beg your excuses if all I can say is that your wit had no occasion for half this apology.
Zechiel. Sir, your very servant. *Toby*, come, let's to the tavern. Upon honour, I'le make thee drunk to night. Give me thy hand. What, dull——flat——like a poet in a church. Prithee, hold up thy head and laugh, man, and let us sing, and roar, and drink away the night like sons of thunder. To morrow will be time enough to see my father. Hey, come along, Boy. [*To* Flaile.] *Bandog,* Sirrah, you shall go too. You shall drink bumpers out of your custard-cap, you rogue, and be drunk for the honour of your countrey——(*Strikes off* Flaile's *hat.*)
Toby. Yes, yes! He's mad——
Flaile. 'Slid! For ought I see you need no wine. Prating will in a short time make you too drunk for any civil mans company.
Zechiel. Well said, *Ploughshare*! (*To* Toby.) Why, how now, *Bully!* Still in thy dumps! Not a word to save a mans longing? Prithee look up and speak like a man of worship. 'Sdeath, I must new mould you e're we part. I perceive that you'l degenerate else. Upon honour, he's no kin to me that is not as brisk as a dancing-master. Give me the spirit of conversation, a man that sings, and talks, and laughs, and stares——and comes aloft thus with agility, hah—— (*Vaults.*)
Harry. Like a taylor o're a washing-block. Well, I must leave 'em, for the disease of folly is as catching as that of the plague.—— Gentlemen, your servant.
Zechiel. Ah Sir, you will not leave us. Shall we not break a jest together o're a glass of *Burgundy*! Upon honour, a man of wit is to me as welcome as a beautiful woman. *Toby,* address your self to the gentleman your friend.

Toby. Sir! The truth is, my brothers a little off o' th' hooks; but 'twill quickly away. 'Tis only the over-flows of wit. You know the old saying, *Sine aliqua [dementia] nullus Phoebus!* This wit is plaguy troublesome.

Harry. Right, Sir. Therefore to prevent, I'le take my leave till some other time.   (*Exit* Harry.)

Zechiel. Is he gone? Dam him, he has no money now, not a souse—— I know it. Upon honour, in this age a man knows not who to bestow his gallantry upon. If he gets among persons of quality, they are so critical, that he has not matter enough to work on. If amongst the vulgar, 'tis lost upon 'em, for the sence of paying a reckoning makes them as dull as a *Cantabrigian* newly enter'd into orders.

Flaile. Ay, this *London*'s a wicked place, that's the truth on't. Che' have gone 3 mile about, and can hardly see ought but ale-housen and taberns.

Toby. Nay, the worst is, one can hardly know a church from a tavern, but only the church has ne'r a sign.

Zechiel. A good observation! Gad, I'le pinch thee for that. [*To* Flaile.] Pinch him, *Bandog*; leave your church, you dog, and execute my mandates. (*Kicks away his staff; he falls down.*) Ha, ha, ha.

Toby. Ha, ha, ha. Up again, *Flaile*; there's no harm done. Udshash! *Zechiel*'s grown an arch wag.

Flaile. Arch, quoth a! 'Slid, he has broke my nose. D'e laugh? Ah, you may be asham'd o' your actions. Your worshipful father wou'd ne'r ha' serv'd me zo.

Zechiel. Nay! No anger, *Flaile*! No anger! What's a fall to a man o' thy parts. Upon honour, 'tis customary here to give or take a fall from any man, especially amongst frends.

Lord Bellamore, *Mr.* Manley, *and* Footmen
pass over the stage.

Bellamore. Sirrah, take this letter, and do as I command you, away—— You shall find me in the Mall—— (*Exit* Footmen.) Come, *Manley,* let's away—— How now? Who's here? My fop of the *Temple, Jack?* This is he I told thee of. I won 300 Guineys of him t'other night at Back-gammon.

Manley. 'Twas well you won 'em. They might else have been thrown away upon one of far less merit, for I see he has a kind of a losing face—— He'l ne'r thrive at play.

Zechiel. My Noble Lord! I kiss your Lordships great toe. Worthy Sir, your adorer. Upon honour, my Lord, you had the most victorious chance t'other night I ever knew. But since it was my fortune to lose, Fate did me a great honour in choosing your Lordship for my conquerour.

Bellamore. Sir! The most worthy are still more subject to ill chance, and 'tis as absolutely impossible for me to excuse my own good fortune, as to enlarge upon your merits.

Zechiel. Ah! Your Lordship o'rewhelms me in the deluge of your gallantries. Be pleas'd to know my brother, my Lord. 'Tis true, he's meanly apparel'd, because newly come from the blessing of 1500 a year in the country, to spend a month or two in town; but else, upon honour, of a good stature, straight back, and a head of most hopeful expectation.

Bellamore. He seems no less, Sir. I wish I had leisure to comment upon his perfections.

Zechiel. Ah! Your Lordship o'rewhelms me in the deluge of your gallantries. Be pleas'd to know my brother, disputed which was the better bred, he or his oxen! Upon honour, a second *Hobson,* my Lord, an everlasting *Plough share*—— Do but view him! Stand forth, o Man of

Motley! Ha, ha, ha—— He blushes, upon honour, he changes countenance.

Manley. [*Aside.*] Not for a worse I hope.

Bellamore. (*Aside.*) No, not unless he should steal one off the poles at *London* Bridge. But come, prithee let's away. Such another description would induce me to beat this fellow for spoiling my stomach to my dinner——

Zechiel. What's that? Dinner! Will your Lordship dine with me? A dish of partredges, and a jowl of salmon (my Lord.)

Bellamore. But your sawce is scurvy, and will doubtless corrode upon my nature.

Zechiel. Gad! The best sawce in the world. This fellow was cook to the King of *France*, and, upon honour, is the most ingenious in his function of any man in Christendome.

Manley. But, Sir, our intrigue lies another way.

Bellamore. Sir, we are to day men of great business, and there is a pressing affair that requires instant performance. Therefore, adieu.

(*Exeunt* Bellamore and Manley.)

Zechiel. This is the bane of our nobility. Pride—— Sloth and ill manners undoes the nation.

Toby. A Lord, quoth a! If all Lords have no more breeding than this, the nation is like to have a hopeful House of Peers. Udshash, I could have carried matters better than so my self. For with reverence be it spoken, and under the rose, my Lord was as unmannerly a fellow as I ever saw.

Flaile. Ha, ha, ha—— He a noble man, and punctilio no better. By th' Mass, the Maior of our town has more manners by half.

Zechiel. Pshaw—— What's matter? Let 'em go. Upon honour, I scorn their ignorance, and to let 'em see the power of a man of wit, thou and I will lampoon 'em. I'le teach thee within this three days to be a Man of Mode; and thou shalt talk, and roar, and fight, and sing even with the best, nay, cocks of all the bullies. I'le teach thee the most new and dextrous way of picking wenches up. Then thou shalt know their tempers, constitutions: whether they are i' th' boat or may be boarded. Thou shalt know every thing, Boy. I'le be a true brother to thee.

Toby. Hoy, Boys, then I'le warrant I'le learn quickly. Nay, Udshash—— I'm very quick at any thing I give my mind to.

Zechiel. No more blowing of noses on your sleeve, nor twirling of band-strings, d'e hear? But when you are in company, cock your hat, place your arms thus, look like the Son of *Thunder,* and cry Hoh.

Toby. Hoh——Udshash! I'le warrant thee I'le do't.

Zechiel. Then we'l have our names alter'd. Let the old Prophets keep their appellations; we'l be new Christned. Mine shall be——*Filloflorido;* thine *Rounsivell.* Hey, *Rounsivell!* Upon honour, it sounds rarely——and then for humour.

Toby. Ay, ay, I warrant thee, Boy! If I can but get a little wit into this pate of mine, let me alone for humour.

Zechiel. Then my *Pithagoras,* shall thou and I make a Transmigration of Souls. Thou shalt marry my mistress, and thy wife shall be my gracious *paramour.* [Seventeen] puncks shall be thy proportion. Thou shalt sleep in the comfort of clean linnen, wench with a safe conscience, and eat no more fresh beef at supper; but the flesh-pots of *AEgypt* shall fatten thee, and the grashopper flourish in thy summer.

Toby. Hoy! Rare, rare *Phillorolido*! Prithee, give me a note o' thy name; Udshash, I shall ne'r hit on't else——

Zechiel. Come away then, we'll go presently and 435
practice——
    And to the tavern door make our approaches,
    Like hect'ring gallants rushing from gilt coaches.
(Exeunt.)

Finis Actus Primi.   440

ACT II. Scene 1. *The [Mall]*.

Enter Lord Bellamore *and* Manley.
Bellamore. A fool is a vacuum in nature, a prolix story without marginal notes, in whose company a man neither gets credit nor profit. If he be rich his greatest perfection is avarice. If poor, he is altogether despicable, and unfit for society.

Manley. I am not of your mind, for if profit turn the scale, there's certainly most to be got by half-witted people. And as to the disgrace, the notion of a fool is so general, and there's so many sorts of 'em, that a man loses not an inch of reputation, but rather gets credit by their defect.

Enter Page.
Bellamore. Now, Sirrah! What news?

Page. I deliver'd your letter as your Lordship directed, and she desires your visit to be as speedily as you can; for she has a kinsman that about an hour hence has ingag'd himself to wait on her, whose company she fears may be very prejudicial.

Bellamore. I'le be with her [presently. *Jack,* I] must beg thy pardon.

Manley. What, an assignation, my Lord! A love-challenge, I warrant.

Bellamore. Even so, i'faith, and I must thither instantly. Where shall we meet at night?

Manley. At *Lambs* with the fiddles and a talboy.

Bellamore. Agreed. I will not fail thee. *Jack,* farewell. [*To* Page.] Sirrah, follow me——

(*Exit* Bellamore *and* Page.)

Manley. So! I am glad it happens thus. I should else have been put to the trouble of excusing my absence from him. Let me see, 'tis now five a clock! At six I promis'd *Celia* to visit her, and his absence gives me a happy opportunity to perform it. I'le take a walk round the park, and by that time 'twill be very near the hour. (*Exit* Manley.)

Enter Zechiel *and* Toby *in a new suit.*

Zechiel. Splendid and Gent. Upon honour thou art metamorphos'd: a courtier of the first edition. Thou hast the town air already, and wearst thy clothes with a boon mene. Walk a little! Walk! Ah—— Observe always to keep your toes outward, and your elbows as far back as you can. That's right! Give me thy hand; upon honour thou art a modish fellow.

Toby. Udshash—— I must quarrel. I shall not be a right gallant till I have beaten some body, or am beaten, it's all one. Hah! *Philloromine.* Plague on't, I shall never hit of thy name.

Zechiel. Thou shalt beat a Constable to night. Thou and I will scour through the Flannel *Mermidons,* and come off conquerors. Nay, rather than fail thou shalt beat me. But I'le ha' thee flesh'd. Stand here! Suppose me now a drawer, and that I had been tardy in procuring a wench according to your order. What wou'd you do oth sudden?

Toby. Do! Why thus. (*Strikes him.*) A box o' th' ear for a Prologue. You know that's but reasonable——
Zechiel. Right, upon honour. 'Tis necessary—— But forward.
Toby. Hoy! *Scaramouchi, Rascal, Poltron, Popinjay*! Son of 20 fathers, besides out-liers, comers and goers! Must a man of honour wait your leisure, you dog, and miss his necessary diversion, through the negligence of such a scarab? Udsbores, I'le beat thee into a tripe. No haste? No attendance? (*Beats* Zechiel.)
Zechiel. Hold, hold! Ha, ha, ha! The right town-humour, *Ned*, flesh to the life—— Ha, ha, ha! Let me kiss thee for this. If thou canst but get the art of gleaning from plays, and remember'st but my rules for picking up wenches, upon honour in a short time not a bully rock of 'em all can come near thee for gallantry.
Toby. Ay, but they say the best way of picking up wenches is to speak bawdy to 'em, and the truth is, I am a little shame-fac'd at present. But I shall quickly come to 't.

    Enter Arbella, Constantia, *and* Page.

Arbella. So pleasant and so inconstant a temper till now I never knew. Her carriage is so graceful and obliging, that 'tis infinitely delightful to all companies. And if she happens to speak of love, methinks there flows a sweetness from her language that charms the ear.
Constantia. And yet she's false as Hell! So strangely wedded to inconstancy, that the town begins to take notice of her and speak the more loudly, as being ignorant of her quality. [*To* Page.] Sirrah, carry that letter as I directed you.   [*Exit* Page.]
Toby. Udshash! Here's women, Brother! [Good-bye]! I'le begone; my heart fails me already. I shall never be able to speak to 'em.

Zechiel. Not speak to 'em! Upon honour thou shalt, bravely too. What, flinch in thy first charge! Come back, for shame. Observe me, I'le begin. I'le introduce thee—— Ladies! The Devil take me if it be not a maxime against reason and civility for you to walk thus without servants. But obliging Fortune, a particular friend to your sex, has sent hither for that employment my brother and my self; and if your pleasure——

Arbella. Sir! You will add very much to our pleasure to leave us; for we are in so ill a humour that the overtures of your imaginary wit will be lost upon us.

Zechiel. Leave you! Shall I leave a lady to the tyranny of melancholly, that may be diverted with the pleasure of my company? Madam, I know more of the punctilio's of civility than so; therefore as I was saying, my brother and my self——

Constantia. [*Aside.*] Oh heavens, Madam! This is the very fool that my father designs me to marry.

Arbella. It seems he knows you not.

Constantia. No; he never saw me but once, and then 'twas at a window.

Zechiel. My brother and my self, Madam, two of the most accomplish'd sparks ith' town——

Arbella. Two of the most conceited fops ith' town——

Zechiel. That shall be punctual in observing your commands.

Constantia. That shall be beaten most unmercifully, if you stay a little longer.

Zechiel. Beaten, Madam! What rash presumer, careless of his life, dares think a thought like that? Beaten!

Toby. Udshash, she has quell'd my courage already. Wou'd I were at home again.

Zechiel. But I see, Madam, you are disposed to rally. Beaten! There goes more to the beating of a man of parts than you imagine. Upon honour, I was my self once so well skill'd in beating people, that the Herald had like to have given me a battoon for my crest, thereby to have signaliz'd my valour to posterity.

Arbella. I wonder you miss'd so decent an honour, for I am of opinion 'twas an excellent device, and very suitable to your new-coin'd gentility.

Zechiel. [*Aside.*] New-coin'd! Damme, this comes of walking without a footboy. Brother, prithee come and espouse my quarrel. These eternal talkers have made my throat as dry as a spunge already. Come! Address, address! They tell me that ours is a new-coin'd gentility.

Constantia. [*To* Toby.] Well, Sir, and what has your large quantity of wit to say on this occasion?

Toby. I say! Why I say—— Say you what you will, the family of the *Tilburies* is an ancient family, God bless the Royal Family, as any family in Christendome, and he that says the contrary is the son of a whore, and my brother here shall cut him into steakes——

Zechiel. Well said, *Rounsival.*

Arbella. 'Slight! Prithee let's away; this angry fool will beat us.

Toby. [*Aside.*] So, so—— Now they begin to fear me; I shall do well enough. [*Aloud.*] The coat of the *Tilbury's* new-coin'd—— Udshash, 'tis as old as *Tilbury Camp,* and that was in the same year with *Noahs* flood.

Constantia. Insufferable impertinence! They may well be brothers, for their united folly out-vies their consanguinity.

Enter Manley.

Manley. [*To* Arbella.] Madam! The [*Mall*] may now boast of a happiness unparallel'd, enjoying the sweetness of your company.

Arbella. Still your rhetorical vein, Mr. *Manley.* You consider not the weak capacities of women.

Manley. Yes Madam, I may consider it, but am sufficiently satisfied in my knowledge of your capacity to think it mean. But me thinks your looks are not so lively as 'tis usually. Your eyes have lost part of their fire. No late loss I hope, Madam, has caus'd this alteration?

Arbella. None, Sir. Only a little molested with the present heat, and the continual buzzing about of flies that haunt me.

Manley. Flies! I understand you, Madam.

Toby. [*To* Zechiel.] Come, I think we had best go. Here's some mischief hatching.

Zechiel. I'le not stir, upon honour. What a pox, he dares not draw in the [*Mall*].

Manley. Sir! I see your presence has the misfortune to be distastful to these ladies, to whom I have the honour to be known. Therefore 'twill become you and your brother fop there to leave 'em, and retire to your better conveniences.

Zechiel. Brother fop, Sir! Upon honour, you licence your tongue by the priviledge of the place. Such an attribute should not have pass'd unreveng'd else. But, Sir, a time will come——

Manley. When I shall cut your throat, Sir. Come, Ladies, I'le be your guardian. Let these mushrumes stand if they dare. The respect I bear the noble company that usually walk here ties up my sword; but if they sleep on't, hang me.   (*Exeunt* Manley *and* Ladies.)

Toby. Udshash! I'le go hire a coach, and into the country immediately.

Zechiel. The country! Such another word and I'le renouce thee for ever. Prithee think no more on't. He'l be hang'd before he'l challenge us.

Toby. I see he has a murd'rous intention, and 'tis an act of prudence to be careful.

Act II Scene 2

Enter Flaile.

Flaile. Oh have I found you at last? I wonder where the Dickins you ramble! Ch' have search'd all the coffee-housen and taberns 'twixt this and *Westminster* for you. What, by th' Mass, my young Mr. *Toby* turn'd gallant too. Whoop! By Coxounty, what a change is here. Come, you must go to Sir *Arthur Oldloves* to your father. By th' Mass, he's almost out on's wits for you.

Zechiel. Go, *Bandog*; tell him we come. And, Sirrah, bid him get a bottle of Claret, and a neats tongue ready. Go—— Brother, come, cheer up. Pox ont, a rencounter is nothing when thou art us'd to't. Prithee, let's be merry.

Toby. If this man had not come to disturb us, I could have been very merry—— Udshash, I could have beaten the woman into a jelly. But no matter; time and experience shall mend all. *(Exeunt.)*

Scene 2. [*Madam* Fickle's *chamber.*]
Enter Madam Fickle *and* Silvia.

Fickle. Is he come! Give me the glass.

Silvia. Yes, Madam, and I've led him into the parler. I protest he's a handsome man, and one that in my opinion little deserves the cruelty you intend him.

Fickle. Call you affection cruelty?

Silvia. Flattery in affection is extreamest cruelty. I know you love him not; I have heard you often confess it. And to possess him with a belief you do, and at last dash his hopes with a denial, is a horrid torture.

Fickle. I am glad he moves your pity. Do you love him?

Silvia. I commiserate his fortune; his love is a happiness too high for me. But, good Madam, let me presume to ask the reason why you use all your lovers thus?

Fickle. Well, in hopes to make thy diligence the surer, I'le tell thee why.

>'Twas my unhappy fate some three years since to fall in love,
>To give away my heart, and throw my self into the arms of
>One of mean descent, and also slender Fortune. Yet had Destiny
>So link'd my soul with his, that each kind glance
>Shot from his darting eye, me thought went through me.
>I lov'd, nay, and ador'd with so much zeal,
>I cou'd have dy'd——nay, willingly been tortur'd.
>I thought he could not wrong my innocence; for then I
>Swear I was so innocent I knew not what sin was.
>Yet this deluding wretch! this base seducer, although
>I slighted all for him, laught at my fervent
>Passion, scorn'd and left me. And when I thought his heart
>Was mine for ever, 'twas then most treacherous, and farthest
>From me. Therefore I've made a strict and solemn
>Vow, on the whole sex to execute revenge——flatter and
>Wheedle all I can——and ever
>To practice to ensnare, but to love——never.

Silvia. The strangest revenge I ever heard; but I doubt not, Madam, in a short time love will alter your condition.

Fickle. I'le venture that. Go and conduct him hither, and fetch thy lute and sing.   (*Exit* Silvia.)

SONG.

>*Beneath a shady willow, near*
>*A rivers purling streams;*
>*Astrea, careless of her sheep,*
>*With folded arms lay fast asleep,*
>*Possess'd with golden dreams;*
>*Her working faculties supply'd*
>*[What] drowzy sleep deny'd;*

For oft she'd sigh, and smile, and grasp the air,
Thinking her much-lov'd Celadon *was there.*

But as this sleeping harmless maid,
Lay rap'd in silent joy,
Possessing all that could be sought,
In fetter'd sense or happy thought,
Her swain came fishing by;
He eager of such rapting bliss,
   Awak'd her with a kiss,
She blushing rose, and cry'd, unhappy Fate!
Ah Celadon *thou now art come too late.*

            Enter Bellamore.

Bellamore. Mirror of Beauty! Abstract of perfection, Sweeter than banks of roses, and more Glorious than the bright empress of the ruddy Morn; when early *Titan* rises——

Fickle. So early in your florid vein, my Lord. I thought that 12 at night had been always your facetious hour. For Heavens sake, no more of this. You'l lose your self in these hyperboles.

Bellamore. To lose my self in you were to find Heaven —— Hah—— Gad, me thinks I have express'd my self in as decent a whining method, as 'tis possible for a lover to do. Come! Shall we abroad; my coach is at door. Prithee, let's to the park; 'tis a fine evening.

Fickle. No, I am oblig'd to stay at home to receive the visit of a kinsman, that sent word he would wait on me.

Bellamore. A pox on kinsmen! Gad, we have other business than to mind relations. In these cases an assignation disappointed with one of them is no more than the telling of a lye, or an ordinary frailty. But to spoil an amorous intrigue, when persons are not at all times provided, i'gad, 'tis a most inhumane offence, and merits condign punishment in the world to come.

Fickle. Ay, Sir, but this is such a kinsman——

Bellamore. Such a kinsman? Why the nearer he is re-

lated to you, the better he may stay. The cold business
of consanguinity is seldom ty'd to an hour; once a week,
or a month, will serve the turn well enough. But the
pressing affair of love brooks no delay. The minute
must be watch'd that guides our souls to perfect joys,
and they who neglect are fools.

Fickle. Well, if impudence be a grace in a lover, I
swear, my Lord, you have as large a portion as any one
I know. What man but you durst contradict his mistress
thus?

Bellamore. What woman but you durst provoke a lover
thus? Nay, one that is to marry you, and consequently to
have power to tyrannize over you; to lie with you but
once a week, and then with an ill will too; to send you
into the country to look to your dairy; to keep a mis in
town, and live three times beyond my estate, according
to custom.

Fickle. Is it not also in my power to be false? Is my
beauty so mean, think you, that no one wou'd make addresses? Lies it not in my ability to wheedle you into a
belief of love, and at last to forsake you? Assure your
self it does—— But Heaven knows I am too constant.

Bellamore. A miracle in nature! A notion of so strange
an extravagance, that the very sound is incredible! Constancy in woman is a second maidenhead: 'tis lost e're
they know they have it. And your constitution, Madam,
certainly tends that way, and the truth were known——

Fickle. (*Aside.*) He little thinks how right he guesses——

Bellamore. But since you are in so ill a humour, and
are resolv'd to spend this afternoon here like a turtle,
solitarily in your cage, I'le leave you, and strive to divert
my self with other company. I have a present here, too,
which I intended to dedicate to you, but to the melancholly all things are distastful.

Fickle. [*Aside.*] A neck-lace of pearl! I must not lose that so—— [*Aloud.*] Use your pleasure, my Lord. The vertue of a present seldom makes me fond of any mans company.

Bellamore. You think, I warrant, this indifference becomes you extreamly. That modish turn of your head and glance of your eye, you imagine, was infinitely taking. But, Madam, I am now in a more serious humour, and not to be fool'd with such dilatory motions; so begging your pardon for my obstructing your kinsmans visit—— I take leave——

Fickle. Well! I am the very'st fool. I swear, my fondness makes you insult over me. Another woman wou'd have made you comply, and be glad to ask her pardon, but my good nature makes you slight me.

Bellamore. No, this action has indeer'd my soul to thee, and I am faster thine than ever. Oh, I could live for ever in thy arms——feed on thy lips, and surfeit with thy kisses.

Enter Silvia.

Silvia. Madam, the gentleman is come.

Fickle. Unlucky minute! Sweet my Lord, away; I wou'd not have him see you for the world.

Bellamore. The Devil blow him hence in a whirlwind! I will obey you; but, by Heaven, with as ill a will as ever coward faught a duel. But since it must be so——adieu. Nay, do not smile upon me; by the Lord I shall tire your kinsmans patience and stay if you do. Farewell. A pox upon him, I say—— Farewell, Madam.   (*Exit.*)

Fickle. So, there's one dispatch'd. I was fain to tell him 'twas a kinsman, to get him gone the sooner. Stay! This is my passionate lover, one that wooes by method, and speaks blank verse. Now must I change my temper suitable to his tone, and speak in the same stile. Let me see:

When Sapho *lov'd! Oh Heaven! What throngs of woes oppress'd her harmless breast?* Very well—— I have it rarely. Now to my posture—— This book—— Languish- 155
ing eyes—— So—— And necessary handkerchief to wipe imaginary tears off—— So—— The Devil's in't if this is not melancholly enough. Here he comes. *(Sits at the table.)*
Enter Manley.

Manley. Life of my soul! Bright treasure of the world, 160
  Queen of perfections, and the best
  Of all thy charming sex—— What dismal fate
  Has caus'd this alteration? Why are thy eyes,
  Late the extreams of glorious light, now clouded,
  Adding more trouble to the frighted world, 165
  Than when the sun eclipsed threatens a chaos?

Fickle. Pardon my frailty, Sir. I have not learn'd
  The power to dissemble. Who cou'd read
  The hapless fate of wretched *Ariadne*?
  Hear *Theseus* falshood, and the piercing mones 170
  Of a distress'd maid, by love undone,
  Left all alone within a desart isle,
  And not pay tribute of a tear or two, to grace the story?

Manley. 'Twas a horrid act,
  And I confess deserves it; but in us, 175
  That love and glory in the passion, 'tis
  Not fit despair should tyrannize.

Fickle. Let them despair that merit no return;
  My passion has been permanent.

Manley. And mine, 180
  The truest heart that e're obey'd the dictates
  Of Loves Imperial Power. From that hour
  That first obtain'd my eye the happy object
  Of your perfections, my poor fetter'd heart,
  Proud of the chains of such a conquering beauty, 185
  Resolv'd to grace the long wish'd victory
  With a perpetual constancy.

Fickle. And mine,
  Bless'd with the pleasure of your loves addresses,

Grew proud of such a fortune. Happy *Celia*! 190
Wou'd I oft cry, if thou canst purchase him,
Thy race is finish'd, th' abstract of all love,
Vertue and valour. Then with my minds perspective
Wou'd I survey your soul, and sigh, and covet.
Love to my sense such pleasing motions brought, 195
That I was lost in my own various thought.

Manley. Sweet Creature! Oh my soul, how I adore thee,
The transport of whose touch has power to kill!
If I shou'd visit often, speak sweet charmer,
Will you be always true? Always thus constant? 200

Fickle. Constant! Alas! What power have I to change
When you possess my heart?

Manley. My soul!
Fickle. My heart!
Manley. My life! My vital spirits! Oh Heaven, I fool my 205
self in too much love, and dote on my own happiness. (*Kneels and kisses her hand.*)
Fickle. [*Aside.*] He's finely caught! Wit, where art thou now?

Manley. Erring philosophers, that knowledge prais'd 210
Above the bliss of women——women, delicious
Women——women, the
Quintessence of Nature: Heavens treasures
Fram'd to enrich mankind, and make 'em deities.
Travel, fond cynick, through the spacious globe; 215
Dive through the sea. Thence through the airy region
Soar, to find out new pleasures; and at last,
When thou hast known the joys of Earth and Heaven,
Believe with me it terminates in women.

Enter Silvia. 220

Silvia. Madam, your kinsman is below, and desires the favour of your company.

Fickle. Unfortunate minute! For Heavens sake, Sir, begone. I am undone if he sees you. Heark! He's coming up. 225

Manley. Was ever fate like mine—— Wear this, sweet creature, and remember me——(*A ring.*) So! Adieu, divinest, sweetest, kindest! O Heaven! Must I be gone?—— (*Exit* Manley.)

Fickle. Ha, ha, ha! I think I did it to the life! *Silvia,* didst thou hear our court?

Silvia. Yes, Madam; and I swear I pitty the poor deceiv'd gentleman.

Fickle. Pitty him! Prithee, talk no more on't. But who is that below?

Silvia. The young brisk gentleman that fell in love with you yesterday: he that your Ladyship gave the song to.

Fickle. Tell him I'le come to him. (*Exit* Silvia.) Now for a brisk airy humour to agree with the temper of this fool. This is the most easie fop of all my pretenders. There needs no net for him; his own actions are his best betrayers. The other two I confess have more wit, but what then? Love makes a dunce of a councellor, and their fondness proves as prejudicial as t'others folly. O men! Silly men, that fetter'd with a smile, forget the business of their creation, the motives of their honour, and the safety of their countrey. Thus far my revenge is prosperous; and I'le forward. My panthers breath shall draw 'em to the snare; my tongue shall charm; my smiles kindle loves fire in their amorous souls, till they'r scorch'd severely. Then forsake 'em whilst in my breast my heart, obdurate flint, shall hear, and yet not pitty.

> Thus all shall know that were like me refus'd,
> No serpent like a woman when abus'd.
> [*Exit.*]

Finis Actus Secundi.

ACT III. Scene 1. [*Sir* Arthur Oldlove's *lodging.*]

Enter Sir Arthur Oldlove (*ridiculously drest, hung with medals*), Tilbury, Jollyman, [Friendlove, *disgused as*] Dorrel.
(*A table with scull, sword, vial, shooing-horn, box and picktooth,* cum caeteris.)

Sir Arthur. [*To* Jollyman.] Sir, 'tis no matter what the world thinks. The world think? Why let it think, I say, once agen. 'Tis such as we redeem lost time from its chaos of confusion. Is there any thing more pleasant than antiquities? The knowledge of the distinction of ages, or the deeds and manners of the ancient: I say, is there any thing more pleasant?—— Oh, happy *Romans,* that took this into consideration; for my own part I am nothing, a man of ignorance, a meer reptile in these rarities.

Jollyman. Every man in his humor, and let the world rub. Appetite and fancy are two great monarchs that sway mortality, and hang pinching, udsbores, 'tis fit they shou'd be satisfi'd. But good *Sir Arthur,* what are these? Doubtless these are rarities too.

Sir Arthur. Right, Sir, and such rarities that, were their worth valu'd, the *West-Indies* were too small to purchase them.

Tilbury. I warrant this has been some princes or great mans scull. 'Sbodikins, he looks still with the face of authority.

Sir Arthur. Fie, fie, Sir, your hat on! This relique shou'd be toucht with reverence, but your ignorance must excuse all—— Pray stand a little back, and give attention. This scull, this noble prudent politick scull, once belong'd, or as I may more properly say, was pertinent to the body of *St. Gawaine,* a Knight of the Round Table.

Tilbury. St. *Gawaine!* A *Dutchman,* was he not? I believe I know some of his relations.

Sir Arthur. A *Dutchman!* Oh, insupportable—— Sir, did you ever know a relique made of the scull of a *Dutchman?* No, he was a *Britain,* Sir, a hardy *Britain,* and nephew to the famous King *Arthur* of happy memory. And this scull was late resident in *Dover* Castle, brought thither by a fam'd Antiquary, whose name time has outworn, and since purchas'd by me, to illustrate this city, amongst the rest of my memorable antiquities.

Jollyman. Very well, Sir, proceed.

Sir Arthur. And this here is the fam'd hero, *Sir Lancelot du Lake's* sword.

Tilbury. I'll warrant this has been the death of many a constable. But methinks, *Sir Arthur,* the rust has been a little too bold with it.

Sir Arthur. Ah, Sir! Rust adds to an antiquity; 'tis our friend. And we that are skill'd in these matters, can by the rust on a sword tell how long it has been durable.

Jollyman. Hang pinching, 'twas well discover'd. I see a man may live and learn, tho' he be never so old. Good Sir, forward.

Sir Arthur. This here is a shooing-horn, d'mark me——Hats off still—— Pray observe it—— A shooing-horn.

Jollyman. 'Tis so——

Sir Arthur. This shooing-horn, Gentlemen, the first that ever was invented, was, with reverence be it spoken, the necessary implement of the Queen of *Sheba,* and left by her careless chambermaid at *Jerusalem,* after her visit to King *Solomon.*

Tilbury. By St. *Jago,* an admirable discovery. 'Sbodikins, who would have thought so much ancient honour could depend upon a shooing-horn.

Jollyman. Very strange! Very strange! By St. *Jago,* as you say. But the stranger the merrier, the merrier the better company, and so hang pinching, let the world rub.

Sir Arthur. This is the silver-box that *Nero's* beard was kept in; 'twas in the *Vatican* 300 years, and lately presented to me by a friend of mine, a man of great authority in *Rome.*

Tilbury. Somewhat like a tobacco-box——

Sir Arthur. No comparisons, good Sir. But observe, this is the rubbing-brush of *Silvius Otho,* and this the picktooth of *Heliogabalus.*

Jollyman. Carefully preserv'd from the ruines of time, to grace your study, *Sir Arthur.*

Sir Arthur. Lastly, this last——tho' most precious and best of all my reliques. This vial is full of the tears of St. *Jerom,* in former years pendant upon the spire of St. *Sepulchres* steeple, but by my indulgent care and great charge redeem'd from thence when the city was on fire.

Tilbury. A thing of moment, Sir, and worth your diligence.

Enter Servant.

Servant. Sir, there's two gentlemen below desire admittance.

Tilbury. 'Sbodikins, my sons, my sons. *Sir Arthur,* I order'd them to come hither, that they might see the ladies you writ me word of. Friend, shew 'em the way up—— *(Exit* Servant.)

Sir Arthur. You did well, Sir. *Dorrel,* go see if my neece be at leisure, and bid my daughter come hither.

(Exit Dorrel.)

Jollyman. Ay, ay, come, hang pinching, let's see the lady. Let women make up the consort, and then let the world rub. There's mirth and frolick in't, but without women, udsbores, 'tis prolix, 'tis impertinent, 'tis every thing ill, and nothing well. Hang pinching, women, women, I say.

Tilbury. Well said, 5-and-50. By St. *Jago,* thou grow'st young agen; thou'rt a very boy.

Jollyman. Not frozen, not frozen. Heart whole, and warm enough to keep out weather. Udsbores, when I was 1-and-20, I was the sprightly'st fellow. I cou'd have sung and danc'd, and leapt and jumpt—— Hey troll—— Faith—— But 'tis past now. However I am sound—— Hem—————— Not so old, but I am a jolly man still, and hang pinching, let the world rub.

Sir Arthur. Well, I say still, there's nothing so becoming as gravity.

Enter Zechiel, Toby *and* Flaile.

Tilbury. Zechiel, my boy, how dost thou? Kiss me, Sirrah—— 'Sbud, I am glad to see thee; they tell me y'are grown an arch wag. *(To* Toby.) Hah——how now! What *Metamorphosis,* Sirrah! Where got you them cloaths?

Toby [*Aside.*] Now must I give him a private item, or this ignorant old fool will disgrace me before all the company. *(Takes him aside.)*

Tilbury. Oh! Are they so, Sir? Well, God give ye joy. But *Zechiel,* prithee, what news in town? Dost thou thrive—— Hah——'

Act III Scene 1

Zechiel. Thrive! There's a *Salisbury* question already. Upon honour, 'tis pity my father was no better bred. Sir, the nourishing fecundity pertinent to our sphere, has bestow'd a better talent on me than can be possibly acquir'd by Fortunes donation, and therefore—— Noble *Sir Arthur,* I sue to kiss your hand. I was so bury'd in my fathers caresses, that I protest my eyes were traytors——

Sir Arthur. Sir! I hope you and I shall have a nearer affinity and knowledge of one another ere long.
      (Toby *surveys* Sir Arthur's *cloaths.*)

Tilbury. [*Aside.*] By St. *Jago,* my pains were ill employ'd else! Why I came to town for that purpose——

Sir Arthur. But where's your brother, Sir?

Zechiel. Here, Sir, taking a particular view of your habit. Upon honour, *Sir Arthur,* methinks your cloaths are not made according to mode.

Sir Arthur. Mode—— Ah good Sir, no more o' that. No modes I beseech you. My habit is the mirror of my mind. Little do you know the value of this outside. Sir, in brief, 'tis more than the Kings three dominions can purchase.

Toby. [*Aside.*] Udshash! I'd like to have spoil'd all; I took him for a Morrice-Dancer.

Sir Arthur. To display my meaning more plainly, Sir, this medal was the Badge of Peace 'twixt *Scanderberg* and the *Turks;* this was the doublet of *Gustavus Adolphus;* and these breeches, renown'd be the tatter'd linings, were the breeches of *Pompey the Great.* He was call'd *Pompey the Great,* by reason of these great breeches.

Jollyman. Peace be to the ancient cobwebs betwixt the seams. *Sir Arthur,* your servant. I must go seek my son. Odsbores, here's the lady—— I'll stay a little longer now, and let the world rub.
    Enter Constantia.

Sir Arthur. How now, where's my neece?

Constantia. Gone to the park, Sir, with my Lady *Arbella.*

Sir Arthur. Park! What, without my permission? Passion o' me, I shall have her stol'n. Huswife, this is your fault; you are still prating to her of the pleasure of intrigues, as you call 'em. Well, these new damnable customs utterly undo the nation.

Constantia. Sir, I am not her guardian, tho' you are; nor do I think it a particular of my duty to pry into her actions.

Jollyman. [This certainly's the Lady *Harry* told me of.] Udsbores, a merry mushrum, I'll warrant her.

Sir Arthur. Well, since 'tis so, we must practise patience, and Mr. *Tilbury,* it shall be my care hereafter to have her ready for your sons addresses. In the mean time, pray, Daughter, know this gentleman, whom I have elected for your husband. (Zechiel *hides his face, and goes backward.*) And let it be a mark of your duty to use him kindly. [*To* Zechiel.] Come, Sir, along, along! A young brisk fellow, and so backward—— Fie!

Zechiel. [*Aside.*] The very same woman I affronted in the *Mall.* What shall I do; she'll discover me.

Tilbury. Why, how now, Sirrah, what, flinch? Recreant, dastard—— Bodikins, thou art a disgrace to th' family. Th' *Tilburies* have been good holders-forth for above this 90 years, and shall they now be dash'd like a knight at a bear-bating? For shame. To her, to her agen I say. By St. *Jago*, I'll cudgel thee forward if thou dost not.

(Toby *breaks the vial.*)

Sir Arthur. Mercy a'me, what's that?

Toby. No harm, no harm, only a little vinegar bottle, an accidental mischance, as I hope to be sav'd, *Sir Arthur.*

Sir Arthur. How! The vial! Oh Heav'n! The vial! What, *St. Jerom! St. Jerom's* tears! Oh Hell! Fate! Death! Destiny! I'm undone, lost, ruin'd for ever. The vial! *St. Jerom's* tears spilt; the Holy relique spoil'd! Oh I am miserable; oh insupportable loss! Out of my doors, thou varlet! Away! I abominate thee, detest thee and thy whole race for this deed. Away I say! *St. Jerom! St. Jerom!* Oh dismal accident!

Tilbury. Good Sir, have patience; I'll make restitution.

Sir Arthur. Patience! Restitution! 'Sbud, both the *Indies* cannot do't. Hadst thou burnt my house, murder'd my wife and daughter, stol'n my plate, any thing but this, I cou'd have forgiven, but to disoblige *St. Jerom, St. Jerom!* O insufferable! Insufferable! 'Tis a capital crime, and not to be forgotten! (*Exit.*)

Tilbury. Sirrah, this is your unlucky hand. Come, we must go and comfort him; he'l run mad else——

(*Exeunt* Tilbury *and* Jollyman.)

Constantia. [*Aside.*] So I hope this accident, and my fathers anger, will be a means to keep me from the future impertinences of this fop. [*To* Zechiel.] Lord! How you look, Sir! What's the matter?

Zechiel. Nothing, Madam. Onely a little troubled at my brothers late miscarriage, and the disturbance of the company.

Constantia. You may repair that inconvenience in the *Mall* to night, Sir. There will be variety.

Zechiel. [*Aside.*] A pox on her, she has discover'd us! Well, Madam, I guess your meaning; and, though my behaviour express'd a little too much the freedom of the age, [yet] I can give my self this satisfaction, that I did nothing but what was courtly, and like a gentleman.

Constantia. A gentleman of the first rate, I grant, Sir. That is, an insignificant squire, whose addresses are so

formal and common, that your *Fleetstreet* prentices have 230
better, whose head, hands, and body are diversly
imploy'd in fashioning a bow; and, when he speaks, he
might be call'd a walking bagpipe, being oblig'd to his
nose for gracing his utterance.

Toby. Nay, if you talk of noses, here's a nose, and 235
Udshash, under the rose, another manner of nose than
yours is, if you go to that.

Constantia. Suitable to the owners person, I confess;
and were my judgment askt in this particular, I shou'd
guess your nose and understanding to be much of a 240
length; onely there is this difference, your nose is more
visible, but both very equivalent to your person and behaviour.

Toby. Madam, let me entreat you to be so much your
own friend, as not to question my behaviour. The shame 245
will be yours, if you do, I assure you that. 'Sbud, I knew
how to behave my self, before you knew how to——
(mum, I had like to have spoke it——) to discern behaviour.

Constantia. Your brisk air, bone meine, and gentile 250
garb expresses it, Sir. You are the exact picture of your
brother there; Nature drew you from its copy. And, Sir,
she has furnisht you, as the world may see, and you
your self doubtless imagine, with all graces pertinent to
your sex. But we are seated in so relentless an air, that I 255
protest I am blind to your perfection, and you appear to
me a very ordinary person, considering the advantages
you have of impertinence, impudence, and good clothes.
What your brother may be in my Lady *Fickles* eyes I
know not, but if she desires his company as little as I 260
yours, we shall both sleep without dreaming.

Zechiel. Damme, I'le be gone. This eternal fleerer will
jear me to a consumption. Come, *Toby,* let's to the

tavern, and rore to night. I'le warrant thee, I'le procure
a couple of females, that shall be good company, and   265
glad of ours. This is the most everlasting repertee.
Ounds, she has given me the griping of the guts in
studying an answer. Come, come away.

Toby. [Well], I am certainly the unlucky'st fellow in the
world. [*To* Constantia.] Why should not I be now as witty   270
as thee? But onely Natures a son of a whore, Destiny's a
slut, and Fortune's a bitch; or else men had had pre-
dominance in talk, not women. Well, the Devil will have
'em for't one day, that's my comfort.

(*Exeunt* [Toby *and* Zechiel].)   275

Constantia. Hard fate of women, that bestow your
hearts where is no return, and that often hate such as
love 'em. If *Manley* knew I lov'd him, I question the success, and yet without a hazard nothing is perfected. I
wonder I have no answer of my letter. I'm sure he had   280
it. But I must have patience; I expect th' event, as time
gives opportunity.

Enter Jollyman.

Jollyman. Your servant, Lady. Your father's in an extravagant rage yonder about breaking his viniger bottle.   285
His relique, as he calls it. Nothing can pacify him. He
swears he will fill another with his own tears, and never
stir abroad till 'tis finisht.

Constantia. 'Tis what pleases his humour, Sir. I hope
he had gain'd so much of time to satisfie himself in   290
every particular, without disgracing his quality, or re-
proaching his years.

Jollyman. Prettily exprest, that. Udsbores, Madam, you
speak well, pithy, and to the purpose. My son *Harry* has
a love-intrigue with a lady that lodges in this house, and,   295
pardon my presumption, at first I thought you to be the
person.

Constantia. No, Sir! I am not the person; and because I am loath to see good nature abus'd, I'le tell you a secret. Therefore know, this person your son loves is at this 300
time engag'd to twenty besides this old gentlemans son you saw here.

Jollyman. How! Twenty pretenders!

Constantia. At least, Sir, all which she wheadles for revenge or profit, without the least design of love or mar- 305
riage; for, to tell you the truth, Sir, (however secretly she carries it) she's marry'd already.

Jollyman. Why then my son is wheadled.

Constantia. Very near the brink of a precipice, assure your self. 310

Jollyman. I'le go instantly and disingage him. This was a lucky discovery. My son gull'd! No, my caution shall secure him from the danger, and then let the world rub.

Constantia. Sir, I had not presum'd to so free a relation, had I not known how nearly it concerns you, who 315
bear an estimable character amongst the greatest Grandees. Sir, I beg your pardon; I must visit my father.

(*Exit* [Constantia].)

Jollyman. Udsbores, a woman of pretty parts, and methinks of an excellent humour—— Hah—— Old 320
Harry, not so old yet, but such a nut may be crackt. But more of this hereafter. Now to my son. I'le get his neck out of the noose, and then follow my own designes as occasion serves. (*Exit.*)

Scene 2. *Covent-Garden.*

[*Enter* Harry *and* Manley *with a*] *letter.*

Harry. Melancholly is either the dregs of sickness or love, and may properly be term'd the poison of life and the odium of society; for a man of wit that is melan- 5
cholly, and sayes nothing, is in my opinion as unneces-

Act III Scene 2

sary a creature as a man that wants wit, and sayes everything.

Manley. I have as few pretensions to melancholly as to the wit you speak of; the one disagreeing with my constitution, and the other surpassing my capacity. 'Tis true, I am somewhat troubled at the receipt of a paper here, which is the reason my face is not drest in my wonted aire; but I think 'twill hardly induce me to be very melancholly.

Harry. A paper! Prithee, what is't, a challenge?

Manley. No, Sir, I have good fortune seldome to look on such missives as challenges with a clouded brow. 'Tis a letter from a stranger that knowes my amours, and takes the confidence upon her to tell me here my mistress is the most inconstant of women.

Harry. I'le lay my life, a malitious design of some jilt or other, that intends you for her particular use.

Manley. The letter discovers some affection in the writer, but my thoughts can never carry me to a belief it can come from any of my former mistresses; for I know none of 'em is acquainted with my present intrigue. Here, prithee read it.

Harry. (Reads.) *If your sex had as great a value for sincere affection as for inconstancy, you wou'd not be so ignorant of your present condition, nor cherish a serpent that delights to sting ye. I mean your mistriss, who, to my knowledge, hates ye, as much as another loves you, whom your self-will'd indifference has made miserable.*

I confess this is mystical, yet carries a greater resemblance of truth [than] first I imagin'd.

Manley. An oracle, by heaven. And the Devil is so cunning, that with imaginary doubts, it adds an intollerable addition to my misfortunes.

Harry. 'Tis certainly a general plague, pertinent to all mankind; for I have a mistriss that I mistrust too, and were she not extremely [obliging when I am with her, I shou'd] be more dubious. For I never come to visit her, but some kinsman or other comes to interrupt us; so that certainly she must have a world of relations, or else I have this misfortune, to come just at their hours for business.

Manley. My fate to a tittle; by Heaven, just so I am tormented. I am scarce yet within dores but I am molested with some uncle or other.

Harry. She calls her self *Cleio,* one of the Muses, and to pursue that humour, I went to visit her last night, and ingag'd three or four friends to entertain her with a dance, where we were fain to stay an hour ere we cou'd get admittance.

Manley. I hope at last your patience was well rewarded by her kind acceptance of your gallantry?

Harry. Indifferently. She appear'd to be very merry, and exprest a gracefull thanks for the diversion I gave her; for the truth is, I accosted her in this manner, the more to endear her to approve my passion, I having that very morning spoke with one that ignorantly confest his father brought him to town upon design to marry her.

Manley. That was a lucky discovery. I hope you was not idle in your endeavour of supplanting him——

Harry. No, gad, I did make the best on't I cou'd, for I went instantly to her, and with the best rhetorick I had, endeavour'd to weed the fool out of her thoughts. 'Twas fortunes bounty also to me, to find her at leasure, and alone; for had her guardian unckle, Sir *Arthur,* been at home, it had been impossible to have had any access to her.

Manley. Who, Sir! Who? Pray that last again.

Harry. Sir *Arthur Oldlove,* the Antiquary here in *Bridges-street;* she's his niece, a widow, an approv'd fortune.

Manley. [*Aside.*] Hell and the Devil! The very same woman I have so sigh'd for. But I see he's ignorant that I am his rival, and I'l get all I can out of him, that I may have the more to upbraid her with. Well, Sir, you made a happy conclusion; I doubt not she was kind without scruple afterwards, hah——

Harry. By Heav'n, kinder than I expected. She told me I had the largest share in her heart, and spoke the sweetest, softest things; 'twould melt a man to hear. I presented her a pair of diamond pendants, which she unwillingly receiv'd; and, as a crown of my courtship, told me at parting she had just before thrust away an impertinent suitor that came to make addresses, purposely to make room for me.

Manley. [*Aside.*] Very well. Dam her, she entertains a legion. I'l visit her instantly, and with the extremest sentiments of rage and jealousie, show'r my afflicted thoughts into her perfidious breast.

Harry. What say'st thou, was it not pleasant? What a pox, not a word? Methinks thou dost not rellish my discourse.

Manley. As well as a rival can, Sir: one that has the fate to follow the wheel of your chariot, whilst you triumph in Loves Empire. Hark'ee, for your further satisfaction, this woman you speak of is my mistriss too, the very same person intimated in this letter, one that I have courted this six moneths, and was in hopes within a week more to have marry'd.

Harry. How, Sir, marry'd to my mistriss?

Manley. Ay, Sir, to our general mistress; for, as far as

reason imbellishes my judgment, I am apt to believe you, and I come but in the reer of twenty more.

Harry. Now the plots unravell'd. I begin to have a knowledge of the visitant kinsman that us'd to molest us.

Manley. One of which I'm of opinion often usurp'd your shape. All will out at last, Sir. And, I'm resolv'd I'll not rest till I'm resolv'd that I may be in a capacity of revenging my self in the blood of him that dares usurp my right in her affection. (*Exit* Manley.)

Harry. Fortune was a damn'd jilt to make me discover my intrigue, nay, to my rival: the onely man I shou'd conceal it from. Well, I must not sleep in this business. If she be false, my loss is the less, but if constant,

> *My sword my rival's claimes must strait remove,*
> *Bravely he dies that victim falls to love.*

(*Exit.*)

Enter Lady Fickle, Arbella, *and* Friendlove *disguis'd.*

Arbella. So much beauty and so many attractive graces, I know, cannot want adorers; but too many lovers, Madam, in my opinion, is like too much money: the abundance of enjoying takes away the pleasure of possession.

Fickle. What you call much beauty in me is so little, that this complement you make me argues, Madam, a defect in your judgment; and as to my servants, which you call my adorers, they are so few, and those so meanly fetter'd, that I am beholden to fortune more than beauty, for the credit I have got in the world.

Arbella. Fy, fy! I swear you wrong your self; your perfections are the general discourse of the town.

Fickle. The impertinence of fops and citizens. A man of wit can find a better subject.

Arbella. I hope you think my Lord *Bellamore* a wit; and

to my knowledge, you are the onely saint he adores. A pretty man, by Heav'n, tall, strait, and well proportion'd, onely a little vain, an intollerable talker; that's his worst fault.

Fickle. (Aside.) Now is this, to my knowledge, a lye of her own invention; the monstrous effects of envy and jealousie.

Arbella. The happiness I wish you, you may guess in the contentment I shall receive in seing you so well marry'd.

Fickle. If constancy and immaculate affection may merit happiness, I doubt not but to have as large a portion as another; but want of desert makes me suspect th' event, although I know he loves me. (*Aside.*) This searches her——

Arbella. (Aside.) Insufferable! Confession! Oh I cou'd kill her.

Fickle. Happy chance! See, yonder he comes.

Arbella. I'll take my leave.

Fickle. Oh fy, by no means, Madam. Pray stay a little longer.

Arbella. I will not for the world. Some other time I'll give you a reason. Till when, your humble servant.

Enter Bellamore, *as she goes out, meets her.*

Bellamore. Madam! The park's unhappy, so soon to lose the pleasure of your company.

Arbella. Your ear, my Lord—— (*Whispers.*)

Fickle. Here is certainly some plot contriving; her wheadling me and whispering with him sufficiently declares it. And, by Heaven, I'll search into the depth of magick, but I'll find it out. I am already sufficiently prepar'd with arguments, and the more difficulty lies in the matter, the better 'tis often perform'd. Hard shifts and dangerous plots suit womens wits better than dull adventures; and whilst in tedious search dull men run on, arm'd by one minutes thought, the thing is done.

Bellamore. To morrow, Madam, I will not fail——

(*Exit* Arbella.)

Now if you had so much divinity in you as wou'd amount to a scruple of conscience, you'd be in a continual fear of future ill, for drawing me from the innocent conversation of this lady.

Fickle. The innocent conversation!

Bellamore. Ay, Madam. She's a soul-saving creature, a female-moralist. Her discourse is a continual sermon, and has the same influence that an ague has upon me, I do so tremble.

Fickle. I imagin'd it a kind of quaking zeal, never durable an hour.

Bellamore. Jack [Manley], thine, dear rogue!

Enter Manley.

[*Bellamore.*] What, melancholly! Qualmish! The sting of a debauch last night I warrant.

Fickle. [*Aside.*] By Heav'n, my t'other suitor. 'Twas happy I brought my masque. This will disguise me——

(*Puts on her masque.*)

Manley. In one sence you are right, for loves grand influence consider'd nearly is but a debauch, and we our selves the parasites that sooth it.

Bellamore. 'Tis so; and therefore why shou'd men of honour, that practice the distinction, and know better, resent its treachery? Prithee, what is it, *Jack*?

Manley. A thing of nothing, and yet every thing that cou'd torment me! Oh that dull appetite shou'd make a monarch of the slave of Nature, to tyranize over that noble soul that gave it first its being.

Bellamore. Dangerous resentments, by Heav'n, *Jack*. But prithee discover, come, be genuine.

Manley. I receiv'd a letter this morning from a stranger, skill'd it seems in my amour, full of invectives against my *Celia*, especially of her inconstancy. This I confess troubled me, for the reasons urg'd. It had some appearance of truth. And afterward conferring with young *Jollyman,* whose misfortune seem'd to suit with mine, he made so ample a discovery, that I found we were rivals, and that this false one carrest him more than me, and, in all probability, entertains several others. This put me into so extravagant a rage, that had not my curiosity of knowing the truth ty'd my hand, my sword had pleaded my interest. I am going now to her lodging to be resolv'd——

Fickle. (Aside.) If he had seen me now, here had been fine work! How near are my plots to discovery?

Bellamore. Gad, 'tis a business of importance.

Manley. So much that, by Heaven, I am resolved to search it through. *(Exit.)*

Fickle. [*Aside.*] So! Now will I instantly home, and perswade him that all is false, and onely the motions of envy. Come, my Lord, shall we go. *Dorrel,* bid the coachman come round to *St. James's* Gate.

Bellamore. What is that fellow? I never saw him before.

Fickle. Sir *Arthur* entertain'd him in his service to day, to look to his accompt.

Bellamore. And brush his antiquities——ha, ha, ha!

Fickle. Never was man so besotted; he dares not sleep o' nights for fear of thieves.

Bellamore. Dam him and his old imaginations. Let us mind our own business. Come, let's to the Mulberry Garden; I ha' not treated you this week. Methinks we live already as we were marry'd: not a word of love in a whole scene of discourse.

Fickle. 'Tis better i' th' heart than in the tongue; be-

sides, from a man of quality, love has so strange a sound. No, in my opinion, the eyes are the best orator, and now and then the serious look, with a short sigh for a prologue.
Bellamore. Thus! Ha! [*Sighs.*]
Fickle. And sometimes the exalting the hand to the lip, with a short kiss, and away.
Bellamore. Thus. (*Kisses her.*)

Enter Manley.

Manley. Now I consider better, I shall have occasion to be punctual to an hour. My Lord, prithee lend me your watch. Hah——blood and death, what do I see?
Fickle. [*Aside.*] Return'd agen! This was a curs'd trick of fate.
Manley. Ungrateful traitress! Now I plainly see (all I have heard is true.) Perfidious *Celia,* more false than crocodills, that mourn the slain, and yet delight to kill 'em. Do you not blush? Are you so arm'd with impudence, this object cannot startle? Yea, this beguil'd object, that bath'd his passion in warm tears of blood, and laid it at your feet, deceitful *Celia.*
Bellamore. Celia! What a mistake is this; by Heaven, my friend's mad.
Fickle. [*Aside.*] Now wit assist me, or I'm lost. Mad! Why, d'ee not see't? Look, look how his eyes rowle, how pale his lips are. See how his perriwig stares with his wild passion; his hands and body tremble. Oh, this *Celia*'s a cruel wretch.
Manley. Ah, perfection of ill! Wou'd you convert your infamy? Disguise your falshood in my shroud of madness? No, no; it shall not do. Madam, all shall out, assure your self it shall.
Fickle. So handsome, so well compos'd a man. Oh Heavens, what pity 'tis! Run, my Lord, run to the gate,

and call your footman to fetch a doctor! Two houres in such a fit will kill him.
Manley. Stay, my Lord, and hear me; I'll discover all. This lady——
Fickle. (Shreeks out.) Ah, delay not a minute, as you love his life! My Lord——away, away.
Bellamore. Poor *Manley,* thou shalt not dye for want of so small a courtesie. *(Exit.)*
Manley. Well, Madam, what's your design in this? What new plot is contriving?
Fickle. Oh Heav'n! Am I thus requited? Sir, I never expected such an action from you. Was there no way to augment my misery but this? *(Weeps.)*
Manley. Your misery! Ha, ha, ha. Your misery!——
Fickle. You know well enough that this is the person my uncle designs to marry me, and that 'tis impossible for me ever to see you, if he knows you are his rival.
Manley. [*Aside.*] Hah, this may be true; for he has formerly told me something of an intrigue like this. Well, suppose this true, Madam. I am sure Mr. *Jollyman* is a person not interested in your uncles favour, though in yours.
Fickle. In mine! That an impertinent serenader, only accepted for the company's sake he brought with him, shou'd have the impudence to talk thus.
Manley. He protested it to me a truth, and swore your extravagant favour exceeded his hopes.
Fickle. And you believ'd it. Well, I'll take care with whom I trust my heart agen—— *(Weeps.)*
Manley. [*Aside.*] Ugh, I can hardly believe this; yet sure these tears are real, it must be so—— Come, I do believe thee. Forgive me *Celia*; and consider how insupportable is jealousie lodg'd in a lovers breast.
Fickle. If I had not hit of this plot, what shou'd we

have done then? I warrant you won't believe I love you yet.

Manley. By this I do; thou hast confirm'd it in me.

Fickle. He'll come back immediately, and I wou'd not have him see you for the world; therefore be gone. I'll expect you this evening at my uncles. 315

Manley. I will not fail you, Sweet. I am glad it happens thus. *(Exit.)*

Fickle. Ha, ha, ha!
> Thus with the snowy veil of innocence, 320
> Contriving women cover their pretence;
> When women weep, look, Gallants, for surprize,
> For all deceit lies drencht in wat'ry eyes.

Enter Bellamore *and* Footman.

Bellamore. There's a coach ready at the park gate. How now, where is he? 325

Fickle. Ah! gone, gone. All my entreaties could not stay him, frighted, I believe, at my naming a doctor. I saw him cross the *Mall,* but in such a strange posture, that caus'd both pity and admiration in all that beheld him. 330

Bellamore. Poor *Jack.* I see the fits of madness are as sudden as those of love, and commonly work the same effects. Fate keep me from the tryal of it; for excess in any thing is a perfect torment, especially this modish passion we men so hunt after, and which is so generally admir'd, though conducing to madness.—— 335

> *He that of loves ripe joyes takes over measure,*
> *Abates his bliss, and loses half the pleasure.*
>
> *(Exit.)* 340

The end of the Third Act

ACT IV. Scene 1. [Sir Arthur Oldlove's *lodging.*]

Enter Sir Arthur, Tilbury, Jollyman, *and*
Friendlove, *alias* Dorrel.

Sir Arthur. Urge me no more, Sir. You have my answer, my final and my punctual answer. I will proceed no further in this business; nor shall my neece join issue with a man so wild, and so unfortunate: *St. Jerom*'s tears spilt, my treasure, my chiefest treasure lost, a blessing which this forty years we cherish'd, snatcht from me in an instant! Oh unparalleld misfortune! I say, let him forbear my house.

Tilbury. [*Aside.*] Well, of a knight, and a Justice of Peace, this is the simplest man of worship I ever saw. Good Sir, let it not so nearly concern you; you shall have restitution. By *St. Jago* I'll sell half my estate, but I'll make you amends. What a pox, d'ee think I'll be ungrateful?

Sir Arthur. Half your estate! A pretty proposition! 'Sbud, Sir, the Grand Signior's revenue would not purchase a drop on't.

Jollyman. A very costly liquor, by *Mahomet.* I think that *Turkish* oath sounds well——hah——

Sir Arthur. Old oaths are not to be despis'd, Sir. Therefore, by *Melchizedech,* which, I conceive, was well thought on, my resolution's fixt; your son shall be a stranger to my house. My daughter is not for him, tell him so. 'Zlid, shou'd he come here, within a week I should have my ancient medals of the *Romans* plaid off at gaming-houses.

Tilbury. Sir, upon my reputation, he knows not what belongs to a gaming-house. Alas, Sir! You are ignorant of his principles; he's countrey-bred, Sir——countrey learning, countrey manners, and countrey wit. 'Sbodikins, he knows nothing of the town.

Sir Arthur. But he may know every thing in time, Sir; and I'll harbour no person within my doors, whose future knowledge is more dangerous than his present.

Jollyman. Udsbores, a necessary maxim.

Sir Arthur. Trouble your self no more, Sir, my will is my law; and tho' I am a Justice of the Peace and *Quorum,* I think my proceedings in this both necessary and judicial. My neece is an heiress, and there is great care requir'd in her bestowing; nor shall my daughter match into a family, when I give such evident proofs of my dislike. Mr. *Tilbury,* you, as being my old acquaintance, shall be welcome to my house; but give me leave to tell you, my eyes are open'd to your sons folly; you understand me, I do not like their tricks, Sir.

Tilbury. Tricks, Sir!—— I find 'tis you have your tricks, Sir—— But by *St. Jago* I'le go fee my lawyer immediately. Force shall compel what good words cannot persuade; and I've a bag of old *Harry-Groats* have lay'n by me these twenty years, which I'll scatter amongst the gownmen, rather than be thus abus'd.   (*Exit* Tilbury.)

Sir Arthur. Old *Harry Groats*! What pity 'tis so meritorious an antiquity should be so ill employ'd—— Is he gone?

Dorrel. Yes, Sir——just turn'd the corner of the street, in so hasty and discompos'd a manner, that it argues him plotting some business of importance.

Sir Arthur. Wou'd he were here agen. Now wou'd I rather his son should have my daughter, than that he should waste any of that precious money.

Jollyman. Let it go, let it go, there's enough to be had in *Lumberstreet*. But *Sir Arthur*, to my present affair; since you have been so generous to deny him your daughter, I hope my address may be successful.

Sir Arthur. Troth, Sir, hope is very necessary in this affair; and if you can but hope my daughter will like your person and years, as well as I like your estate, your hope will have as ample a field to range in, as any mans I know.

Jollyman. My person and years—— Why, Sir, 'tis impossible she shou'd dislike it; whatever my years are, I assure you my imagination is but one-and-twenty.

Sir Arthur. But, Sir, in the space of a week, the strength of your imagination will be worn away, and your person will be left to the deliberate age of eight-and-fifty, a month or two over.

Jollyman. No, 'tis three months under, by my faith, *Sir Arthur,* and what then? With me 'tis an age of 21. Look in my face, Sir; observe how the blood mounts. Here, here's your complexion, without art, *fucus,* or any thing. Then, Sir, peruse my person—— Hah—— I think I am well set—— Hem—— And as sound as another man—— Besides, I can talk well, walk well, and make water well, which, udsbores, is as provoking a quality as any man is master of.

Sir Arthur. Sir, in a young man I confess these are additions; but a man that has the misfortune to decline into the vail of years, were he really master of all this, wou'd not get credit with the world; he would not be believ'd.

Jollyman. Not believ'd! Sir, my actions shall give continual demonstration, I am not in the catalogue of your infirm persons. My back, Sir, is strong, my body active; nor has my infirmity been so much my foe, to abate any part of my vigour. But I can run, wrestle, fight, or play a game at tennis with any spark i' th' city, and let the world rub. To confirm you, you shall see me do't—— (Not believ'd!) Udsbores you shall see me ride the great horse, or jump over a stick for the King of *England*.

Sir Arthur. Well, Sir, I will consider on't. In the mean time address your self to my daughter. Come, you shall sup with me. *Dorrel,* if any one ask for me, I am not at leisure. Be careful, and let no eye be spectator of my rarities without my knowledge. Come, Sir——

(Exeunt.)

Dorrel *manet.*

Dorrel. The uncertain dice of Fate thus far run well, and my designs are prosperous. My disguise, shrowd to my troubled mind as well as person, secures me yet from knowledge; and my eye attains the liberty to gaze at all her actions, and yet pass undiscover'd. Oh curs'd Jealousie, how crooked are thy paths!

Enter Bellamore *and* Arbella.

Bellamore. Unconstant, and to me! By Heav'n 'tis so strange a notion, that methinks 'tis incredible.

Arbella. And why incredible? Lord, how you men are deceiv'd in your opinion! You term your selves princes and lords of nature, imagining the easie tempers of women slaves to your nobler quality; and yet for all your pretences, to my knowledge some of you are often mistaken.

Bellamore. Well, if she be false——

Arbella. What then?

Bellamore. Why then she's damn'd; that's one comfort however. But, Madam, this extraordinary favour in you, obliges me in gratitude to a return. Shall I wait on you to your lodging? By Heav'n I hate ingratitude. Come, Madam, what satisfaction?

Arbella. Such a question to a mercenary spirit might perhaps be accepted under the notion of gratitude, but you having a perfect knowledge of my quality and obliging temper, give me leave to tell you, my Lord, 'twas very unbecoming, especially from the mouth of a man of honour.

Bellamore. Igad, I mean it cordially, and if my service——

Arbella. Hold, Sir, y'are observ'd. Yonder's *Sir Arthur's* man; from him you may doubtless learn the truth of all. My presence will be unnecessary, therefore I'll withdraw. [*Aside.*] So, I hope this will wean him. (*Exit.*)

Dorrel. This is one of her suitors; now for a new discovery, and I'm resolv'd to be prepar'd for him.—— Your Lordships humble servant——

Bellamore. Dorrel, come hither, I've some business with thee.

Dorrel. 'Tis too much honour, my Lord.

Bellamore. I long have lookt on thee as on a man above the common pile of menial servants; and since I know thee such, I dare request a secret from thy tongue, to me of great importance. Come, I'll bind thee to me in golden fetters; shall I trust to thee?   (*Gives a purse.*)

Dorrel. I am your Lordships creature, and if my ability extend to serve your Lordship, I am proud on't. (*Aside.*) Sure he has not discover'd me.

Bellamore. I'll try thee instantly. The truth is, *Dorrel*, I am grown jealous of my mistriss. Several reports declare she is unconstant; and tho' I do not positively believe 'em, yet Gad, I must confess they trouble me. Now I know thou hast a catalogue of all her suitors, and know'st all her intrigues, prithee disclose 'em. Am I the man or no, or has she others?

Dorrel. This is so dangerous a point, my Lord, I know not how to answer.

Bellamore. Fear nothing, but speak to th' purpose; I'll be so much thy friend, thou shalt not need to fear the frowns of any.

Dorrel. My Lord, there is one Mr. *Manley* comes hither often.

Bellamore. So, who else?

Dorrel. And one Mr. *Jollyman*; I heard her sware one night she'd marry him.

Bellamore. Very good, prithee proceed. (*Aside.*) Oh perfidious traytress!

Dorrel. [*Aside.*] Now has he a fretting feaver on him. Several others there are, my Lord, that visit her as pretenders, but with what success I know not. One of 'em I heard her appoint to visit her to night; and because your Lordship shall see how willing I am to serve a person of so much worth, follow me, and I'll place you where you shall, unseen, hear all their courtship.

Bellamore. Do that, I am thine for ever.

Dorrel. More than that owes tribute to your bounty. Come my Lord—— (*Exit.*)

        Enter Manley *and* Constantia.

Manley. Can this be real, Madam?

Constantia. True as Heav'n;
  I swear she is the falsest of her sex,
  Designing love upon fallacious terms,
  Without a spark of passion or desire
  To possess him that courts her——

Manley. Perjur'd creature!
  Oh Heav'n, that Providence gave man a heart
  To lose in such abyss of treachery!
  But, Madam, is there no ocular proof to be given of this?

Constantia. There is, Sir; and to that purpose I brought you hither. My chamber joins to hers, whence from a private closet door you may hear all. One of her suitors is now with her, and by their discourse you may soon guess the truth of her treachery; for doubtless 'twill be amorous enough, and very sutable to such an adventure.

Manley. O dam her! Dam her! Is this her constancy! Madam, the debt of gratitude I owe you for this discovery, is so far above my present ability——

Constantia. Good Sir, no more of that, but follow me——

Manley. All her feign'd caresses come to this! A curse upon the sex—— Madam, I wait your leisure.

(*Exeunt Ambo.*)

[Scene 2. Madam Fickle's *chamber*.]
Scene discovers Lady Fickle *in a morning gown,*
and Harry *sitting.*

Fickle. And cou'd you credit so ridiculous an asseveration, knowing how tender my caresses have been to ye? I thought my actions might have given you sufficient demonstration of my constancy.

Harry. By Heav'n, I never doubted it. I confess I was a little surpriz'd to hear him say he was at the expence of six months courtship, and within a week more it was to terminate in marriage. But now you have told me his intrigue with Madam *Constantia,* I am very sensible of the mistake——

Fickle. Had I not told you, I'll lay my life you wou'd ha' been jealous.

Harry. No, no, faith, I shou'd not—— Jealous!—— I know I have no cause; thou art the Heav'n of truth, and in thy breast *Astrea* reigns and triumphs. Suspect thy faith! What fiend cou'd be so envious? I'll prove thy constancy as firm as fate, and against all defend it.

Fickle. (Aside.) So, I think I have carry'd matters rarely.

Harry. But, Madam, pardon me if I presume to ask you why our interview is to be thus i' th' dark?

Fickle. 'Tis because Sir *Arthur's* coming often into the next room, seeing a light here, will be very apt to come and disturb us.

Harry. 'Sdeath! I've ignorantly left my sword and gloves upon the table there, which shou'd he come in, would infallibly discover my being here. I'll go fetch 'em immediately. *(Exit* Harry.)

Enter Nurse *(with a light) in a morning gown.*

Fickle. How now, what's the matter?

Nurse. Oh sweet Madam—— Ugh—— I am so out of breath. There's the basest plot contriving——

Fickle. A plot! Prithee what plot?

Nurse. Where's the gentleman? Get him into another room, or you'll both be discover'd immediately.

Fickle. How, prithee? By what means?

Nurse. Madam *Constantia* has watch'd you all this night, with an intent to betray you; I saw her bring Mr. *Manley* into her chamber, I'm confident with design to place him where he may hear the discourse 'twixt you and the gentleman.

Fickle. Manley brought hither by *Constantia*! Her envy now is apparent. What shall I do, *Nurse*?

Nurse. Alas! I know not—— Fire the house, I think, and say you call'd him in for help.

Fickle. No, so dangerous a remedy must not be try'd. Humm—— I have it! Sit you down, and personate me; our gowns are alike, and in the dark there can be no difference in faces. He's in the next room, looking for his sword. When he comes, feign my voyce, and caress him like a lover; in the mean time I'll go, and with a counterplot deceive both *Manley* and *Constantia*.

> Prosper designs, and by this act I'll try
> Which is the *Witty'st False One,* she or I——
> *(Exit with the light.)*

Nurse *sits in the chair.*

Nurse. Well, I've known the time when I've employ'd my self in such an adventure with a better will. But, however, I'll warrant I'll fit him with a repertee. I am not so old, but I can repertee as well as another, if occasion serve.

Enter Harry *with a sword.*

Harry. 'Tis so dark, that igad I could hardly find the table. Where art thou my dear?

Nurse. Here my dear.

Harry. I have been often thinking on the products of time, and have often wonder'd how they employ'd themselves before the deluge, when love was like the storming of a castle, attain'd by violence, not as now, with fair words, address, and insinuation. Men were not then such fools to kiss a glove, fall on their knees and sigh. Igad, they were wiser in those dayes——

(Kisses and embraces her.)

Nurse. Fie, fie, I protest you are not civil—— D'ee know who I am——

Enter Manley *(peeping) and* Constantia.

Constantia. D'ee hear 'em, Sir? They're yonder in th' alcove.

Manley. I do, Madam, and am sufficiently confirm'd in her treachery. But hush—— Let's observe.

Constantia. Sir, I'll go and get a coach to the garden gate, that you may get away undiscover'd. [*Aside.*] I think this was well plotted. (*Exit* Constantia.)

Nurse. I protest! Methinks your carriage is too licentious, and in my opinion you treat me ill. Your love shou'd still be cloath'd with a respect due to my youth and beauty, but I vow you'r so wanton——

Manley. (Aside.) Very well. She'll deny this anon——

Harry. Can any ill arrive from so much love? I swear there cannot, Madam; your charms are ingraven in my heart, and in my soul your virtues. I die when you are absent, and 'tis your influence that raises me from death to new-born life, and makes me currant from the dross of Nature.

Nurse. Give me no cause to doubt what you have said, I then shall be contented. But I protest you men are so subject to flatter, and we poor tender young creatures are so apt to believe, that it often proves very prejudicial——

Manley. She doubts his love. Oh death—— I shall want patience——

Harry. To flatter thee—— By Heav'n 'tis a thing so far from me, I hardly know its meaning. Let parasites, such as get bread by fawning, flatter their patrons. Let the empty fopp, that's sensible of some defect in Nature, and sees the little beauty in his mistriss, flatter her to exalt it. But in me it wou'd appear a crime unpardonable. Your lustre wants no foiles; but like a diamond in his native rock, you shine without the aid of art or flattery.

Nurse. Now by my quondam maidenhead this is very pretty. Well, Sir, you shall find my heart—— *(Coughs.)*

Manley. (Aside.) And lungs, pray Heaven—— Wou'd she might cough 'em out. She has catch'd cold with sitting up so late. Oh damn'd incendiary!

Harry. Could I live out *Methusalah*'s long age, or number years with the old patriarchs, and every day study new themes of virtue, I could not merit half so great a blessing. Brightest of women, fresher than the dew that early sits on roses—— Oh I'm rapt with my own happiness!

Nurse. [*Aside.*] Well, as I'm virtuous this is fine. I see I shall not be able to hold out long. I shall grow bold with him. I hope, Sir, my love deserves this from you. You have entire possession of my heart, and tho' I have broke my faith with all my other suitors, I've kept it firm for you.

Enter Lady Fickle *behind* [Manley.]

Fickle. Sir, Sir! *(Pulls him.)*

Manley. Limb of the Devil—— I hear her, Madam, I hear her.

Fickle. You should not hear 'em, Sir. Pray come back, they are lovers——

Manley. Lovers, dam 'em—— Have a little patience; I'll wait on you immediately.

Fickle. I swear you're uncivil, Sir, thus to disturb 'em. For Heaven's sake come away——

(He turns back, sees her, and starts.)

Manley. Wonder of wonders—— Is there two *Celia*'s, or am I in a dream?

Nurse. Yonder's a light. Let's step in here—— I fear

Sir *Arthur*'s coming—— (*Exeunt* Harry *and* Nurse.)

Fickle. What ailes you, Sir? For Heav'ns sake, why d'ee stare so! D'ee not know me!

Manley. By Heav'n I know not. Are you *Celia*?

Fickle. What strange questions are these? You know I am.

Manley. And is that yonder *Celia* too?

Fickle. Heav'n! What a humour's this? That *Celia*? No, 'tis a lady that lodges here, one that Mr. *Jollyman* courts.

Manley. Young *Jollyman*!

Fickle. Jollyman? Yes. What d'ee wonder at? If this humour hold, you need not counterfeit a madness.

Manley. By Heav'n you are right—— I am mad! Stupid, insensibly mad, and have been so these three hours. 'Sdeath, was ever any thing so strange as this? Sure I've been enchanted. Pray Madam, give me leave to question yee. Where have you been all this night?

Fickle. In my chamber, Sir, expecting you.

Manley. Who told you I was here?

Fickle. Constantia. I met her coming up stairs; and seeing me, she brake into a violent laughter; and asking her the reason, she told me she had put a pleasant trick upon you; and then fell a laughing till she shook agen.

Manley. I'gad I have been trickt, that's the truth on't—— Oh the Devil! Am I thus abus'd?

Fickle. This from a woman that lov'd yee, is very strange—— Who did you expect to find?

Manley. You. She told me you was in that *alcove*, and plac'd me to hear you, where I have stood this half hour in the most insufferable torture——the agony of jealousie and despair——that 'tis impossible to express it.

Fickle. Me! Did you expect me there? And after all my actions to declare my unspotted constancy. Are you still jealous, ingrateful man? Was ever woman so unhappy? *(Weeps.)* Will nothing make you credit me? I swear I am

the most unfortunate of women! How has my soul and heart been fetter'd to you? How have I dreamt of you, and thought a look to any other man was an offence to love; slighted the oaths of gallants, shun'd their presents, despis'd their persons, and refus'd their gifts, all——all for you! And do you still suspect me? Would I could be unconstant! Wou'd I had the power to be so, that I might revenge my self—— Oh misery! Still suspected!
(Weeps.)

Manley. [*Aside.*] If she be false, there's no such thing as truth. I'll credit it no more. Madam, I see my error, and thus low sue for pardon. 'Tis my last tryal, and I will henceforth more adore thy vertues than ere I did suspect 'em. Thou art the soul of truth; so excellently good, Nature is proud of her great work. Nor will I ever be betray'd agen into the gulf of jealousie, but live blest in thy love, the prince of all content, and dye old in thy armes.

Fickle. You will relapse agen.

Manley. Never by Heav'n—— By this kiss I'll never——

Enter Constantia.

Constantia. Come, Sir! The coach——

(Sees Fickle *and starts.)*

Manley. May return agen, if it please, Madam—— Your servant. You see your plot han't took——

(Exit Manley *and* Fickle.*)*

Constantia. This Devil has outwitted me——nay, in this plot, which I thought so securely laid, it was impossible to break it. Her cunning is so prosperous, that I believe Hell designs her for the onely person to wheadle souls with:

I'll try once more——
And if my next plot hit not right, give o're.

(Exit Constantia.*)*

Enter Harry *and* Nurse——Bellamore *after.*

Bellamore. [*Aside.*] Here they are. I have from yonder dore, now too late, resented her treachery—— Dam her! Was mine a heart to play with? Was there not fools enow to feed with hope, but she must flye me? But I'll revenge my self immediately——

Harry. Here's some body coming towards; let's retire, my dear.

Bellamore. Sir! I have a message first——

(*Strikes him.*)

Harry. Such messages are thus to be return'd.

(*Drawes and fights.*)

Nurse. Ah help, help! Murder, murder—— Help, help——

Enter Lady Fickle *with a candle.*

Fickle. What's the matter, Nurse? Oh Heav'ns, my Lord *Bellamore!* And Mr. *Jollyman!* How came you hither at this time of night?

Bellamore. 'Sdeath! What a mistake is this? (*Looking amazedly at* Nurse.) Have I fought for this pippin?

Harry. Zounds! Have I bestow'd all my caresses and courtship to night upon this beldam?

Nurse. Well, Sir; I shall find a time to requite your favours for all your jesting. (*Exit* Nurse.)

Bellamore. Gad, I thought it had been you, Madam——

Harry. And so did I, by Heav'n. I durst have sworn 'twas her voice.

Bellamore. Your thoughts were ill imploy'd, Sir, in a thing that so little concerns you. I hope you have no pretences here.

Harry. How, Sir, no pretences! Has any man?

Fickle. (*Stops his mouth.*) 'Buz! 'Sdeath are you mad! Why this is the person my uncle designs me to marry—

([*Aside*] *to* Harry.)

Bellamore. Nor is this boldness pleasing, Sir.
Fickle. [*Aside to* Bellamore.] My Lord! For Heav'ns sake, what d'ee mean? Will you ruine all? This is the very gentleman my uncle designs for my husband, and if he knows you are his rival, I'm undone.

Enter Manley.

Manley. Come, Madam, whither do you run? By Heav'n I'm so melancholly without you— Ha, my Lord *Bellamore* and *Jollyman!* 'Sdeath! What new intrigue's this?

Fickle. (*Aside.*) O Fate! Is he come too? What a spiteful minute is this? [*Aside to* Manley.] Why, Sir! What d'ee mean? D'ee not see my Lord there; unknown to [me] he supt with Sir *Arthur* to night, and has chosen this minute to accost me. Stare, stare! Counterfeit your self mad, or we are lost. Then leave the rest to me. (*Aloud this.*) Pray, Sir, to bed, to bed. Fye, what mean you by this unseasonable rambling? Sir *Arthur* will be very angry if he knowes it. [*Aside to him.*] Stare! Stare!

Bellamore. Jack *Manley* here at this time of night—— Hark'ee, Madam, what makes him here?

Fickle. Sir *Arthur*, seeing him in his mad fit, brought him hither to night, with intent to administer a potion, which he had made for lunatick persons; and, it seems, they left his chamber dore open, and he is got out. Look! Look how he stares!

Harry. Gad, 'tis a miracle to me to see him thus. I have often heard him say, love is the parent of dullness, and wine of madness. Madam, how came his misfortune?

Fickle. Love, Sir, love. Passion for one *Celia*, a lady i' th' town here, an obdurate, inconstant person I have heard. And it seems she has wheadled him into this condition.

Manley. She shall be drest in flames! Pendants of ice

shall hang at either eare, and cool her as she burnes——
Whiz—— Buz—— Shugh—— Bough—— She's gone,
ha, ha, ha—— Ah *Celia!* How sweet were thy amours?
Dam her! She eates onions——and her blue veines are
all but colour'd lute-strings, in which she hangs her
Cupids, Sir—— Sir, I would have your nose par'd
less—— Adieu, adieu pop—— Let me hear no more
on't——   (*Exit* Manley.)

Bellamore. Had I not seen this, I should have thought
it incredible; a man of the town, and run mad for love.
By heaven 'tis above the common rate of wonders, and
doubtless portends some visible calamity that threatens
the nation.

Harry. [*Aside to her.*] Madam, a word with you.

Fickle. [*Aside to him.*] No whispering, Sir; 'twill cause
him to suspect us. You know my promise. Visit me to
morrow morning, and then by an unexpected choice, I
shall declare the man I think most worthy of my love.

Harry. [*Aside to her.*] Enough, I will not fail. I guess the
night far spent, and in staying longer I may obstruct
your rest. I'll take my leave, Madam. Your faithful
servant—— My Lord, your Lordships devoted. (*Aside.*)
He little thinks what pollicy's in this——   (*Exit* Harry.)

Fickle. Now, am not I extreamly kind, thus to send
him away, that I may have the freer discourse with you?
I hope you will say this is very obliging.

Bellamore. I confess it weighs somewhat more than a
common favour; but, Madam, I am not yet satisfied in
his proceedings. His coming hither so late must be upon
some design; and, how that old woman shou'd interpose,
is to me a mistery——

Fickle. Oh dull, dull man! Why d'ee not see 'twas by
my plot? I order'd the light to be taken away, and laid

her a bait for him, purposely to keep my self free from his troublesome impertinences.

Bellamore. Was that it? By Heav'n, 'twas a witty one.

Fickle. Was that it? What else cou'd it be? I wonder what recompence I shall have for this care in preserving my love intire. I swear, my Lord, you'll be ungrateful.

Bellamore. No, by Heav'n, I'll heap together as much love and strong imagination as wou'd serve forty men, but I'll be out of thy debt. Prithee do not censure till the tryal is made. I'gad, I'm sure I never fail'd yet. But, when shall be the day?

Fickle. To morrow, Sir! A sudden thought has so ordain'd it. Visit me in the morning, where I suppose will be the rest of my amoretto's, and you shall see what sentiments of private passion my heart retains for you.

Bellamore. To morrow! I am rapt with the thought on't! To morrow.
> Call up the Sun! Black Shades away;
> Bid *Phosporus* go fetch the day.

As my friend *Cowley* has it. Madam, I'll be as early as the lark. Nay, by Heav'n, I'm very passionate! You see your beauties pow'r, Madam. And, I'll go and prepare my self——

Fickle. And I'll go and think of my purpose.

Bellamore. Think on to morrow night; a pox on purposes.   (*Exit* Bellamore.)

Fickle. You shall have reason to curse it when you know what purpose I mean.
                    Enter Manley.

Manley. Are they gone, Madam?

Fickle. Both gone, Sir, and full of different hopes. I swear the love I bear you makes me commit strange frailties.

Manley. Oh my dearest; my heav'n of love, how shall I recompence thee? My life's service is nothing, if consider'd. When, when, my Sweet?

Fickle. To morrow, Sir.

Manley. Happy accent!

Fickle. You carry'd the plot so well, in counterfeiting madness, that I were ingrateful, should I not recompence it. Visit me to morrow morning, Sir; and by a happy choice, receive what you have so long sigh'd for.

Manley. Oh transport of delight!
> By Heav'n, I fear I shall not live till then;
> Excess of joy will kill me. Best of women——
> Best! 'Twas too vilely said; thou art so good,
> By Heav'n, thou art a miracle; and I
> The happy man elected to possess it.
> Till the morning comes I will employ myself
> In thinking on thy beauties——and then dy
> In the possession of so sweet a joy. (*Exit.*)

Fickle. Ha, ha, ha, ha——
> That Heav'n shou'd give man so proud a heart,
> And yet so little knowledge—— Silly creature,
> That talkes, and laughes, and kisses oft that hand
> That steales away its reason; as if Nature
> Had play'd the traytor, and seduc'd the sex,
> Without the aid of destiny, or women.
> Ah! With what pleasant ease
> The bird might be ensnar'd—— Set but a wanton look,
> You catch whole covyes. Nay, there is a magick
> Pertaining to our sex, that drawes 'em in,
> Tho' in the Long Vacation. And, by Heav'n,
> I am resolv'd to work my sly deceipts,
> Till my revenge is perfect. Thus far I've done well,
> And I'll persevere in the mistery.
> Wheadle 'em to the snare with cunning plots;
> Then bring it off with quick designing wit,
> And quirks of dubious meaning. Turn and wind
> Like foxes in a storme; to prey on all,
> And yet be thought a saint. Thus Queen I'll sit,
> And Hell shall laugh to see a womans wit.
> (*Exit* Lady Fickle.)

ACT V. Scene [1]. *The Street.*

Enter Zechiel, Toby, Flaile, Jollyman, *Linkboyes, and Musicians playing and singing.*

Zechiel. Hey! Rare boyes! Rare boyes. Done like sons of thunder: true heirs of mirth and jollity. Upon honor we have outdone example in our frollick to night; the town shall talk of us with admiration, and call us children of the night: the night, the happy night. Pox o' your day-debauches, the dull and insipid common-way of frollick. Give me the night to roar in——

Jollyman. 'Sbud, well said; the night or nothing, I say. Give me thy hand; I love thee; thou art a merry wagg. I am pleas'd with't, udsbores I am. I thought I had a son here too, but I see now he's grown a serious rascal; he never seeks good company, such as thine is. No matter, hang pinching, I'll be even with him, and let the world rub.

Zechiel. Banter him, banter him, *Toby.* 'Tis a conceited old scarab, and will yield us excellent sport. Go play upon him a little; exercise thy wit.

Toby. Not I, udshash—— I had like to have had my head broke with his halbert just now, for going about to exercise my wit.

Jollyman. Come, another song, another song, my merry wags, and hang pinching. I'll make a third man—— Hem—— *(Sings.)*

> *And underneath the greenwood tree*
> *This youngster laid her down a,*
> *And there he kist her once or twice,*
> *Sing hey derry, derry, derry, down, a.*

Zechiel. O brave old Signior—— *Flaile*! Sirrah, *Bandog*, what a pox, dreaming? Sing, Sirrah, to entertain the company.

Flaile. I sing, zing, what d'ee mean, Sir! I sing! Lord save us; alas, I cannot sing, Sir. Ich was ne'r so well bred.

Zechiel. Whistle then, you dog; do something for diversion——

Flaile. Whistle! By Coxbones, I cannot whistle neither. Bless us! Must I never go to bed? Bless me from *London*, if this be the trade.

Zechiel. Trade! Thou son of *Assafoetida!* Call a gentlemans divertive custome a trade! Come, all hands, wee'll go pump the rogue.

Jollyman. Ay, ay; a dull drowsy rascal. Pump him, I say——

Enter three Wenches.

Zechiel. A prize! A prize! Petticoats, upon honour; stand there! Come before a man of authority—— And why thus early my Lady of the Lake? Whither are you going?

1st Wench. To Hell! Will you follow me?

Zechiel. Not I, upon honour. There I'll leave you——

Toby. (*To 2nd* Wench.) By your favour, Madam, what's a clock?

2nd Wench. I am sorry the pawning your watch, Sir, forces you to ask so necessary a question——

Toby. Now will this damn'd bulking quean be too witty for me; o' my conscience, if I shall ask her any more questions! Udshash! I'll ee'n proceed to the business and say nothing.

(Jollyman *goes to the other, and she slights him.*)

3rd Wench. Fy, fy, Sir! An old man and talk thus!

Jollyman. An old man! 'Sbud, you'r a whore. An old man! Call a gentleman, in the midst of a night debauch old—— Hem, hem—— Sound lungs and heart-whole—— Old, quoth a!

Zechiel. Come, upon honour, ye shall all to the tavern with us, and we'll compleat the nights debauch with credit. But first a song. I know you have your parts in the last new verses, made of the nights ramble. 'Tis a part of your function; a new song is as necessary for a town woman, as a sute of knots, or a new gown—— Hey! Strike up there!

Song.

Happy the man that takes delight
In banquetting the sences;
That drinks all day, and then at night
The height of joy commences.
With bottles arm'd, we stand our ground,
Full bumpers crown our blisses;
They rore and sing the streets around,
In serenading misses.

Chorus. *With bottles arm'd, &c.*

Pleasures thus free and unconfin'd,
No drowzy crime reproaches;
No Heav'n to a frollick mind,
No pleasure like debauches.

Whilst rambling thus, new joyes we reap,
In charmes of love and drinking, 90
Insipid fops lye drown'd in sleep,
And the cuckold he lies thinking.

Chorus. *Whil'st rambling, &c.*

Zechiel. Rarely done of all hands. Come, now let's to the tavern; I am resolv'd to make a night on't. 95
Jollyman. Well said, agen, Boy. To th' tavern! To th' tavern—— Hah—— Merry rascal—— Hang pinching. 'Sbud, thou'rt a brave fellow——
Toby. Come my little pignies; you and I will go and be drunk together. Hey—— You shall see me performe 100 rare exploits, i'faith. Nay, Gad, now my hands in, I shall pepper you with wit. I feel it growing in my head like a bunch of parsenips.
Zechiel. Agen! Igad, pinch him agen; but come, of this at the tavern; we lose time. Strike up there— Sing. 105
Whilst rambling— (*Exeunt singing.*)
Enter Lady Fickle *in mans cloaths, and* Silvia;
Dorrel *at a distance.*
Fickle. So, is all fit? Prithee how do I look? May I pass for a bully of the first rate amongst dablers in the mys- 110 tery? How fit my cloaths?
Silvia. Decently I swear, and well become you; you have as masculine an air as any man. I mean any man that has no more beard than you.
Dorrel. (Aside.) This gives an end to my suspition; the 115 plot's unravel'd, and my late doubts have now their period.
Fickle. Away then, and be sure you miss not a tittle in the charge I've given you, but with a feign'd sigh, and a tear or two, tell *Sir Arthur* I went away unknown to you, 120

and supposing it to be discontent, relating to his designs
of marriage. Do this handsomly, and I'll come in person,
and prosecute the rest. This habit will, I am sure, disguise me, and I intend to invite my self to another banquet of wit with the suitors, ere I have done with 'em.
Away—— A day or two's time will make all quiet, and I
shall be in readiness for as many more.

Silvia. Madam, I have my lesson perfectly, and am so
much your creature, as not to dispute your commands.

(*Exit* Silvia.)

Fickle. Now am I in my opinion a second *Machiavil*.
My wit has finish'd works as strong and great as *Hercules*
12 labours! Oh I cou'd hug my self for my inventions,
they are so prosperous; as if Fate meant to make my wit
a miracle for men to wonder at. To betray in me's a virtue, being first betray'd, the thought of which does like
an eating canker prey on my heart and vitals. Therefore, sweet Revenge,

> Thou art my darling. Thus I'll blind their eyes;
> 'Tis on the neck of wit Revenge must rise.——
>
> (*Exit.*)

Enter Dorrel.

Dorrel. Can this be true! Oh Heav'ns, what have I
heard! Is't possible she shou'd be thus affected to him
that basely so deserted her? If so I am a Devil, and my
jealousie the sin of all corruption—— I'll redeem it,
watch all her actions, and discover all, lest she shou'd
lose her self in her revenge.

> 'Twas well I overheard her—— Happy day!
> That does all former fears with bliss repay.
>
> (*Exit* Dorrel.)

Scene 2. *The street. A tavern bush hung out.*
Enter Bellamore, Zechiel, Toby, Jollyman,
Three Wenches, and Musitians, drinking.

Zechiel. 'Twas well, my Lord, your valor interpos'd betwixt me and the danger; by Heav'n I had been stockado'd else.

Bellamore. I am glad, Sir, Fate guided me that way, and made me capable of doing you so good an office. Pray how came your quarrel?

Zechiel. Why one of the rascals would needs take the wall of me, nay, tho' I told him in *French* I was drunk, and had a whore with me. Was ever such an incivility? But I think I am reveng'd, for if I may believe my eye, my last full pass pierc'd his *diaphragma*. I'm sure I kill'd him.

Jollyman. How, kill'd him! Not so, I hope, my merry wag, not so.

Zechiel. Not so! Upon honour I am sure it is so. Whoo—— Pox, 'tis accounted nothing now in Termtime. The killing a man's no more lookt on in a nights debauch, than getting a clap in a mornings ramble. The town's full, the town's full.

Toby. I hope the consequences are no worse than he makes 'em; but, udshash—— My heart goes a-pit-to-pat.

Bellamore. [*Aside.*] Tho' I hate this fellows impertinence, yet for diversion sake I'll make one in the debauch to night. (*To his footman.*) Sirrah, bid the coach go home; tell *Raines* I have no occasion for him to night.

Zechiel. Come, musick, strike up there. Damme you sleepy dogs. Come, we'll have a song and a dance, hey—— Drawer.

Enter Drawer.

Drawer. Will you not be pleas'd to take a private room, Sir?

Zechiel. A private pox, Sir. (*Strikes him.*) What, I warrant you take us now for some of your serious brood of aldermen, d'ee Sirrah? But such another word, and I shall make a private room in your guts for this engine here.

Toby. Sirrah, you shall be hufft and cufft, and flip'd and kick'd, Sirrah, if you talk of private rooms— Now am I as valiant as a Hector; methinks I cou'd beat this drawer into a wicker bottle.

Zechiel. Sirrah, as a reprieve for life, bring out the butt; we'll have the triumph of *Bacchus* to night, my Lord. You shall be spectator now of one of my frolicks. I invented it in *Paris,* for the benefit of all lovers of the grape, and cherishers of *Burgundy,* and I hope you'll speak it a facetious one; 'tis call'd a triumph to *Bacchus,* my Lord.

Bellamore. A good theme, Sir. (*Aside.*) Worthy of your wits invention; no doubt a great piece of ingenuity.

Zechiel. (*To three* Wenches.) Come my witty devottees of *Venus,* you must be assistant here. Hey—— Drawer, where are you Sirrah?
    Enter drawers with an empty butt.
Come hither, *Toby;* thou shalt personate God *Bacchus*—— Give him a wreath there——and a bumper—— Come, up, up, advance into the throne—— (*Toby gets on the butt.*) So, now Ladies kneel, and pay obedience to your emperor—— My Lord, I must beg your Lordship to bear part in the ceremony—— There, on that side, my Lord. Drawer, give every one a glass. Flourish musick and drink! Hey!   (*Flourish; all drink.*)

Toby. How do I present it, ha! Methinks it becomes me very well.

Zechiel. Look big, look a little bigger; you know the effigie.

Jollyman. By the Lord *Harry*, I'll kiss thee for this, my darling of the dark. Well, I am resolv'd to disinherit my son, and adopt thee—— Hang pinching, I'll do't Boy, and let the world rub.

Zechiel. Come, now to the song——and let all parts be ready for the *Chorus*.

Song.

Bacchus, thou mighty power divine,
Great God of mirth, and sprightly wine,
Behold us here that kneeling show
    The duty that we owe——
We through thy influence rejoyce,
And thus with free and chearful voyce
    The fame and praises sing
Of Bacchus, *our great God and King.*

Chorus. *'Tis wine, 'tis wine, that still controuls,*

And fame and love must both strike sail;
There lies such vigor in full bowls,
The fate of princes can't prevail.
The wreaths of great heroes his altar shall crown,
Whil'st the grave and the prudent bow down.

When beauty darts a smiling beam,
Our souls are [slain] by loves extreme;
But one brisk glass takes care away,
    And yields us back the prey.
No fate of love or piercing dart
Can wound when wine surrounds the heart;
    Still guarding it from care,
It baffles Fate, and slights the fair.

Chorus. *'Tis wine, 'tis wine, &c.*   *(Dance.)*

Jollyman. Spark, let me embrace thee. 'Udsbores, thou art the mirror of our age, and hast the best principles of *English* gallantry I ever saw—— Ah would I were but 5-and-20 for thy sake—— But come—— Hang pinching—— 'Tis well it's no worse, as my friend *Hearty* sayes.

Zechiel. What think you my Lord? Is it not modish? By Heav'n 'tis new, that's one good property, and I believe 'twill take very well.

Bellamore. Sir, if you will take my opinion in this business, I think it an excellent invention, and were I you, I wou'd have books printed, that the world may not be ignorant. I'gad you have this encouragement: the press has been troubled with matters of less consequence.

Toby. [*To* Wenches.] I tell you I have 200£. a year. I've my lands free and unmorgag'd, and am resolv'd to keep a miss, according to the mode; therefore speak now, or for ever hold your peace.

1st Wench. But which of us would you have, Sir?

Toby. Either of you—— Udshash I'm a right countrey squire; any thing will serve my turn, if the properties be not wanting. What's your price?

1st Wench. Why in truth, Sir, I have had 40 *s.* a week, but in kindness to a man of your complexion, I'll abate a crown.

Toby. My complexion! Ah wheadling queen——

Jollyman. Come Sirrah, Drawer fill each his glass. Hey—— Let the world rub, and let's have t'other song.

Enter Flaile.

Flaile. Zong, quoth a—— Lord zave us, a zong——
Pray, pray, good folks—— Pray—— Oh, oh——

Zechiel. How now *Bandog,* what makes you howl thus? Ha!

Flaile. Howl! By Coxnowns, you'll howl too, if you stay longer; y'have kill'd a mon yonder, he that you quarrel'd with about your crack there. 'Slid she have a good mind to crack her for't; and God save his soul, they think he's dead. The Constable and a regiment of beggars, I mean bilbo's, are searching for you, and just coming up the street. Uds diggers, up you go, if they can catch ye. Oh that ever the ancient family of the *Tilburies* should come to such disgrace!

2nd Wench. Nay then, this is no time for merchandizing. (*Exeunt* Wenches.)

Zechiel. Malicious fortune! Heav'n what shall I do! If I am taken, I shall certainly be hang'd.

Bellamore. Pox, not for killing a man in Term-time, Sir; you know the town's full.

Jollyman. Hang'd! Heav'n defend, my merry wag, is't come to that? Hang'd! Gentlemen your servant. I've a little earnest business——

Bellamore. Nay, Sir, leave not your friends in adversity; for my part I'm resolv'd to stick to't if we are hang'd.

Toby. If we are hang'd, quoth a? Ah Lord! The very word has put me into an ague.

Bellamore. If we do miscarry, Sir—— Why let the world rub, as you say.

Toby. Ay, ay, you need not fear; you are a Lord. You'll come off well enough; 'tis we shall stretch for't. Udshash nothing vexes me, but that I cannot stay to perform my bargain with Mrs. *Juniper* there. (*A noise without.*) Hark, they come; the Devil take the hindmost.

(*Runs into the tavern.*)

Zechiel. And so say I. [*Exit.*]

Bellamore. Dam 'em! Are they gone? What scarabs are these, to trust a tavern security beyond a sword. [*To* Flaile.] What, Sirrah, are you creeping away too? Turn back and help to defend, you dog, or——

(*Noise within, follow, follow.*)

Flaile. O Lord, Sir! I defend, Sir!

Bellamore. Fight, Sirrah, and fight valiantly too, or by this steel——

Flaile. Well, Sir, I will, I will; oh what will become of me!

Jollyman. Come my Lord, have at 'em, since it must be so. Here's old Madge, has not seen sun these 20 years, shall be scowr'd in some of their guts, rather than I'll be taken. Udsbores, I have been valiant in my time.

Bellamore. [*Aside.*] I must quickly dispatch, for fear of a disappointment with my *Corinna*— [*Exit.*]

Enter Constable *and Watch.*

Constable. Oh here they are. Caitiffs, rogues, murderers! Down, down with 'em, my men o' midnight; fall on in the Kings name, fall on——

(*They fight;* Constable *and Watch are beaten off.*)

Enter Toby.

Toby. No hole; ne'r a corner to creep into? This is the worst contriv'd house I ever saw. Hang'd did he say? Marry, Heav'n defend, I am too raw a bully to venture hanging yet. Oh, well remember'd, ifaith—— Here's the butt, the throne of *Bacchus,* as *Zechiel* calls it; this will be a rare place to secure my self in. (*Gets into the butt.*) The Devil's in 'em if they search here. I'll stay till the cry is over, and then home to my lodging. I love a debauch, till it comes to fighting; but then, methinks, it grows troublesom—— Hark, here they come; now close like a coney in a burrow.

Re-enter Constable *and* Watch.

Constable. Why, Neighbors, we were mistaken; these were none of those that hurt the man. I am told 'twas two brothers, and that they were dog'd to this tavern. Come, come——they must be here still. Let's in and see.

(*Exeunt.*)

Enter Zechiel *above in a balcony.*

Zechiel. Was ever poor night-walker in such distress? What shall I do? They are searching within, and the damn'd rogues are so curious in the discovery, that they miss not an augur-hole. I found this ladder of ropes upon a shelf, but dare not venture down yet, for fear some prying rascal shall snap me between Earth and Heav'n. 'Sdeath, I'll creep into this bush; it may be this may secure me. *(Gets upon the tavern bush.)* Hah! Upon honour I grow chearful; this is so modish a device, that I've great hopes of good success.

Toby. They're all gone in, and now I'm in a tub of troubles about vent'ring out. If some of 'em should watch at the gate, I shou'd be snapt; if snapt, hang'd. Udshash, my stomach cannot relish that word. Yet I'll couch a little longer, and see what will come on't.

Enter Tilbury, *drunk, with a torch.*

Zechiel. Here comes a man with a light. Now sit close——

Tilbury. A son of a whore to question a man of 1500£. a year, and dispute the family of the *Tilburies*. By *St. Jago*, he deserves to be mortifi'd. Constable—— What's a Constable, to a man of worship! A man of drunken reeling worship! A worm! A scarab! 'Tis fit he should be carbonado'd. Let's see, where am I? What tavern's this? Oh 'tis the *Rose*. I'll take another dose of sack here, and then——home. Ho—— Within there, Drawer, gives a cup o' sack here——

Zechiel. Ah Lord! 'Tis my father, and drunk as a wheel-barrow. I shall be found out, for he holds his torch so high, that any one that comes by must needs see me. *(Takes orange-peals out of his pocket, and throws at* Tilbury.)

Tilbury. Why, rascals! Poltroons! Sons of popinjayes, what d'ee mean, hah! Dare you affront a man of quality—— I mean a man of countrey quality—— Hah, Puppies, by *St. Jago* I'll break all the windows—— I'll teach you to be civil. Now, now cannot I find e'r a stone.

This is the great enormance of this city——here's 240
wenches in abundance, but not a stone to throw at a
dog. No matter—— I'll set fire on your bush, 'tis all one.
I'll mortifie your owls nest, by *St. Jago.*
(Offers to burn the bush.)
 Zechiel. Oh! I shall be burnt! Why, Father, Father, I'm 245
here! I'm here! Your son! Your hopeful son—— Oh
Lord, if I cry out too, I shall be hang'd. What shall I do?
Fire! Fire! Fire!
Enter the Constable *and Watch.*
 Constable. How now! What's here, one going to fire the 250
house? Away, away with him to the lodge; here's fine
work indeed! Come, bring him away. Stay some of you
here and watch; the rest must be hereabouts.
(Exit Constable *with* Tilbury.*)*
 1st Watch. But is't possible, Neighbours, this house 255
should be haunted, and yet folks live in't?
 2nd Watch. Possible? As sure as you are there, Neighbours. They say the Devil appear'd to 'em every night in the likeness of a hog.
 1st Watch. Lord bless us, Sirs! A hog! But see what the 260
Devil can do.
 2nd Watch. Set down the lanthorn, *Patch,* and come let's sit down on this butt. I'll tell you the story.
 3rd Watch. Ay come, silence ho! Let's hear neighbour
Cobble. *(They sit.)* 265
 2nd Watch. Why look you, Sirs, one winter-night, the maid here sitting up late in the kitchen, and busie about her houshold affairs, who should come in at the window but this hog——
 Omnes. So! 270
 2nd Watch. And you must know the Devil's a cunning hog, when occasion serves, kept such——such a grunting and shuffling, and jumping, that the poor wench was even out of her wits; she wou'd have pray'd but her

memory being very short, and her prayer-book out of the way, she could not. In short, Sir, this hog, or this Devil, or this Devil of a hog, for'ts all——having thrown down several pewter dishes, and swallow'd a whole porridge-pot of brewis——takes me his way into the cellar——there makes such a wrack among the butts and bottles, such havock among the glasses——

(Toby *puts out the candle in the lanthorn.*)
How now, who puts out the candle there?
1st Watch. Not I.
2nd Watch. Nor I.
Toby. (*Grunts like a hog.*) Ugh! Ugh! Ugh!——
Omnes. Oh it comes! It comes! The Devil, the Devil—— (*Exeunt.*)
Toby. Udshash! This ugh, ugh was a rare invention. (Toby *comes out.*) I think I have outwitted the rogues. Now give me a man that can help a danger at a pinch; for tho' I say it, *Machiavil* was an ass to me at a nights intrigue. But I'll away, for fear of insurrections—— (*Exit.*)
Zechiel. That was *Toby's* voice; I believe he's gone. What the Devil was't scar'd the watchmen so? No matter now, the coast is clear—— I'll venture down—— so—— (*Gets down the ladder.*)
Upon honour, I have been severely frighted to night. But the uncertain fate of a night-walker seldom meets better success. I have escap'd two eminent dangers, burning and hanging, the thought of which has made me as dull as a rifl'd cully.

> *Thus with the brawny crew of suburb roches,*
> *We swim the brackish ocean of deboches,*
> *Without the sense of honour or reproaches.*

(*Exit.*)

Act V Scene 3

Scene 3. [Sir Arthur Oldlove's *lodging*.]
Enter Sir Arthur, Silvia, Arbella, Constantia.

Sir Arthur. Come, come, I say, there's a trick in't, some cunning scurvy lewd design, I know it; have I not foster'd her with tenderness? And before she could write woman, bred her carefully! What cause has she then to desert my house? Answer me that, what cause?

Silvia. Only fear, Sir, you should match her against her will. Heav'n knows I know no other cause.

Sir Arthur. No, no, there must be more in't. 'Twas your pleasure, Mistriss, often to quarrel with her; it caus'd your envy to see her so belov'd, hah. But bring her agen, and quickly too, or see my face no more. Out of my doors, by *Jacobs* pantible——a relique of renown'd memory. Thou art no more my daughter, unless my neece return.

Arbella. Indeed, *Sir Arthur,* you are a little too severe in this, for I am confident Madam *Constantia* knows nothing of her going. She always kept her intrigues from her knowledge, and consequently this, being, it seems, of more importance than any of the rest; what her design is Heav'n knows, but a day or two's time will doubtless discover all.

Sir Arthur. Madam *Arbella,* you are one I respect; your father *Sir Andrew Swipplethrop* is my intimate good friend, a man I love and honour, and by *St. Augustines* night-cap—— Madam *Arbella,* you are welcome to my house, but seek not to defend an ill argument. I say once more there's a trick in't, and give me leave, Madam, I will persevere in my justice. Therefore, Minion, look to't.

Enter Dorrel.

Dorrel. Sir, there is three gentlemen below, suitors to Madam *Fickle,* that desire admittance.

Sir Arthur. Conduct 'em up; I hope here's some discovery.

Enter Bellamore, Manley *and* Harry.

Bellamore. [*To* Manley.] Though I was ignorant, Sir, you were my rival, I thought I had known you for a gentleman, one that wou'd not have carry'd a design under the disguise of counterfeit madness; but assure your self, Sir, such an injury shall require satisfaction.

Manley. And have it, my Lord, when you dare demand it. All falshood I deny; nor can I condemn my self with carrying on a love intrigue with policy.

Harry. 'Sdeath! I see I am baffled at last. These are two of her suitors——I, it seems, the third. But I hope her choice will dissipate all doubts——

Sir Arthur. My Lord and gentlemen, your humble servant. May I request to know what bus'ness brings you hither so early?

Bellamore. I suppose my business is not unknown. I come, *Sir Arthur,* to pay my devotion to the charming *Corinna.*

Harry. And I mine to the glorious *Cleio.*

Manley. And I the particular tender of my heart to the adorable *Celia.*

Sir Arthur. Corinna! Cleio! Celia! They are names of antiquity, I confess— But for Heav'ns sake express your selves more largely, Gentlemen. I know none of the persons.

Arbella. [*Aside.*] Now the plot begins to be discover'd; now we shall know all.

Constantia. [*To* Arbella.] Prithee do but observe the alteration of countenances; oh this was a subtle Devil!

Bellamore. Your neece, *Sir Arthur,* the rich widow—— I have had the honour to be long interest'd in her favour, and she commanded me to wait on her this morning, and promis'd publickly to make choice of me.

Manley. By Heav'n, she promis'd to make choice of me.

Harry. Nay gad, she promis'd to make choice of me.

Bellamore. Was ever such insufferable impertinence? *Sir Arthur,* I protest, by my honour, all I say is true; and by virtue of her premeditated choice and election, I am the man.

Manley. Death! What impudence is this? I say, by virtue of her choice I am the man.

Harry. Hell and Furies! I say I am the man.

Sir Arthur. Hey day! What, are all of ye the men? By the threshold of *Mahomet's* temple, this is very fine! Has she a tripartite husband, a threefold father of children? But hark ye, Gentlemen, let us come nearer to the business; for as far as I can perceive, you have mistook the house. Here are no *Cleio's*, nor *Celia's*, nor *Corinna's* under my roof, I can assure ye. 'Tis true, I had a neece, a widow, and such a fortune as you describe, who is this day gone, I think, to seek her fortune. Her name is *Fickle*. Sure she cannot be the person you seek after?

Bellamore. 'Tis so! We are all most finely gull'd, I find it! Oh! 'Sdeath, now could I eat my flesh for madness, dull blockhead, not to perceive her wheadling.

Manley. Fickle is her name; dam her, she has been fickle enough I see. Oh Hell! Hell! Were ever hopes so frustrated? 'Tis plain now she has entertain'd us all with equal caresses, and by taking a several name has thus long kept us ignorant!

Harry. Sure there must be some plot in this, *Sir Arthur.* Pray be particular in the narration; is she certainly gone, Sir?

Sir Arthur. Why, Sir, upon my honour, and the honour of our family, I protest, Sir. She is certainly gone, Sir.

Harry. The Devil go with her, Sir. Oh confusion seize

her; after all my hopes, and fears, and doubts, am I thus abus'd?

Arbella. Oh Heav'n! Was it possible your Lordship shou'd be so deceiv'd? Nay, by a person that shou'd ha' been proud of the honour she receiv'd in the amours of a man of quality, who was unsensible of any beauty but the charms of *Corinna*. Nothing cou'd penetrate but the eyes of *Corinna!* Nor nothing appear attractive, but the person and mein of *Corinna!*

Constantia. I protest, Sir, I pity you. Heav'n knows how constant you have been——how ador'd *Celia*, dreamt of *Celia*, sigh'd for *Celia!* Mourn'd out the tedious night in meditations, and visited the light with thoughts of *Celia!* And now to have so strange a metamorphosis, an ungrateful *Fickle* instead of a constant *Celia*, by Heav'n 'tis great tyranny in fortune.

Manley. Well, Madam, well!

Enter Lady Fickle [*disguised*].

Fickle. Sir Arthur, your servant. Permit a stranger somewhat interest'd in your present affair, the liberty of speaking a word or two.

Sir Arthur. Sir, any man that wears the presence of Gent. has liberty to express himself here.

Fickle. Then briefly and boldly thus—— My Lord and Gentlemen, I know you better than you imagine; you are all pretenders to my *Lady Fickle,* a person to whom my private inclinations have been long devoted. And having last night the honour of kissing her hand, she in tears told me, she had deserted *Sir Arthur's* house, only to be rid of your troublesom impertinences; she also did me the favour to desire me to give you this assurance: that she hated you all three, and her former proceedings with you have been only to divert herself with your ceremonious addresses.

Bellamore. Sure 'tis impossible a woman shou'd be such a devil? Dare you prove this?

Manley. Dam him, this is the impudentst young Hector I ever met with.

Harry. Hark ye, dare you fight, Sir?

Fickle. Yes, Sir, with you if you dare, Sir! Fight! Blood of the heroes, d'ee question it? There's my glove. I'll fight you all three; appoint your place and time.

Manley. The soul of a gyant by Heav'n, a very Devil *in decimo sexto.*

Fickle. I scorn to win a lady of her perfections, with the loss but of a drop of blood. A river full I say, my veins drawn dry, and on the active gore fierce atoms darting to win my love through streams of death and horror. I'll bathe my lips in gore, kiss bleeding wounds, cleave helmets, stand a breach, and dare a cannon, divide a heart in two, hah! Hah!—— 'Tis done. Soul of *Belona,* I'll exhaust a flood, turn Earth to chaos, oceans into blood. Consume your timorous cringing amorists, that would possess their Heav'n, but dare not bleed for't. Blood is my province; therefore with you all am I resolv'd to fight. A single man's too poor for my revenge. All, all I say, and all at once; 'tis base else.

Bellamore. This is the daringst young rogue I ever saw; I must dash his hopes. Hark'ee, young huffing Sir, no more of this here; follow me, you shall find one of us sufficient to cut your throat.

Fickle. All or none, by Heav'n. I will not fight else.

Dorrel. [*Aside.*] Now is the time, and this mysterious plot shall be no longer hid.—— Fie, fie my Lord! I thought your Lordship cherish'd too much honour ever to draw your sword against a woman!

Omnes. A woman!

Dorrel. Look on her well, *Sir Arthur.* My Lord and

Gentlemen, d'ee not know her? Nay, Madam, blush not; all must out. You must be discover'd. This is the very person you are speaking of, my *Lady Fickle!* Your *Cleio* Sir! Your *Celia!* And your *Corinna*, my Lord!

Sir Arthur. By *Pharoah*, 'tis the same; I know her now. Why how now, Neece!

Fickle. Discover'd! And i' th' end of all my plots. What devil told this fellow my designs? Well, Uncle, 'tis I.

Bellamore. What, in your masquerading habit, Madam? If I may presume, what intrigue to night are you designing for?

Fickle. 'Tis frustrated, my Lord; you might have known else.

Manley. Ungrateful creature! Was I so desertless? Was my hearts passion so far wanting merit, to deserve this return?

Bellamore. Was I not worthy of your favor?

Harry. And was my heart too base to be your slave?

Fickle. By Heav'n, no. All your deserts are boundless, and I am far unworthy your addresses; and since I am discover'd, you shall know why I have us'd you thus. I lov'd, and was betray'd, and for this cause swore a revenge on all that should love me. To make it plainer to ye, I am marry'd. My husband, fir'd with jealousie, forsook me to spend his time in travel; since, I have liv'd a widow in opinion, and wheadled many suitors, but lov'd none.

Sir Arthur. Why then your husband lives!

Fickle. I know not, Sir; I have not seen him since.

Dorrel. Yes, Sir, he lives, and lives to bless the hour he took up this disguise.—— Oh my sweet, consider humane frailty, and forgive my crime of too much jealousie. *(Pulls off his beard.)*

Fickle. My dear *Friendlove!* Can this be true? Am I then once more blest with thy caresses?

Sir Arthur. Hey, *Dorrel* metamorphiz'd to Mr. *Friendlove!* By *Melchizedech,* this is strange!
Bellamore. Marry'd! Gad I have spent my time very finely well! If ever I trust a widow agen, may I wear horns like *Acteon,* and seek for a patrimony *in terra incognita.*
Dorrel. I swear I have been cruel to thy virtue, but my whole life shall sue to make amends. And my noble Lord, and you Gentlemen, whatever presents on this ladies behalf have been receiv'd, shall be return'd with ample satisfaction. And since espousing her perfections, I am bound to have a particular interest in her actions, if any one here holds himself wrong'd, my person shall give him the acknowledgment he demands, and my sword the satisfaction of a gentleman.
Bellamore. Sir, I hope you think I dare fight, and refuse not through fear, but since I see she had some reason for what she did, my particular resentments are not worth a quarrel. (*To* Arbella.) My thoughts now bowing down to this shrine of beauty.
Manley. (*To* Constantia.) And mine to this. Madam! Can you forgive——
Arbella. 'Twere an excellent revenge to use you as my Lady *Fickle* did; I swear, my Lord, you have deserv'd it.
Bellamore. We have all failings, Madam, you must pardon.
Sir Arthur. I like this well. I like this well; win her and wear her. Mr. *Manley,* I like your person and estate well. By King *Pharoah* I am very merry; come, we'll have a dance.

Enter Constable *and Watch with* Jollyman,
Tilbury, Zechiel, Toby.

How now, what's here? Mr. *Jollyman,* and my old friend *Tilbury* in durance. How came this, Friend, hah?
Constable. An't please your worship, these are the gen-

tlemen that wounded the man last night, and they got from us once, but we catcht um again; and we took this other firing a house.

Sir Arthur. Well, leave 'em with me. I'll be bail for their appearance to morrow. I am resolv'd nothing shall hinder my mirth to day. Mr. *Tilbury* and Mr. *Jollyman,* I have heard of all your frollicks last night, both yours and your sons. Let it be so no more. For the present all shall be well. But there is no hopes of my daughter now; she's bestow'd.

Jollyman. Since she's bestow'd, God give her joy. I'll cherish my self with a merry song and a fiddle, and hang pinching, let the world rub.

Tilbury. My sons unmarry'd, and the family of the *Tilburies* thus disgrac'd—— By *St. Jago,* I'll take post and away for *Salisbury* immediately.

Toby. And so will I. Udshash, if these disasters belong to men of parts, as yee call 'em, give me a country life; for though there's less wit, there's more security.

Zechiel. Infamous, impertinent! Canst thou repugne the pleasures of a debauchee, through the apprehension of a walking nightrap, and a guilded truncheon, with the City Armes on't—— Upon honour thou art a libel to my fame, and unworthy to break a glass in my society.

Toby. Udshash, I might ha' bin hang'd in your society for all that, but that Fortune was my friend, and reserv'd me for the future benefit of my family.

Zechiel. Hang'd! A man of parts! An honest nightwalker hang'd! Intollerable impudence! No Sir, assure your self no such fate attends us Brothers of the Bottles. A stockado, a gentile thrust through the lungs or so, might have happen'd, but no hanging, Brother Bullfinch, no hanging.

Toby. Come, come, a word to the wise is sufficient. I

have resolv'd a reformation; I rellish not your stockado's not I, nor is a gentile thrust through the lungs, as you terme it, so agreeable with my nature to persevere. In brief, Sir, I am converted; I will into the country immediately.

Sir Arthur. Come, come, embrace and be friends. I am in a good humour, and by *Melchizedech,* strife shall be a stranger to my house to day. So, so; all, all well—— And though you are not partners in this wedding, you shall be merry at it, and let the world rub, as my old friend here sayes.—— Go call in the fidlers there—— (*Dance.*)

Dorrel. Come, my dear sweet, and let us loose our selves in loves embraces. This is a happy day.

Fickle. Through crooked paths, dark plots, and ways obscure,
Revenge still roves, to make its action sure.
I have been false to night, and purchast hate,
But Ladies, on your smiles depends my fate;
Let me then gain one happy glance from you,
And th' *Witty False One* shall be ever true.

(*Exeunt Omnes.*)

Epilogue.
And now to you gallants that smiling sit,
And with insipid votes infest the pit,
Because the play was by a stranger writ;
The poet sayes, he knowes his merit's small,
And trembles at the thought of a caball;
But since a bully in his play I was,
I am resolv'd a champion in his cause:
Therefore let him that boasts of too much strength,
Appoint the place, and send his rapiers length.
A barb'rous critick shall not walk the street,
Nor from this moment dare to censure wit;
By Heav'n I'll pepper you if once we meet.
You smile, and perhaps doubt my want of skill,
But I'll revenge it, blood and death I will.
I must confess there is a safer way,
You may walk safely if you'll like the play;
But else, if you your censures raise anew,
Fate sends his darts abroad; blood must ensue.

Let him that on that basis honour builds, 20
Meet me to morrow in Lambs-Conduit-*Fields;*
There he shall find a woman now turn'd bully,
Has power to turn a critick to a cully.

FINIS.

NOTES TO
MADAM FICKLE

Epistle dedicatory.

3. Duke of Ormond: James Butler, twelfth Earl and first Duke of Ormonde (1610-1688), one of D'Urfey's early patrons. Both *Madam Fickle* and *A Fond Husband* are dedicated to him.

29. young author: D'Urfey was approximately twenty-three at the time. This was his first comedy.

35-36. imperfection of my speech: D'Urfey stuttered and was, in 1691, the butt of an anonymous lampoon, *Wit for Money; Or, Poet Stutter*.

Dramatis Personae.

5. Antiquary: collector and studier of antiquities. Sir Arthur is drawn principally from the character of Veterano in Marmion's *Antiquary* (1635).

22. Maskers: Their role is not indicated in the text itself; presumably they would participate as supernumeraries in Act V, Scene 2.

Prologue.

5. trader of the town: prostitute.

8. cits: citizens, as opposed to gentlemen. A term of contempt.

9. eighteen-pence: probably the minimum admission to the gallery seats.

16. cabal: clique, coterie.

18. nice: overly meticulous.

24. sifting: scrutinizing, examining closely.

27. colledges have fail'd: one of D'Urfey's many derogatory comments on the universities.

33. swinging clap: a serious case of gonorrhea.

39. friends that sit above: those in the boxes, notably King Charles and his entourage.

40. indifferent censures: impartial judgments.

41. *squibs and crackers*: fireworks, with a possible pun on witty remarks and jests.

Act I. Scene 1.

4. Scene 1: *sic*, though the act is in a single scene.
22. conning: studying, learning.
25. Precisian: Puritan.
28. Speed the plough: God-speed; Good luck to you.
33. *cum privilegio*: with impunity.
52-53. Hang pinching: Down with care.
58. Let the world rub: Let things go as they may.
59. Nay: used here, as frequently, in an affirmative sense.
60. upon design: *i.e.*, for a love intrigue.
62. gone through stitch: done it perfectly.
64. SONG: The song is by D'Urfey and was set to music by Matthew Lock. It is found also in *Catch That Catch Can* (London, 1685), No. 64.
77. *cherishes*: cheers, gladdens.
79. rare woman: possibly the girl who sang the song.
80. wheedle: (also wheadle) to flatter, especially in a love intrigue.
107. St. *Jago*: St. Jacob.
113. let me go: Evidently Jollyman is restraining him.
119. *Chancery*: the court of the Lord Chancellor.
121. fortunes: women of fortune, heiresses.
124. *Temple*: law school.
125. another-ghess: a different sort, a better.
128. brave: excellent, admirable.
129. Hock: Hochheimer, a German wine.
130. *Longs*: a famous tavern much frequented by fashionable gentlemen.
132. Canary: a light sweet wine from the Canary Islands.
137. *Piazza*'s: the Piazza of Covent Garden.
143-44. Udshash: a common oath, probably corrupted from "by God's eyelash."
147. meer: utter.
165. closely: secretly.
166. *Jeroboam*: See 1 Kings 11:26ff.
166. fit: retaliate, match wits with.
208. swinge: beat, thrash; pronounced to rhyme with "hinge."
224. nearly: privately, intimately.
226. horns: Cuckolds were fancifully thought to sprout horns. The allusion is common in Restoration comedy.
242. Common Council: city council.
245. *Flaile*: His name suggests a tall, ungainly person.
248. Beangarson: possibly Zechiel's rendering of *bien garçon*.
251. *Bandog*: Zechiel's nickname for Flaile is a common contemptuous epithet; literally, a bound mad dog.
275. bumpers: toasts. Cf. *A Fond Husband*, I, 489.
276. custard-cap: possibly should read "custard cup." Flaile is identified as Zechiel's cook at line 380 below.
282. *Ploughshare*: common name for a rustic type.

Notes to *Madam Fickle*

283. Bully: used here in an affectionate sense, but subsequently as the term for a bravo, a "hector," a "bully rock."

290. Vaults: performs some sort of leap to prove his agility.

291. washing-block: washboard. The point of the insult is unclear, though it obviously alludes to the staging of Zechiel's leap.

299-300. off o' th' hooks: not himself.

301-2. Sine ... Phoebus: literally, "There is no Apollo (enlightenment) without some madness." The source has not been identified.

303. to prevent: *i.e.*, in anticipation of more foolishness.

306. souse: a pittance; from the French *sous*.

310-11. paying a reckoning: picking up the bill.

311. Cantabrigian: one from Cambridge; another slur on the universities.

314-15. Che ... taberns: Flaile's inconsistent dialect is the west-country or Somerset speech so common in Restoration comedy.

319. pinch: reprove, chastise. Zechiel's speech makes little sense, since the "church" reference occurs in Toby's previous speech. The text well may be corrupt at this point.

323. arch wag: master rogue.

328. parts: talents, abilities.

335. Mall: the popular promenade in St. James Park.

365. a second *Hobson*: probably alluding to Thomas Hobson (1544-1631) of Cambridge, from whom derives the phrase "Hobson's choice." He rented horses and forced his customers to take either whichever horse was nearest the door or none at all. Thus, Hobson's choice is no choice at all, as is a choice between Flaile and his oxen.

366-67. Man of *Motley*: clown.

368. countenance: facial expression; hence, "face" for the following joke.

370-71. steal ... *Bridge*: From about 1305 to 1678, the heads of important executed criminals were affixed to poles on London Bridge for public viewing. Among the more notable were those of Sir Thomas More and Thomas Cromwell.

375. jowl of salmon: a dish prepared from the head and upper portion of the fish.

377. sawce: with a pun on sauciness, or wit.

379. fellow: *i.e.*, Flaile.

394. under the rose: confidentially, secretly. Cf. III, i, 236, below, and L. *sub rosa*, still in use.

396. punctilio: the strict observance of proper, formal conduct; politeness. Used here in a verbal sense. Cf. II, i, 104, below.

402. Man of Mode: clearly a reference to Etherege's comedy, which had been revived at Dorset Garden in the preceding month (October 1676).

404. cocks ... bullies: roughly, "masters of all the swaggering bravos."

407-8. whether ... boarded: evidently a cant expression referring to the availability of a woman of pleasure.

414. band-strings: the laces for tying the collar or "band," which was out of fashion by 1676. Toby, however, still wears one.

420. Filloflorido: probably a fanciful invention of Zechiel's. *Rounsivell*: possibly intended as Rouncival, a fanciful name for a huge, robustious person.

424. let ... humour: Leave humor to me.

425-32. Cf. the following speech from Marston's *Parasitaster* (Act I, Scene 2): Then, my Pythagoras, shall thou and I make a transmigration of soules: thou shalt marry my daughter, or my wife shall be thy gratious mistris. Seventeene puncks shall be thy proporcion. Thou shalt begge to thy comfort of cleane lynnen, eate no more fresh beefe at supper, or save the broth for next daies porrege; but the flesh pots of Egypt shall fatten thee, and the grasehopper shall flourish in thy sommer.
428. puncks: prostitutes.
433-34. give me a note o': write down.
438. hect'ring: *behaving like a hector; swaggering.*

Act II. Scene 1.
8-9. turn the scale: counts for anything.
9. by: from.
20. prejudicial: disadvantageous.
27. Lambs: a tavern, unidentified / talboy: a two-quart container of wine.
39. Gent.: gentlemanly.
42. boon mene: attractive appearance (properly, *mien*).
51. scour: a cant term for the activities of night-roaming bullies, especially their plundering and abuse of the constable's watch. / Flannel *Mermidons*: contemptuous reference to the constable's watch; the Myrmidons were warriors under Achilles.
53. flesh'd: eager for battle.
54. tardy: remiss, delinquent.
65. into a tripe: to a bag of guts.
69-70. art of gleaning: knack of picking up ideas or modes of behavior.
71-72. bully rock: hector or bravo.
75. shame-fac'd: bashful, shy.
96. servants: admirers.
127. battoon: a Heraldic emblem resembling a truncheon; hence, Zechiel's allusion to it as a symbol of bravery. Arbella's rejoinder puns on battoon as *baton sinister*, the Heraldic badge of bastardy. / had like to have given: came near to giving.
149. Tilbury Camp: Tilbury dates back to the twelfth century.
183. mushrumes: roughly, *nouveaux riches*.
185-86. if they sleep on it: *i.e.*, if I don't avenge your honor by nightfall.
203 neats tongue: ox tongue.
204. rencounter: duel.

Act II. Scene 2.
41. SONG: The song is by D'Urfey and was set to music by William Turner. It appears also in D'Urfey's *New Collection of Songs* (1683), p. 4. The emendation in l. 48 is from that source and makes better sense than copy-text's *with*.
85. stay: wait.
99. mis: mistress.
114. turtle: turtle dove.

131. insult: exult, triumph. Cf. *Fond Husband*, II, i, 25.

153-54. When . . . breast: The quotation has not been identified and may be fanciful.

193. perspective: magnifying glass. Cf. *Fond Husband*, I, 167.

239-53. These lines are set as verse in all editions. Such arbitrary composition occurs frequently in the printings of D'Urfey's plays. The present editions retain them only where they scan as verse. Cf. *Fond Husband*, III, 99 (note).

Act III. Scene 1.

5. cum caeteris: with others.

21-23. Cf. Veterano's speech in Marmion's *Antiquary* (Act II): ". . . the whole Indies, seeing they are but newly discovered, are not to be valued with them."

25. still: even now.

42. illustrate: render illustrious, make famous.

52. been durable: lasted, been in existence.

72-73. Cf. Veterano in Act II of *The Antiquary*: "Then there's the great silver box that *Nero* kept his beard in."

74-75. friend . . . *Rome*: possibly a disrespectful allusion to the Pope.

78. rubbing-brush: a hard scrub brush. / *Silvius Otho*: M. Salvius Otho (A.D. 32-69), Roman emperor for three months in A.D. 69.

79. Heliogabalus: Elagabulus, or M. Aurelius Antoninus (A.D. 204-222), Roman emperor from 218 to 222.

83-84. St. *Jerom*: St. Jerome.

86. on fire: the London fire of 1666, in which St. Sepulchre's in Newgate was severely damaged, including the loss of many relics of the saints. It was restored in 1880.

100. make up the consort: comprise the company.

110. Hey troll: an exclamation of exuberance.

122. private item: confidential explanation.

128. Salisbury question: a proper question only for country folk, not for gentlemen.

134. caresses: attentions, favors.

152. Scanderberg: regularly Scanderbeg, from Iskender Bey, the title of a popular Albanian hero (1403-1467) who defeated the Ottoman Turks. The name is frequently used as an oath. See *A Fond Husband*, V, iii, 115.

153. Gustavus Adolphus: Gustavus II (1594-1632), King of Sweden from 1611 to 1632.

155. Cf. *The Antiquary* (Act IV): "He was call'd *Pompey* the great, from wearing of these great breeches."

157. cobwebs: threads, with a possible pun on "cobs" for "testicles," since Sir Arthur is presumably wearing the breeches.

174. mushrum: upstart, in an affectionate sense.

184. discover: expose, identify.

221-22. Constantia refers to Zechiel and Toby's obligation to answer Manley's challenge at II, i, 182-86.

230. Fleetstreet prentices: law students of the Temple in Fleetstreet.

232-34. speaks ... utterance: evidently alluding to the actor Anthony Leigh's comic voice in the role of Zechiel.

235. here's a nose: This and the following speech of Constantia's probably refer to the actor James Nokes's large nose. Both Nokes and Leigh were favorite low comedians, well known to the audience, and such "in" jokes would be entirely appropriate.

250. gentile: gentlemanly.

255. so relentless an air: such a pitiless or heartless social milieu.

262. fleerer: mocker, jeerer.

289-92. The sense is obscure; possibly, "I hope his age is sufficient excuse for his indulging himself in his eccentricity without bringing disgrace or reproach on himself." Such convoluted passages are typical of D'Urfey's attempts at elegant style.

Act III. Scene 2.

7. wants: lacks.

22. jilt: a fickle woman; a deceiver.

24. discovers: reveals.

38. imaginary doubts: unconfirmed suspicions.

51. Cleio: Clio, the Muse of history.

58. Indifferently: impartially, without bias.

87. pendants: earrings.

175-76. and whilst ... done: The sense is unclear; possibly, "while men tediously search for the truth of an intrigue, women, armed only with a small idea, outwit them." Possibly "minutes" should read "minutest"; in Q and Q2 "our" reads "one."

207. resentments: sentiments.

216. carrest: caressed, showed favors or attentions to.

235. besotted: infatuated, doting.

238-39. Mulberry Garden: a popular promenade and pleasure garden, on the present site of Buckingham Palace.

259-60. crocodills ... kill 'em: alluding to the fabulous belief that crocodiles shed tears for their victims.

268. perriwig stares: *i.e.*, even the hairs of his wig stand on end.

299. serenader: suitor, referring to Harry Jollyman.

Act IV. Scene 1.

12-13. Justice of Peace: as today, an inferior magistrate.

13. man of worship: applied to a person of repute and standing.

16. what a pox: a popular exclamation.

19. the Grand Signior: the Sultan of Turkey.

21. by Mahomet: a popular oath; probably from Mohammed II, Sultan of Turkey from 1451 to 1481.

24. Melchizedech: Melchizedek, Old Testament priest-king of Salem. See Genesis 14:18.

40-41. Justice ... *Quorum*: the full title for such a position.

50. fee: hire, retain.

52. Harry-Groats: coined by Henry VIII and taken out of circulation after 1662.

Notes to *Madam Fickle*   141

54. gownmen: lawyers.
65. *Lumberstreet*: Lombard Street, the financial section of London.
81. what then: so what?
83. *fucus*: false coloring, cosmetics.
101-2. ride . . . horse: show skill in horsemanship. / jump . . . stick: jump a hurdle in a steeplechase.
185. More . . . bounty: You deserve more than this for your generosity.

Act IV. Scene 2.

18. *Astrea*: Astraea, Greek goddess of Divine Justice, who became a star in the constellation Virgo.
23. interview . . . dark: a common contrivance in D'Urfey's comedies, allowing a confusion of identities or other intrigues. The audience understood the convention, though the stage would be fully lighted. Cf. *A Fond Husband*, V, iii.
34. contriving: being contrived.
49-51. This device occurs also in *A Fond Husband* (V, iv, 1-13).
95-96. makes . . . Nature: roughly, "makes me genuinely superior to the dregs." There is sexual imagery in the speech.
105-6. parasites . . . patrons: ironically, applicable to D'Urfey himself.
117. incendiary: one who excites men's passions.
216. resented: perceived.
218. flye: rise above, triumph over (?).
233. pippin: slang term of abuse, possibly referring to the crab apple. The Nurse is sour and crabbed.
235. beldam: ugly old woman, hag.
258-66. This speech is set as verse in all editions.
286. lute-strings: variant of "lustrings," ribbons of a glossy, silk fabric.
287. Cupids: lovers.
287-88. nose par'd less: possibly alluding to the facial disfiguration caused by the pox (syphilis); possibly mere nonsense, since Manley is feigning madness.
328. amoretto's: lovers.
333. *Phosporus*: Phosphorus, the morning star.
334. Cowley: Abraham Cowley (1618-1667), poet and playwright. The quotation has not been identified.
353-56. This speech is set as verse in all editions.
377. Long Vacation: summer, the longest term during which the law courts were not in session and during which the young gallants would presumably be out of town.
383. quirks: shifts, evasions.

Act V. Scene 1.

2. *Linkboyes*: torchbearers.
4-17. These speeches are set as verse in all editions.
42. son of *Assafoetida*: probably referring to his odor.
44. pump the rogue: The bullies commonly drenched their victims under the pump.

50. Lady of the Lake: unclear; evidently a cant term for a prostitute.
58. bulking quean: a woman who sleeps on bulkheads; hence, a woman of the streets.
71. nights ramble: a debauch.
72-73. town woman: prostitute. / sute of knots: a decorative accessory to a costume, made of ribbons, bows, etc.
75. SONG: The song is by D'Urfey and also appears in a slightly altered version under the title of "The Epicure" in John Banister's *New Ayres and Dialogues* (1678), pp. 156-57, and in D'Urfey's *New Collection* (1683), p. 36.
86. drowzy: dull, stupid.
99. pignies: variant of *pigsnies*, an expression of affection; roughly, *darlings*, *pets*.
105. Sing: possibly a stage direction.
116-17. late doubts . . . period: recent suspicions are now ended (confirmed).
131. Machiavil: the type of the arch villain in English drama; from the supposedly unscrupulous nature of the ideal ruler in Machiavelli's *Prince*.
142. Enter: i.e., comes forward. He has been on stage since line 108.
143-48. This speech is set as verse in all editions.

Act V. Scene 2.

1. tavern bush: A bush, usually of ivy, was the traditional sign for a tavern.
6. stockado'd: run through with a sword.
10-11. take the wall: force one to pass on the street side of the walk, an insult.
18-22. This speech is set as verse in all editions.
19-20. Term-time: the period during which the courts are in session. The implication is that the courts are burdened with cases of murder resulting from such debauches.
38. engine: his sword.
40. hufft and cufft: scolded and beaten.
42. Hector: bully, bravo.
43. bottle: basket; possibly referring to the custom of hanging a cat in a wicker basket as a target in archery.
45. butt: a large wine cask.
57-64. This speech is set as verse in all editions.
67-68. effigie: i.e., the likeness of Bacchus.
75. SONG: The song is by D'Urfey. The word in brackets is a conjectural emendation, for the space is blank in all editions.
103. Hearty: not identified; perhaps fanciful.
105. modish: i.e., the Bacchus song.
134. crack: whore. / she: dialectal for "I."
137. bilbo's: sword carriers; hence, officers.
159. Mrs. *Juniper*: contemptuous term for a prostitute. See *A Fond Husband*, V, iii, 177.
174. old *Madge*: his sword.
175. scowr'd: thrust.
195. coney: rabbit, hare.
203. night-walker: one who roams at night, especially a thief or prostitute.

203-48. Cf. Jordan's *Walks of Islington and Hogsdon* (IV, ii) for the source of this business.
   205. curious in the discovery: thorough in the investigation.
   208. snap: apprehend.
   223. mortifi'd: slain.
   226. carbonado'd: slashed or hacked.
   227. the *Rose*: a popular tavern, identified in *Wit for Money* (p. 9) as D'Urfey's favorite haunt. Referred to also in *A Fond Husband* (I, 442).
   241. stone: with a possible pun on "testicle," in view of the reference to wenches.
   277. for'ts all: for it's the same thing.
   279. brewis: broth.
   280. wrack: damage, destruction.
   303. rifl'd cully: cheated gull.
   304. *roches*: roughs, bullies (?).

Act V. Scene 3.
   5-6. could write woman: *i.e.*, had attained womanhood.
   14. pantible: corruption of pantofle; slipper, sandal.
   60. largely: fully, at length.
   99. particular: detailed, minute.
   127. Gent.: gentleman.
   147-48. *in decimo sexto*: in the size of a sixteenmo (a very small book); hence, in miniature.
   156. Belona: Bellona, Roman goddess of war.
   163. huffing: swaggering, bragging.
   212. horns like *Acteon*: Bellamore refers to the horns of cuckoldry, though Actaeon, the great hunter of Greek mythology, earned his another way. He was changed to a stag by Artemis after looking-upon her at her bath.
   264. walking nightrap: a night watchman.
   266. break a glass: drink a toast.
   270-75. This speech is set as verse in all editions.

Epilogue.
   1. The epilogue was presumably spoken by Mrs. Mary Lee (Madam Fickle) in her bully's costume.
   21. Lambs-Conduit-*Fields*: in St. Pancras, south of Euston Road; a site for dueling.

*A Fond Husband; or,
The Plotting Sisters*

INTRODUCTION

The initial publication date of *A Fond Husband* has been variously cited as 1676 and 1677, though the latter date is correct.[1] The 1676 citations were based upon the imprimatur of the 1677 text, which reads in part, "Licensed *June* 15. 1676." If this were to be taken as accurate, it would indicate that the play had been performed prior to that date, for plays were rarely printed without having been staged previously. Thus, one finds references to a putative 1676 performance in the Reverend John Genest's monumental history of the English stage, in Forsythe's account of D'Urfey's plays, and in various early bibliographies of the Restoration drama.

These references must be discounted, for they would indicate that *A Fond Husband* appeared prior to *Madam Fickle* (November 4, 1676), an impossibility. *Madam Fickle* was not printed until early 1676/7, yet the dedication to *A Fond Husband* makes reference to Ormonde's acceptance and approval of the dedication to *Madam Fickle*. Thus, *A Fond Husband* could not have been printed be-

---

1. See the editor's "A D'Urfey Play Dated," *Modern Philology* 64 (May 1967): 322-23.

fore early 1676/7 and, in fact, does not appear in the Term Catalogues until November 26, 1677.[2]

Aside from these proofs, there is internal evidence that points to a first printing late in 1677. In the dedication of *A Fond Husband,* D'Urfey refers to his patron's "*departure from* England," a reference to Ormonde's assignment to Ireland in August 1677; and in one of Cordelia's speeches (V, i, 35) a reference to a comedy recently performed can allude only to Mrs. Behn's *Debauchee* (Dorset Garden, *c.* February 1677).

The problem may be solved by assuming that the 1676 date on the imprimatur is a misprint for 1677, which, in view of the carelessness of seventeenth-century printing practices, is not unlikely. In that case, the play was first performed shortly before June 15, 1677, the true date of its licensing, and appeared in print in time to be entered in the Term Catalogues for Michaelmas Term (November). Unfortunately, the play was never entered in the Stationers' Register and the unreliability of the 1676 imprimatur can not be substantiated through that source.

Nicoll has fixed the date for the first performance of *A Fond Husband* as May 31, 1677, based on an entry in the Lord Chamberlain's lists (5/143, p. 162).[3] It was probably performed every night through June 8, the date of the second L.C. entry. Richard Steele, writing in 1713, records that the comedy was "honoured with the presence of King Charles the Second three of its first five nights."[4] The play was evidently fairly successful, because D'Urfey notes in his dedication that "it has indifferently [impartially, without bias] past in the Opinion

2. Ed. Edward Arber (London, 1903), 1: 291-92.
3. *A History of English Drama: 1660-1900* (Cambridge, 1965), 1: 408.
4. *The Guardian,* no. 82 (June 15, 1713).

of the Town." John Downes, in *Roscius Anglicanus,* claims that the comedy, along with Otway's *Soldier's Fortune,* "took extraordinary well, and being perfectly *Acted;* got the Company great Reputation and Profit."[5] It was certainly to become one of D'Urfey's more popular plays, for Day records some twenty-nine productions of it, as late as 1740.[6] In addition, it was chosen for D'Urfey's benefit in 1713.

Historical criticism of *A Fond Husband* is scarce. The anonymous author of *Wit for Money* (p. 13) ridiculed D'Urfey's dependence on artificial plot devices, noting especially "the putting out of Candles, changing of Gowns; Tables and Traps." Sir Richard Steele also pointed out these defects in an ironic statement that D'Urfey "contrives the most natural perplexities . . . that ever were represented on a stage, [and makes] not only the characters of the play, but also the furniture of the house, contribute to the main design." Still, he admitted that the comedy contained "ample food for mirth."[7]

From *A New Theatrical Dictionary* we learn that the play "met with very great applause, and is looked upon as one of Mr. Durfey's best plays"; and Genest agrees that it is "on the whole a good play," though "there is too much of Ranger and Maria" in it.[8] Even Gerard Langbaine, D'Urfey's nemesis, while deploring the playwright's lack of originality and dramatic skill, singled out *A Fond Husband* as his only work of any merit. He wrote: "This is One of his best Comedies, and has been frequently acted with good Applause: tho' methinks the business of *Sneak, Cordelia,* and Sir *Roger Petulant,* end

5. Ed. Montague Summers (London, 1928), p. 36.
6. "Dates and Performances" (Charlottesville, Va., 1950), pp. 4-5.
7. *The Guardian,* no. 82.
8. (London, 1792), p. 91; and *Some Account of the English Stage* (Bath, 1832), 1: 192.

but abruptly."[9] Certainly the comedy was one of D'Urfey's most successful plays with Restoration and early eighteenth-century audiences.

The plot of *A Fond Husband* is typical of the Restoration intrigue comedy and is not derived from any particular literary source. It is one of D'Urfey's most original plots, possibly explaining Langbaine's indulgence toward it. Cuckoldry and sexual intrigue were common fare on the Restoration stage, and D'Urfey's treatment of the themes is entertaining if not entirely skillful. The principal structural weakness of the piece lies in Bubble's repeated failure to see through his wife's and Rashley's trickery. This allows D'Urfey to contrive one deception after another but makes for a highly episodic plot. Virtually all complication is achieved by the end of Act III, and the final two acts are no more than repetitious variations of the basic situation. Nevertheless, many of the individual scenes are amusing and entertaining, at the level of farce. Notable are Fumble's and Sneak's courtship of Cordelia (II, iii), the table scene (IV, iv), and the several scenes involving Old Fumble and his mishearings of innocent remarks.

The characters in *A Fond Husband* are types that recur frequently in D'Urfey's comedies. None is developed in any depth, though as types they provoke their share of laughter. Some may be classed as *humours,* especially Bubble, Fumble, and Sir Roger Petulant. In creating dialogue for these figures, D'Urfey succeeded in assigning them diction that is consistent with their basic traits. Sir Roger, the old-fashioned knight who prefers to live in the past, frequently sounds antiquated, drawing heavily upon the diction of an earlier age. Such phrases as

---

9. *An Account of the English Dramatick Poets* (Oxford, 1691), p. 180.

"in verity," "if thou wert but," and "thou hast been" hark back to former times. Old Fumble, the deaf and nearly blind lecher, exhibits *humours* speech in the repeated use of the oath "ifack," in his lewd puns, and in his constant swearing. The characters of fashion (Emilia, Rashley, Ranger, and Maria) are assigned a style of speech that aims at the verbal elegance often achieved so successfully by other dramatists (*e.g.*, Congreve and Wycherley), but their refined and eloquent utterances are often merely convoluted and confusing rather than witty. The first scene of the play will illustrate this point sufficiently.

The dialogue of *A Fond Husband* differs from that of *Madam Fickle* in its preponderance of obscene puns and wordplay. Much of the lewdness is based upon slang that is no longer current, and the modern reader is apt to miss the sexual meanings. Such words as *nick, snap,* and *stones* are frequently *double entendres;* these have been noted in the present edition.

A Fond Husband was popular enough to have had an influence on subsequent intrigue comedies. Otway's *Soldier's Fortune* (1681) employs the device of the feigned rape for preventing discovery of a love intrigue. Two Shadwell comedies also owe some of their action to events in *A Fond Husband*. In *The Volunteers* (1692), a comedy for which D'Urfey wrote a prologue, the chance discovery of a love intrigue in a darkened room suggests the actions of Bubble in the present text. In the fourth-act playhouse scene of *A True Widow* (1678), Shadwell offers a brief satire of *A Fond Husband* that ridicules the convoluted dialogue typical of D'Urfey's Rashley-Emilia scenes, as well as the putting out of candles, concealments beneath tables, and discoveries via skeleton keys.

The structural fabric of *A Fond Husband* is thin stuff,

but the comedy is fast moving and entertaining, if for no other reason than the variety of situations D'Urfey is able to draw forth from the one central intrigue. Though its fashionable characters are rather colorless, the eccentric figures of the subplot provide some truly amusing business, making this one of D'Urfey's more diverting comedies.

A Fond Husband:
OR,
The Plotting Sisters.

A COMEDY:

As it is Acted at His *Royal Highness*
THE
DUKE's Theatre.

Hæc, dum incipias, gravia sunt, dumque ignores, ubi cognoris, facilia, Terent.

Written by *THO. DURFEY* Gent.

Licensed *June* 15. 1676.
    ROGER L'ESTRANGE.

LONDON:
Printed by *T. N.* for *James Magnes* and *Rich. Bentley*, in *Russel-street* in *Covent-Garden*, near the Piazza's. 1677.

TITLE PAGE OF THE FIRST EDITION OF *A FOND HUSBAND*. The Latin epigraph is from Terence's *Self Tormentor* and is a piece of advice from an old man to a young man who is about to be married. It means: "These things are hard when you begin until you come to understand them; when you understand them they are easy." The 1676 imprimatur probably should read 1677. See the Introduction to the text.

To His GRACE, The
Duke of Ormond,

Lord Steward of His Majesties Houshold,
Knight of the Noble Order of the Garter,
One of His MAJESTIES most Honourable
Privy Council, &c.

May it please your GRACE,
 The arrogance a poet may be guilty of in a Dedication, often brings him more terror, than his fear for the success of his play; and I always thought the frowns of an offended patron a greater punishment than the censures of the partial criticks. But the sin of confidence is so natural to a young poet, and so suitable to his character and business, that an excuse, or reproof (as it would be extreamly unnecessary, so it) might perhaps be a hinderance to his fortune. My sence of this, has encourag'd me to present this comedy to your Grace; with this humble suit, that as it has indifferently past in the opinion of the town, it may have the honour to stand as neuter in your Graces favour. The greatest confidence of a poet can ask no more; nor can you, (My Lord) govern'd by your excellent temper, grant less. This I know I need not repeat, nor urge a second time; for who ever yet made an humble address to your Grace, that went away unsatisfied? You are so far from singularity, so nobly just, and so unwearied in doing good, that to pen your applause, were as impossible a work, as to pen the actions of your life, every hour

producing some memorable thing as an addition to the volume. My Lord, 'tis not only my particular grief, but every ones for your Graces departure from England. *And though the great place of trust conferred upon you by His* Sacred Majesty, *(and which none can be more worthy of) gives us proof as well of your pious loyalty, as unequal'd grandeur; yet such an influence you have gain'd on all hearts, that they had rather the Kingdom of* Ireland *should lose its preserver, than they so good a patron. This I confess I am most sensible of, perhaps having as much cause as any; which relation I'll smother, lest it is thought interest more than gratitude makes me resent it.*

If I have presumed too much, I have this excuse, that a Dedication to such a person cannot be writ without it; and 'tis the only honour a poet is ambitious of, to have a great name before his play. I confess I was guilty of this; and have only this excuse for the arrogance of a Dedication, that your Grace was pleas'd to favour my last, and that this was writ with the same integrity. For the play I can say nothing, only that it was my own, though some are pleas'd to doubt the contrary, (the Scotch Song *excepted, a part of which was not mine; nor do I desire any reputation from it.) Be pleased,* My Lord, *to forgive this prolixity; and believe my sence of the honour I have in addressing to your Grace, almost equals the ambition I shall ever own, in stiling my self,*

           My LORD,
           Your GRACES most Humble
           and most Obedient Servant,
                         THO. DURFEY.

DRAMMATIS PERSONAE.

Rashley, a Gentleman, friend to *Emilia*.	Mr. *Smith*.
Ranger, his rival.	Mr. *Harris*.
Peregrine Bubble, a credulous fond cuckold, husband to *Emilia*.	Mr. *James Nokes*.
Old Fumble, a superannuated Alderman, that dotes on black women. He's very deaf and almost blind; and seeking to cover his imperfection of not hearing what is said to him, answers quite contrary.	Mr. *Anth. Leigh*.
Sir *Roger Petulant*, a jolly old Knight of the last age.	Mr. *Sandford*,
Sneak, nephew to Sir *Roger*, a young raw student.	Mr. [*Jevon*].
Spatterdash, servant to *Fumble*. *Jeremy*, servant to *Rashley*.	Mr. *Richards*.
Apothecary.	Mr. *Percival*.
Emilia, wife to *Bubble*.	[Mrs. *Barry*.]
Maria, sister to *Bubble*.	Mrs. *Marshall*.
Cordelia, niece to *Bubble*. [Mrs. *Snare*.]	Mrs. *Hughes*.
Betty, woman to *Emilia*.	Mrs. *Napper*.
Governess.	Mrs. [*Norris*.]

Servants and Attendants.

PROLOGUE.

If plot and bus'ness comical and new,
Could please the criticks that sit here to view,
The poet might have thought this play would do.
But in this age design no praise can get. 5
You cry it conversation wants, and wit;
As if the obvious rules of comedy,
Were only dull grimace *and* repartée.
Such, Sirs, have been your darlings prov'd of late.
The author therefore careless of his fate, 10
And knowing wit a chattle hardly got,
Has ventur'd his whole stock upon a plot.
He says a mock-song, or a smutty tale,
Can please the town; and why not this prevail?
I friendly told him, all that I could say, 15
Was, that your fancies lean'd the other way;
And you lov'd wenching better than his play.
For th' body still you luxury prepare;
But let the mind be desolate and bare.
Thus lose your selves in the worlds prudent thought, 20
Then strive to get reprieve by finding fault.
A critick is a monster that can sway
Only o'er ignorance, and yet dares prey
Upon that power that form'd him out of clay.
Adulterate age, where prudence is a vice, 25
And wit's as scandalous as avarice.
Yet in despight of this, —y'are poets too;
And what two fops rail at, a third shall do.
Upon our priviledges you incroach,
And with dull rhimes the noble art debauch. 30
For writing plays you scorn a poets name;
A bawdy song's enough to get you fame.
Where midst the reputation that is due,
You will be sure no man shall censure you.
Yet though your faction does infest the town, 35
There is a wise cabal dares judge and own
Desert and wit, and our endeavours crown.
To these we humbly dedicate our plays,
Whilst at their feet our poets throw their bays.

[A]
FOND HUSBAND;
OR,
The *PLOTTING SISTERS*.

Act I. Scene 1. [Bubble's *lodging*.]

(*A dining-room, a table,*
Shuttle-Cock and
Battle-Dor's.)

Rashley *and* Emilia *sitting*. Betty *sings*.

In vain, cruel nymph, you my passion despise,
And slight a poor lover that languishing dies.
Though Fortune my name with no titles endow'd;
Yet fierce is my passion, and warm is my blood.
Delay in affection exalts an amour;
For he that loves often will soonest give o'er.

2.
But vigorous and young I'll flee to thy arms,
Infusing my soul in Elizium *of charms.*
A monarch I'll be when I lie by thy side,
And thy pretty hand my scepter shall guide;
Till cloy'd with delight you confess with a joy,
No monarch so happy, so pleasant as I.

[*Exit* Betty.]

Rashley. By Heav'n, there's nothing so dear to a free

and generous spirit, as this roving and uncontroul'd way
of love. Me thinks we live like angels, and every kiss
brings a new life of pleasure.

Emilia. You have reason to believe I think so, for suffering this early visit from you in my husbands absence; who, poor man, went from me by break of day to see a horse-race a mile beyond *High-Gate.*

Rashley. Nay, I confess, 'tis a sign of your kind resentment of my passion. Oh Heav'n! That happy thought has made me all rapture. I'll cherish it, Madam, as I would my youth, or the best of all my sences, the sence of feeling.

Emilia. Cherish it rather as the means of keeping our love from my husbands knowledge. Well! I swear the thought of my indirect plot sometimes makes me very melancholy.

Rashley. Melancholy?—— Fie, Madam, banish such thoughts for ever from your breast. If you are melancholy now, what would you have done, if I had not known you, when the clog of your conscience (I mean your husband) would have been your perpetual plague, and given you cause for more melancholy than the contrivance of the plots you speak of?

Emilia. Ay, but to break a vow, Sir, a vow! Little do you think what 'tis to break a vow.

Rashley. Little do I think? Madam, I thought you had known me so much a gentleman, to imagine I know what belongs to the breaking a vow as well as another man. To undeceive you, I have broke twenty vows, that is, unnecessary vows, (such as yours are!) nay, and without a scruple of conscience. I thank my stars, I'm of a tougher constitution.

Emilia. Besides, you consider not the other inconveniences; you know my husband's sister *Maria* loves you, and is of that untam'd, malicious nature, that she'll revenge my invading her propriety in your heart by discovering our love to my husband. I know she plots it hourly; and tho' her pretence is the honour of our family, her real design is through her love to you.

Rashley. Never doubt your husband, Madam; he has so strange a confidence in my fidelity, that to possess him otherwise, were utterly to take away the little sence is left him. You know he brought me to lodge in his house, which prudently I refus'd at first, and seemingly fled from the heav'n I desir'd, to make him more importunate. Since I came here, you know how he has carrest me; and to colour my design, and divert you, have I feign'd a mistriss in this quarter of the town; and then, as if I spoke of her, have told him all that has past betwixt my self and you, at which the good-natur'd creature has laught extreamly, and wisht me good luck a thousand times; and can we now doubt further success? By Heav'n, we cannot Madam.

Emilia. Then you know there's another great obstacle; *Ned Ranger* has long profest a passion for me, and doubtless is not ignorant that my love for you is the cause of his no better success. A jealous man sees more than twenty others; and 'twill be very necessary for us to be careful of so dang'rous an enemy.

Rashley. Dang'rous? Not at all, Madam, never think him so; success, which animates the hero, and leads him on to greater enterprizes than before he durst attempt, has cherisht hopes in me. Let me alone with him; and for thy part, Igad I'll turn thee loose to any female-devil on this side *Lapland*, either for plot or repartée.

Emilia. Yet still I fear the worst.

Rashley. Fear nothing, Madam. Fear is the worst of passions, and incident to base, not noble hearts. Besides,

our love, consider'd rightly, is a second-rate innocence, where affection, not duty, bears prerogative; 'tis the great and primitive bus'ness of our souls; suspition and fear came in by the by.
Enter Betty.
Betty. Madam, Mr. *Ranger*, in spite of my resistance, has rudely prest into the house, and is just coming hither.
Emilia. Call up the footmen. Lock the door.——
Enter Ranger.
Ranger. (*To* Betty.) Stand still, Mrs. Jilt, or I shall spoil your door-keeping hereafter. *Jack Rashley*, here—Hell and the Devil——
Emilia. What insolence is this? Pray, Sir, your business? [*Exit* Betty.]
Ranger. Only my zeal, Madam, to give you notice of an approaching danger. Your husband has so intangl'd his horns yonder in a hawthorn-bush, that 'tis to be fear'd without immediate help he will lose the decent and commodious ornament of his forehead.
Emilia. Most impudent of men! How dare you talk thus?
Ranger. Most infamous of women! How dare you do thus?
Rashley. Do what, Sir?
Emilia. Hold, and as you love me, move no farther. Basest of men! Have you the folly to believe this way can prove beneficial to your love? No, I hate thee mortally, nor shall thy malice from henceforth be successful; I'll disarm it; and when thou thinkest thy plots are surest laid, be sure of a surprize.
Ranger. O infamy!—— 'Sdeath, is your forehead steel? And is your skin of that obdurate temper you cannot force a blush into your cheeks at the confession of your

obscene crime? How great a friend to Hell is impudence!

Emilia. Pray, Sir, forgive him; 'tis an insipid fellow that I am often troubled with, and believe his insolence for the future shall be prevented. In the mean time, to express my gratitude, give me leave to present you with this necklace; this ring too will fit your finger—— Nay, and swear you shan't refuse 'em; my husband gives me often such as these; 'tis all the good I get by him.

Ranger. Very well; the blessing of a wife let all men judge. What envious fiend to plague me makes me love this creature?

Rashley. I will preserve your favours as my life; your memory shall possess my soul, and all your charms live ever in my sight. My kindest, sweetest, dearest——

(*Kisses her hand.*)

Ranger. Death and damnation, must I stay and see this? Madam, this modest carriage before a jealous lover makes——

Emilia. Little for your contentment I doubt not, Sir. But 'tis a fate proper enough for such busie and inquisitive persons.

Rashley. (Sings.) Fa, la, la, la, la.——

Ranger. Go! You are a devil; so far from being a woman, that I begin to doubt whether Nature had any hand in your creation. Is't not enough, vile creature, that I know you abuse your husband, but that you dare give me an ocular proof? Dispence your favours to the man that horns him before my face? Oh unparallell'd impudence!

Emilia. Incorrigible fool, think'st thou to daunt my will? The little ill I do can raise no infamy, nor will I ever doubt it.

Rashley. [*Sings.*] Fa, la, la, la.

The joys of a lover in passion remains,
In passion that's fervent and free, &c.

Enter Betty.

Betty. Oh Madam, my master's just come home and coming up.

Ranger. Blest minute! Now I hope his eyes will be unseal'd, and through the right end of the perspective see you. Madam, assure your self there shall want nothing in me.

Emilia. I know, Sir, and am prepar'd for the worst of thy malice. [*To* Rashley.] Here, take this Battle-dor, and let us play.   (*They play.*)

Rashley. Out, out, Madam—— Y'are out.

Enter Bubble.

Bubble. Ha, ha, ha.—— Chicken; good morrow, Chicken.—— Morrow *Tom.* Chick, prethee let me kiss thee. What, in the mumps?—— This morning, pop—— No more of that—— Hoh—— What my old friend *Ranger* too! Morrow *Ned.* Faith! Would you had been with me this morning; I have had the rarest sport yonder at *High-Gate* with two or three country-fellows—— Harkee, Chick, I have invited 'em all to dinner one day this week; good blunt course fellows, faith, but damnable rich.—— As Gad jidge me, I past for a brave fellow amongst 'em.——

Emilia. You need boast of applause from such clowns.

Bubble. Clowns? What, honest, tough, hard-fisted, plain-dealing farmers, clowns?—— Pop—— I say, you are an inconsiderable varlet, Chicken, and know not what belongs to such good company.

Ranger. She is so well diverted at home, Sir, that all rural society is distastful to her.

Emilia. [*To* Ranger.] I guess 'em to be much of your

humour, Sir, owners of a great deal of dull, insipid noise, and very little or no sence.

Bubble. Well said, Chicken.—— *Ned.* To her.—— To her agen, *Ned*; 'tis a raging Turk at repartée.—— Invent, invent; strike her home; prethee try her wit.—— Thou art a scholar.—— For my part I dare not; (as Gad jidge me!) she's always too hard for me.

Ranger. And me too, I assure you, Sir.—— But there's a gentleman that has the good fortune to be more intimate; his address is far more pleasing than mine.

Bubble. Who, *Tom!* Come, I'll hold a Guiney she's too hard for him too! Why, 'tis the readi'st, witti'st, jeering'st, flearing'st quean—— 'Sbud she's one of the pearls of eloquence.—— And pop,—— By the way, let me tell you, there's ne'er an orator in Christendom has more tropes and figures, take her when her hands in——

Ranger. Nor knows the Art of Wheadling better, I'l say that for her.

Bubble. Gad, thou art in the right, she's a *non parelio* at it. But now you talk of wheadling, prethee, *Tom,* how goes thy love-affairs? Thou look'st but ill upon't.—— Any plots? Adventures of late? Hah!

Rashley. None that can make me frown, Sir. My stars have allotted me so mild a destiny, that I can caress my friend with my wonted air, without being discourag'd by my success in love-affairs.

Bubble. I'm glad on't, faith. Come, prethee let me be partaker of thy good fortune; when wert thou with her?

Emilia. Tell him, tell him, Sir. Lord, you never used to be so cautious in these matters.—— Pray tell him and tremble.—— (*To* Ranger *aside*.) Now observe.

Rashley. Why, Sir, I was with her this morning.

Bubble. So! And what success prethee?

Rashley. Why at my first coming she entertain'd me with a song, softly expressing the delights of love in an excellent air, and added to it a thousand kind words and kisses. I had all the priviledge imaginable, and 'twas my good luck to come at a very happy hour, for her husband went out early i' th' morning a fowling as far as *Holloway*.

Bubble. Holloway? A pox on't. What damn'd luck had I? If it had been *High-Gate* I should have met the fool; for I have been there all this morning.

Rashley. Ah! 'Tis no matter, Sir; his company can add little to any ones credit, for he is but a kind of a softheaded, a half-witted fellow.

Bubble. A ninny, a fool.—— Ha, ha, ha.

Rashley. Ay, and the most credulous of all the cuckolds I ever met with.

Bubble. Poor animal! Faith I pity him, but there's a number of 'em about town ifaith,—— We men of wit should want diversion else.

Ranger. [*Aside.*] We men of wit, quoth a! Dam him, he's duller than a justices clark.—— To be made a property all this while, and not discern it. Oh insufferable stupidity!

Emilia. Observe, Sir, observe.

Ranger. Yes, Devil, I do observe; I doubt not but my observation shall add little to your quiet. Oh curse of——

Bubble. Why how now, *Ned*? What, grinning like a monkey eating of chesnuts? Prethee what art thou thinking on? As Gad jidge me, I think thou art grown insipid, as my wife says. How dost like *Tom*'s intrigue? Ha,—— Is it not pleasant?

Ranger. Very pleasant, Sir, and, faith, in my judgment represents as nearly as any character I ever saw——

Bubble. Represents?—— Whoo pox, you're at your quirks and quiddits, your *Cambridge*-puns and *Westminster*-quibbles are you?

Emilia. Pray forward, Sir; me thinks 'tis very divertive.

Ranger. Very divertive! Dam her, she was sure the off-spring of *Belzebub*.

Rashley. After a thousand other caresses intermixt with kisses and smiles, and a world of happy thoughts and fancies extravagantly rendred upon so happy an occasion, she oblig'd me in a new and most sensible way, presenting me, with a sweet and incomparable grace, this gold watch, and this diamond ring.

(Ranger *looks amaz'dly.*)

Bubble. Prethee observe *Ned* there; he's grown a strange whimsical fellow;—— Ha, ha, ha, look how he stares.

Ranger. Was ever such an impudence? Sure I dream! And this is all delusion.—— Harkee, Sir, are you irrecoverably blind?

Bubble. Blind? What, I blind?

Ranger. Methinks that watch looks very like one I have seen your wife wear often.

Bubble. Ha! As Gad jidge me, and so it does; but much good do thy heart, *Tom,* I'll warrant it right.

Ranger. Me thinks that ring too much resembles yours.

Bubble. The square is right, but I think my stones were a little bigger.

Ranger. (Aside.) Now the Devil take thee for a dull rogue.

Rashley. But the best jest was, before she gave me these, there happen'd to come rudely into the room a wild, young fellow, that I found afterwards to be my rival, and one she hated for his ill nature and impertinence; but to see how pitiful he lookt to see me so presented before his face, would have made you die with laughing.—— Ha, ha, ha.

Bubble. } Ha, ha, ha.
Emilia. }

Ranger. Hell and Furies, what's this I hear? Am I made a property too? If I bear this, may I be posted for a coward, and my infamy known to all nations.—— Harkee, Sir.

Rashley. Well, Sir.

Ranger. By your ridiculous fleering behaviour, I guess I was concern'd in your last description, an affront that requires instant satisfaction; and believe, Sir, you shall not carry it off so clearly as you imagin'd. Tho' he is such a fool to be bubbl'd out of his reason, I am not—— Follow me, Sir, if you dare.

Rashley. Dare! Lead on, Sir,—— You shall see how much I dare.

Emilia. Hold, Sir, you shall not go.

Rashley. Dare follow you?

Ranger. Ay, Sir, 'twould be a doubtful question if your protection there were out of the way.   (*Points to* Emilia.)

Rashley. What's that? Protection?

Bubble. How now? What, jokes? Hard words? What's the matter, *Tom*? I must have no quarrels here.

Emilia. 'Tis Mr. *Ranger's* ill humour; prethee, love, speak to him; he's always disturbing good company. Tell him he's impertinent.

Bubble. Gad, and so I will.—— What a pox, a man cannot be a little jocose in his own house but he must disturb him; you shall see me go and huff him.

Ranger. [*Aside.*] His horns I am sure are large enough—— Horns of sufficient growth, substantial horns; horns visible, large, craggy-brancht, rough horns, and yet he may not believe it.

Bubble. Believe what, *Ned*? Ha, ha, ha.—— He's mad. Downright out of his wits. 'Tis a thick scull'd fellow, God knows, but we were not all born to be wits.—— What dost believe, *Ned*?

Ranger. Why, Sir, I believe you are mad.

Bubble. I mad? Damme *Ned*, you're an impertinent fellow. Now observe, Chicken.

Ranger. How, Sir?

Bubble. I say, Sir, an impertinent fellow, Sir, and deserve to be cramb'd into a powdering-tub.

Ranger. Dam this fool, how he tortures me! But my revenge lies another way; I'll instantly go to his sister *Maria,* who I know loves *Rashley,* and will willingly join with me in my revenge. This must [I] do, and I'll about it instantly. (*Exit.*)

Bubble. Ah——he's gone. I thought when I began to roar once he would quickly vanish. I warrant I have frighted him into an ague.—— Poor fool, he'll hardly trouble us again this good while.

Rashley. An uncivil person, first to intrude into our company, and then to hinder our discourse, especially of so pleasant a narration. Gad! 'Twas too much.

Bubble. Too much? Why 'twas the Devil and all; and as Gad jidge me, he's the son of a whore, and I'll make him an example.

Enter Footman.

Footman. Sir *Roger Petulant* with his nephew, and old Mr. *Fumble* are come to visit you.

Bubble. Gads so!—— Sirrah, wait on 'em up, and call my niece down. This is the man, Chicken, I told thee that I intend for *Cordelia's* husband. He's very rich, I am told, and his father's a knight, and Sheriff of the county.

Emilia. But who is the other, Sir?

Bubble. Why, dost not know him? 'Tis old Alderman *Fumble.* He's a little deaf, but ifaith very good company, and will so fumble about the women.—— You shall see he's a very jolly follow, and repartées, and talks, and chats at all rates. But the Devil a word he hears, for he always answers quite contrary. He'll make us all laugh ifaith.

Emilia. I've heard he dotes on all the women he sees, and is as passionate and inconstant at his age of seventy three, as the brisk sparks of our times are at five and twenty.

Rashley. He says (the Devil take him that believes him) nothing fails him but his eyes, which defect he has lately amended by a pair of Venetian spectacles.

Bubble. Ha, ha; 'tis a pleasant old fellow.—— But here they come.

Enter Sir Roger, Sneak, Fumble.

Sir Roger. Cob! Come, *Cob,* come! Along, I say, and hold up thy head. Fie, fie, be not so bashful, Child. Nay, *Cob*— What, dost think I'll forsake thee? Pish, in verity I will not. Wipe thy eyes, I say.

Enter Cordelia.

Bubble. He's a little moody-hearted, that's the worst on't. But the young man will show his parts by and by, I warrant ye.—— Come hither, Niece. Sir *Roger,* your most humble servant.   (Old Fumble *pulls out his spectacles, and looks on* Cordelia.)

Sir Roger. Yours, good Mr. *Peregrine.* You see, Sir, I am as good as my word; I have brought my nephew. *Cob,* here's your [mistress] *Cob.*— Look, look up, and go and salute her. I'll shew thee the way. Nay, *Cob,* still in thy dumps? Look upon me, Man! I'll do't first.

Sneak. Well, well! I'll follow you, Uncle. I am a little bashful at present, but I shall come to't anon.

Sir Roger. Well said. Madam! I am your humble servant.—— *(Kisses her.)*

Sneak. And I likewise, Madam!

Fumble. Ifack, ifack! A pretty well-favour'd woman that there! A good eye, good hair, and ifack I think ev'ry thing good—— Ha—— Hem, Mr. *Peregrine,* prethee who is that there? That woman there?

Bubble. Who, she yonder?

Fumble. Hah!

Bubble. (Aloud.) Why, she's a near friend of mine, Sir.—— What an ignorant old fellow 'tis, not to know my niece?

Fumble. A friend? Well I could have heard you, I could have heard you without this exclamation. What, ifack, I am not deaf; I could have heard you. But if she be a friend, I hope an old friend may salute her; 'tis a civility well paid. By your leave, sweet Lady.

(*Goes to kiss* Cordelia, *and kisses* Sneak.)

Sneak. What the Devil does this old fellow mean? Uncle! Did you ever see the like?

Sir Roger. Ha, ha, ha! A pleasant mistake ifaith.

Fumble. Ha! ifack I think I was mistaken, was I not, Gentlemen? Was I not? I doubt my false light guided me to the wrong person. Hah! But come, no matter, I meant it right, Madam, I meant it right. Never the older for a mistake ifack! I meant it right.

Cordelia. I am glad I mist it for all that.

Sir Roger. Mr. *Rashley,* you are not merry; in troth I fear I have disturb'd you, hah!

Rashley. Not at all, Sir; 'tis impossible your free humour can be troublesom to any one.

Sir Roger. You know my old way, Sir, jovial and inoffensive. Pray let me commend my nephew to you. *Cob,* come hither.—— He's a little too modest, Sir, but else I think I may say, a youth of notable parts. Come hither, *Cob.*

Rashley. I can believe no less. Sir, your humble servant.

Sneak. With all my heart, Sir; and I am your servant in like manner.

Cordelia. Bless me! What a figure of a husband shall I have?

Sir Roger. You know, Sir, when I was a batchelor I delighted much in merry songs and catches.—— Ah! *Sawny Broome,* rare fellow! And when a dozen of us Royalists were met at the Miter under the Rose there, the leveller went round, round, ifaith.—— I hold out still, Sir, as well as I can; and tho' I cannot sing my self, I keep those that can.

Bubble. Ay, and so do I. My wives maid shall sing you a Scotch Song.—— Come, sing it *Betty.*——

(Betty sings.)

A Scotch Song.

In January last on Munnonday *at morne,*
As along the fields I past to view the winter corne,
I leaked me behind, and saw come ore the knough,
Yen glenting in an apron with a bonny brent brow.

2.

I bid gud morrow, Fair Maid, and she right courteously,
Bekt lew and sine kind Sir, she said, Gud day agen to ye.
I speard o her, Fair Maid, quo I, how far intend you know?
Quo she, I mean a mile or twa to yonder bonny brough.

3.

Fair Maid, Ime weel contented to ha sike company;
For I am ganging out the gate that you intend to be.

When we had walkt a mile or twa, I said to her, My Dow,
May I not light your apron sine kiss your bonny brow?

4.

Nea, gud Sir, you are far mistean, for I am nean o those, 465
I hope you ha more breeding than to light a womans cloths;
For Ive a better chosen than any sike as you,
Who boldly may my apron light, and kiss [ma] bonny brow.

5.

Nay, gif you are contracted, I have no more to say; 470
Rather than be rejected, I will give ore the play.
And I will choose yen o my own that shall not on me rew,
Will boldly let me light her apron, kiss her bonny brow.

6.

Sir, I see you are proud-hearted, and leath to be said nay; 475
You need not tall ha started for eaght that I did say.
You knaw wemun for modesty no at the first time boo;
But gif we like your company we are as kind as you.

Bubble. How dee like it?
Sir Roger. Oh! I have hundred such as this, Sir. 480
Fumble. A pretty matter ifack, a very pretty matter.
Rashley. I doubt, Sir, you heard it not.
Fumble. Ay, is it not, Mr. *Rashley,* is it not? Ifack I like it well.
Rashley. With all my heart, Sir. 485
Fumble. Right ifack, it was sung well indeed.
Omnes. Ha, ha, ha!
Bubble. Well said, Grandsire *Fumble.*— Come, Sir *Roger,* now let's in, and toss a bumper about.
Sir Roger. I wait upon you, Sir. *Cob,* lead in your 490
mistriss.——   (*Exeunt.*)
(*Manent,* Rashley *and* Emilia.)
Rashley. So! Thus far all is well.—— But what's next to

be done? For I know *Ranger* and *Maria* are plotting mischief.

Emilia. To prevent 'em we must counterfeit a falling out by railing at you to my husband. I'll soon confirm it in his opinion; but be sure you are melancholy enough; and by this means their designs are frustrated, and we still safe in our intrigue.

Rashley. Excellent!—— And I'll warrant you, Sweet, I'll play my part well.

Emilia. The better will be the success. But let's go in for fear we are seen.

Rashley.
 Thus whilst we're equally involv'd in thought,
 That side fares best that lays the wisest plot.

(Exeunt.)

The Second Act.

[Scene 1. Ranger's *lodging.*]
Enter Ranger *and* Maria.

Ranger. Never was an intrigue carried with so much confidence; every word they spoke retain'd a double meaning, but so evident, that any animal but a dull husband could not fail to understand it. For they were so far from hiding their amour, that they openly confest all; only speaking in a third person for a slender security. He stood and heard it, and often would laugh heartily to hear himself notoriously abused.

Maria. An insipid fool! Oh that I had been there to have chang'd the scene a little! But, Sir, cou'd you be idle on such an occasion? Why did not you play your part cunningly, and discover 'em?

Ranger. Faith, I did what I could. But the cunning devil your sister, still as I was speaking something towards the discovery, would interrupt me, and in a minute dash all my hopes by turning what was said into raillery.

Maria. Is she so politick? 'Tis very well; I once imagin'd I could best design, and thought my talent of wit equal with any. But are they so intimate, say ye, Sir?

Ranger. As man and wife.
Maria. Impudent fellow! Dares he insult over my love? Baffle my passion with a sly pretence? I am not fair enough; but he shall find my brain has wit enough to ruine his design, fool as I am.
Ranger. (*Aside.*) Now the Devil in her is working hard for me; we shall have it anon.——
Maria. Fool'd by a brothers wife! A creature that the law makes kin to me! No, 'twas tamely thought, and I as tamely now should suffer wrongs had I a dastard spirit. But in me Nature has shown her master-piece, and to a masculine person Providence has bestow'd an active soul so sensible of wrongs, that to forgive would argue me as base as is their treachery.
Ranger. (*Aside.*) Now she thunders; the Devil has been priming her all this while, and now she scatters like a hand-granado.
Maria. My love refus'd! 'Tis death to the dull fool. Death, double death! Damnation too 'tis likely.—— But why did I name it love? There's no such word; for with this breath I banish it for ever, and in my breast receive obscure revenge, my hearts delightful darling! Oh the pleasure in that slender word revenge!—— I'll plague the fool her husband with a story shall make his gall flow upwards.
Ranger. Plague him with doubts, and make his jealousie break into violent fits of rage and passion. I'll further all, Madam; by Heav'n I will not fail you.
Maria. Enough; and doubt not we'll soon turn the current.
Ranger. We'll catch 'em in his lodging.
Maria. Entrap 'em there, and bring him in to see it.
Ranger. Right! What else? We'll shame 'em.——
Maria. Slight 'em.——

Ranger. Laugh at 'em.——
Maria. Vex 'em.——
Ranger. Ruine 'em.——   60
Maria. Dam 'em.——
Ranger. Hey! By Heav'n 'tis excellent; and now I see the sence of wrongs can arm a female spirit, and make it vigorous.—— Oh I adore thy temper!
Maria. I'll instantly go to her, and first charge her   65
with the fact, then upbraid her; for I am resolved never to let her rest till she deserts his passion.——

> And whilst she suffers that base wretch to woo her,
> I'll plot, and counterplot, but I'll undo her.
>
> *(Exit.)*   70

Ranger. I am glad I met with her; for of all the persons I am acquainted with, she only has enough of the Divil to follow such a business closely; for she'll never rest till she has betray'd 'm, which still will further my revenge; and I am resolv'd to enjoy her sister, if it be   75
but only for the dear pleasure of boasting it hereafter. I'll strait to *Bubble,* and once more infect him with my poyson. *Maria* is my pilot, and her being thus slighted by *Rashley,* will still augment her desire of revenge; 'tis natural to the sex.   80

> For baulk a woman once, and love rebate,
> Not all the devils shall reclaim her hate.
>
> *(Exit.)*

Scene 2. [Bubble's *lodging.*]
Enter Rashley, Emilia.

Emilia. Manage it but carefully, you need not doubt the consequence. I have already possest my husband with a belief of our variance, and I know he's coming up   5
with an intent to reconcile us. I'll not be seen; the rest is your part. Carry it but handsomly, and *Ranger*'s plots

are fruitless. *Maria* has sent also to speak with him; I guess the bus'ness, and I am accordingly provided.—— But remember you are not tardy.

Rashley. Never doubt me, Madam; I am more a lover than to be idle in a bus'ness that so nearly concerns us. Besides, 'tis so well contriv'd, and so easie to be follow'd, that to fail now would demonstrate me as defective in sence as your husband is. But what bus'ness can your sister have with you? The Devil and she have been plotting together about this intrigue.

Emilia. Let 'em plot.—— I am so much her sister, that my part shall never be wanting to furnish the comedy. I'll go to her strait. In the mean time be you sure to play your part with him.—— (*Noise within.*) Hark! I hear him coming. (*Exit.*)

Rashley. Well! I never thought a woman till now so necessary a creature. Intrigues are their master-pieces, and as readily they undertake 'em as a country-lawyer a bad cause from a half-witted client. 'Twould be excellent sport to hear the two she-wolves bark one at another; but since I cannot be there, I'll divert my self with entertaining the fool her husband.—— Here he comes! Now to my studied posture.

Enter Bubble.

Bubble. Why how now, *Tom*? What, all-a-mort? In verity this is foppery, as Sir *Roger* says. Come, cheer up, cheer up, Man, and hold up thy head; in troth thou makest me sad to see thee look so like—— so like a—— gammon of bacon. There I was sharp upon him.—— Ha, ha! A good jest afaith.

Rashley. (*Aside.*) Dam him, what a simile the fool has found out! Sir, it lies not in any mans power to banish serious thoughts at all times.—— Besides, I have some cause for my present melancholy.

Bubble. The cause?—— Come, come, *Tom,* I know the

cause, ha, ha.—— You thought, I warrant, to have carried matters so privately; but if I once go about such a business, there's ne'er a man in Christendom (tho' I say it) can find out a cause sooner than I.

Rashley. You may be mistaken in mine, Sir, for all that.

Bubble. Mistaken? Ha, ha!—— I see, *Tom,* thou knowest not what 'tis to be ingenious. I tell thee once more, I do know the cause, the very cause; I, and more then that, the cause of that cause;—— 'Sbud there's ne'er an attorney in the Inns of Court knows more causes than I do.

Rashley. I doubt not but in the end you'll be brought to confess your self too positive in this particular. But since you have such an excellent faculty, and imagine your self so well skill'd in finding out secrets, come, what is't? What is't?

Bubble. What is't? Why, ha, ha, ha!—— My wife—— my wife, *Tom,* and you're faln out, ha, ha, ha!—— Have I mumpt you now ifaith?

Rashley. I must confess you are in the right, Sir.

Bubble. O must you so, Sir? What a pox, I warrant you thought we husbands had no wit but what our wives lend us? But I would have you to know, *Tom,* that I am a Leviathan at these matters. To be plain, that is as much as to say, a whale.——

Rashley. I am sufficiently convinc'd of your excellent judgment, Sir; and as I have confest to you freely the cause of my sadness to be your wives ill usage of me, so I am continually tortur'd to guess the reason; for I am confident, Sir, you know I always honour'd her, and lov'd her.

Bubble. Faith! So thou didst! I'll say that for thee; and by the Lord *Harry* she shall love and honour thee too, or I'll be very sharp upon her; I'll pinch her severely faith, for all she's my Chicken. Nay, if she'll be still refractory, rather then fail thou shalt pinch her too, *Tom*. I am not like your surly-burly-waspish-cross-grain'd fellows, that fall out and fight about their wives. 'Sbud I'll give my friend leave at any time to chastise my wife if she don't behave her self civilly.

Rashley. You ever load me with your kind expressions, dear friend!——

Bubble. Dear *Tom,* faith thou'rt an honest fellow.

(*Embrace.*)

Rashley. (Aside.) This ever is the fate of cuckolds.——

Bubble. Never doubt; I'll bring you together agen with a vengeance. Nay, I can tell you the reason of her anger too, if I thought 'twere convenient.

Rashley. Convenient! Why, Sir, 'tis the only thing that conduces to my contentment; for I have long studied in vain, and could never yet so much as guess at it. Let me beg it of you, Sir; come, I'm sure you cannot deny so near a friend.

Bubble. Ifaith I cannot, that's the truth on't, and thou shalt have it.—— Why, you must know, *Tom,* one night (when I was examining her about you) she told me very seriously that the cause of her anger was, that you promis'd to give her a squirril that night, and never kept your word; and she loves squirrils passionately.

Rashley. 'Tis true, I confess I did promise her; but as the Devil would have it, I was disappointed utterly of my squirril that night my self; for I got very drunk, and from thence sprung this fatal consequence.

Bubble. Pugh!—— No matter; I'll warrant thee I'll bring all about again.

Rashley. Oh 'tis impossible; I am sure she'll ne'er be brought to't.

Bubble. Not brought to't? Yes, I'll lay my commands

upon her, and I'll have you know she shall be brought to't. I'll lay a wager I'll reconcile you both before night.——
Rashley. Done. Any wager.——
Bubble. What shall it be? 115
Rashley. Why, five Guinneys to be spent in a treat of ven'son and champaine.
Bubble. Agreed ifaith; and we'll drink and sing toryrory. Not reconcile you! You shall be all one before tomorrow-morning.—— I have a spell for that; I'll do't, 120 I say; come along, Boy.—— *(Exit.)*

    Rashley. A petty friend for pimping we applaud
    But of all men a husband's the best bawd.——
                                            (Exit.)

        Scene 3. [*Another room in* Bubble's *lodging.*]
            Enter Sir Roger, Cordelia, Sneak.
Sir Roger. Madam, you, as being the niece to Mr. *Peregrine*, truly deserve the favour I intend you by this alliance. You are a handsom woman, and in verity were 5 I a young man, none shou'd be more forward than I for a place in your affection. I like your air well; and upon my faith you have the right way on't. Ah!—— Madam, I once saw the days when such an eye as yours—— Well, I say no more on't,—— 'Tis for my nephew now I make 10 addresses; you see what he is, Madam. His face is none of the worst, nor his person, I think, any way defective. In brief, Madam, I present him to you, nor shall he want an estate to make him worthy.
Cordelia. [*Aside.*] 'Tis well he nam'd an estate to candy 15 over his bitter pill; my squeamish stomach would else have hardly digested it.—— Lord! How he looks?——
Sir Roger. Cob! Go; prethee go and make your address to the lady. He's newly come from the Colledge,

Madam, and is as the rest of 'em are, a little bashful at
first; but by that time h'as seen a play or two——
Cordelia. Me thinks this silence becomes him very well,
Sir. A student should always be contemplative; 'tis a
great sign of learning.
Sir Roger. 'Tis a sign he thinks the more. But,
Madam, ladies of this age are not to be won with imaginary courtship; 'tis the practick part they love. And he
that can sing well, dance well, talk well, rhime modishly,
swear decently, and lye confoundedly, is certainly the
happy man, whilst others pass unregarded.
Cordelia. I see, Sir, you are well skill'd in modish address; but give me leave to tell ye, perhaps few other
ladies are of my humour. I love words considerately
spoken.——
Sir Roger. And I too, faith, Madam. *Cob,* dee hear that,
Cob?
Sneak. Ay, ay! 'Tis a fine woman, by *Jerico,* and now I
begin to be a little in heart. I shall put up well enough
anon, Uncle.
Sir Roger. Well said! Why now I love thee. And,
Madam, as to his interiour vertues, I dare speak for 'em.
His wit is hereditary. Ah! his father, old Sir *Jeremy Sneak,*
had a notable head-piece, and troth *Cob* comes very near
him. You'll find it, Madam, when he talks with you.
Cordelia. Your character of him, Sir, gives me the satisfaction I should receive in his discourse. I imagine him
to be one of those that hoord up wit for *Plato's* Great
Year, and are very shie of using their talent for fear of
diminishing the value in making it too common.
Sir Roger. In verity, Madam, I always held him so.——
Cob!——
Sneak. Ay, Madam, you may say of me what you
please; I am your slave,——your vassal,——your pigg,

Madam. But as for wit, as my nuncle says, I think I may compare with another, take the Court-Cabal away. 'Tis a blessing thrown upon me. Besides, mine is none of your wheadling wits, that cheat for a livelihood. I am no parasite, Madam; I am a scholar, I!

Sir Roger. In troth he's in the right. Did not I tell you, Madam, he would speak notably? Ah, 'tis a wag.

Cordelia. His disputes in the Colledge have added extreamly to his rhetorick; he speaks with good emphasis, and gives a delightful period to every jest, of which I see he has many. But I would fain have the gentleman speak himself; a little talk I am sure would become him.

Sir Roger. He shall do't, Madam.—— [*Aside to* Sneak.] *Cob*, now's your time; she's wrought finely.—— Madam, I'll take my leave for a minute.—— [*Aside to* Cordelia.] I know his temper, Madam; he'll speak the better for my absence.—— (*Exit.*)

Cordelia. Pray, Sir, what university was blest with your presence?

Sneak. Cambridge, Madam.——

Cordelia. Will you not be angry if I ask you one question more?

Sneak. O Lord, angry, Madam? You do not know me. Angry! You mistake me clearly. We of the Round Cap are not giv'n to't; 'tis your Graduates are the angry people.

Cordelia. Pray, what have you learnt at *Cambridge?*

Sneak. Learnt! What a plaguy question's that?—— [*Aside.*] Where's my uncle now?—— Learnt, Madam?

Cordelia. Yes, Sir, learnt!

Sneak. Why, Madam,—— I learnt nothing.

Cordelia. Nothing, Sir!

Sneak No,——but to wear a daggled gown, as the rest do, and eat dry chops of rotten mutton. We fellow-commoners don't go thither to learn; Madam, we go for diversion, we.

Cordelia. I thought you had gone to learn the Sciences.

Sneak. Right, Madam; but not gentlemen. Your green half-witted pupils, I confess, come thither for some such business; that is, Madam, your priggs that would be parsons. But the Sciences of your persons of quality—— I'll give you a description—— Hum?—— 'Tis to wench immoderately—— To be drunk hourly—— To wear their cloaths slovenly—— To abuse the Proctor damnably—— And to be expell'd the Colledge triumphantly.—— There are sev'n, but I contented my self with these.

Cordelia. [*Aside.*] This is ever found. Your slie fool is in his nature more impudent than the greatest Professors of Debauchery.—— I must shift him off.——

Enter Fumble.

Fumble. Oh!—— Here she is; and ifack I'll put up to her now I have found her. How dost thou do, Girl?—— Hah! How dost thou do? Give me thy hand. Ah, little rogue!—— Well, I have been with my goldsmith about the ring I promis'd thee; thou shalt have it, Bird, thou shalt have it.—— How now, who is that there?

Sneak. O the Devil!—— Now will the old doting fellow disturb us before I have told her half my mind. Who am I, Sir? Why, Sir, I am one that cares as little——

Fumble. Thank you heartily, Sir, ifack; I am very well; only cold weather, cold weather.—— 'Tis Sir *Roger's* nephew! A pretty fellow, a very pretty fellow.

Sneak. Very well, Sir; wou'd you were very sick, Sir. 'Ounds, I must beat this fellow.——

Cordelia. Here's like to be rare sport.

Sneak. Pray, old philosopher, depart in silence for fear of further damage; this lady and I have bus'ness.

Fumble. Ifack, and so she is, Sir, very pretty, very pretty; *bona fide.* Ah that black o' th' top there! Well, I'll say no more. But, ifack, black hair, black eyes, and a black—— (Gad forgive me, what was I going to say?)—— patch or two further generation more than tissues and embroideries.

Sneak. Generation? O Lord! Was ever such an impudence? An old doting impotent fellow, one that was rotten in his minority, and now has lost three of his five sences, to talk of generation! I am impatient. Will you begone, Sir? 'Sbud I will so swinge you else.

Cordelia. Hold, Sir, and pray forbear this rudeness; I like his company very well.

Sneak. How! Like him? Why, he has nothing, Madam. A lady can like no hearing, no smelling, no tasting, no teeth, no strength, no——nothing I say that a man should have? Besides, he's above four-score; and by being a stallion in his youth, has acquir'd to be a baboon in his age, by *Jerico.*—— 'Sbud, like him, quoth a?

Fumble. What does the wag say? Hah! What does he say? He's a pretty spruce fellow, Madam, and ifack knows a hawk from a handsaw, as the saying is.—— But here are those not far off that ifack know as much as he, if that were all. What think'st thou, Bird? Do they not? Do they not, Rogue? Well, still I say that hair of thine. Ah, Rascal!

Cordelia. I am glad it pleases you, Sir.

Sneak. But, Madam, when shall I begin? 'Sbud, me thinks we lose time.

Cordelia. Begin! What, Sir?

Sneak. Why, my courtship. Pox o' this old chatt'ring fellow; if he had not come, I had been out of my pain before now.—— Hark ye, Reverend Sir. 'Bud! What d'ee do prating here? Why don't you go and chat to your

grand-daughter at home, if you love women so well?——
  Fumble. Hah!—— What does the wag say, Madam?
  Cordelia. He says, Sir, he's extreamly in love with your grand-daughter.
  Fumble. My grand——daughter? And ifack she deserves it, Madam. She's a juicy, sprately girl; she'll make a pottle of water of a pint of ale. A chip o' the old block, *bona fide,* and shall turn her back to ne'er a one in Christendom of her inches, I'll say that for her.
            Enter Betty.
  Betty. [*Aside to* Sneak.] Sir, there's one Mrs. *Snare* below desires to speak with you.
  Sneak. Snare! O Lord, what shall I do? How the Devil came she to know I was here? Hark, prethee, Sweetheart, tell her I am gone. Oh! I would not see her for the world.
  Betty. Sir, she says she dogg'd you hither, and swears and rants yonder strangely.
  Sneak. O damn'd quean! What shall I do?
  Betty. And vows if you come not instantly, she'll go into the parlor to Sir *Roger,* and discover something to him, I know not what; but I saw she was a big-bellied woman, and I was loath to discourage her.   (*Exit* Betty.)

  Sneak. Well, well, tell her I'll come. Why, how the Devil cou'd she get from *Cambridge* already?
  Cordelia. What's the matter, Sir? Not well?
  Sneak. Yes, I thank you, Madam, very well, only thinking of a little business I have; I must about it presently. Madam, your servant; I'll wait on you some other time. [*Aside.*] I must go and pacifie this quean. This comes of learning the Sciences with a pox.——   (*Exit* Sneak.)
  Cordelia. Come, sir, shall we go in?
  Fumble. Ifack, and so he is, Madam. But the fellow has

some pretty parts, and will grow better in time. But come, let's go in and see Sir *Roger*.

Cordelia. 'Twas that I askt you.

Fumble. Hah! Dost like me, sayst thou, ifack? I'm glad on't. Shall we not have a word or two in private, my little Queen of Fairies? We must, I say, we must.—— Ah Rogue!—— I'll warrant thou art a swinger.—— But come, let's go.—— (*Exeunt.*)

Scene 4. Emilia's *bed-chamber*.
Enter Maria *and* Emilia *severally.*

Emilia. Now for my talent of women! I see by her looks I shall have occasion for it.

Maria. Sister!

Emilia. Sister!

Maria. The natural love I bear you, and my desire to prevent your growing infamy, has brought me hither to give you counsel.

Emilia. The sence I have of your ill nature, and my knowledge of the little good it will do you, has brought me hither to give you advice.

Maria. Your reputation is lowdly branded by all tongues, and I only as a sister have power to speak indifferently of your life in hopes of your reformation.

Emilia. Your malice and unexampled envy is mortally hated by all people; I only as a sister retaining so much pity as to desire its utter dissolution.

Maria. Why do you eccho me?

Emilia. Why do you question me? What have I done deserves it?

Maria. Done! Recollect your thoughts, and then confess; for my part, shame ties up my tongue. I dare not speak it.

Emilia. Dare not! Nay, that I am sure is false; you dare speak any thing. Come, prethee don't fright me; what is't you mean?

Maria. (*Aside.*) Excellent cunning! She has fitted me.—— Why would you seem ignorant? I confess to a stranger you might be cautious of a nice confession. But this artifice to your sister, fie, *Emilia.*

Emilia. Now I'll lay my life your design is to wheadle something out of me to make your self merry withal.

Maria. [*Aside.*] Rare still!—— No, Madam, this is no such merry matter; the infamy of a family is not so to be jested with.

Emilia. Infamy! Nay, then I see 'tis time to be serious. Come, express it; I suppose 'tis the invention of your envy, some new stratagem to affront me with; I am no stranger to your temper.

Maria. This is an impudence beyond a prostitute. Do I not know you are false?

Emilia. False! How?

Maria. False to your husband; false with *Rashley*. I need not tell you how; you best know that.

Emilia. I know you love him! And am sensible of the intrigues and assignations which you have had, which makes your meaning visible. But me thinks this is so strange a design.

Maria. Design! What is't she means? I hope you can tax me with no such crime with him.

Emilia. Not I; 'tis not my business; I have only liberty to guess. Yet indeed your often private meetings were a little suspitious, and I suppose your late raillery was only a design; but you might have took a better way with your sister. I am not so talkative.

Maria. Exquisite Devil!—— Death, I am incens'd beyond all bounds of reason. I private with him! An intrigue with me! Fury! Thou know'st——

Emilia. I do; and to exasperate thy rage, will now confess all. I do love *Rashley* more than I love fame. Nay, more than you could do, could you die for him.—— But why shou'd that offend you?

Maria. Oh confusion! I am all o'er fire. Dare you be such a devil? Dare you love him?

Emilia. Yes; and to vex you more, dare make you of my counsel.

Maria. Can I indure this? Oh for a look now of a basilisk that I might kill thee.

Emilia. Thou art worse.——

Maria. Expect to find me so; for if there be a strategem of malice in all Hell, I'll have it thence. Ah, I'll be a tender sister to thee.

Emilia. As ever woman yet was blest withal.

Maria. Not all the infernals clad in the secret darkest robes of malice did ever watch a soul they meant to ruine, as I will thee. Thy very sleeps shall be discover'd to me, and every dream I'll trace with so much care, that if thou scapest thou art the wiser sister, and I a poor unthinking creature good for nothing.

Emilia. I slight thy threats, and dare thee to persevere. Manage thy hate with such dexterity, the world may wonder at thee, and confess thou hadst the practick part of policy. Design thy plots so subt'ly, that the Devil shou'd own himself out done in his own mystery; yet in the arms of him I love, I'd laugh to see my wit out-do 'em.

Maria. Thy wit! Thy wit compare with mine, insipid fool?

Emilia. Yes; and my prosp'rous fate shall mount me far above thy shallow strategems.

Maria. I'll pull thee down from that ambitious height, and trample thee in ashes.

Emilia. Do.

Maria. Expect it.

Emilia. And from that low recess I'll forge a plot shall blow thee into air.——

I'll make that devil in thy envy tame.
Maria. And if I fail thee may I sink and dam.

(Exeunt.)

The Third Act.

[Scene: *a room in* Bubble's *house,
adjacent to* Emilia's *chamber.*]
Enter Sneak *and Mrs.* Snare.

Sneak. Nay! Prethee, *Pegg*, have patience.

Snare. Tell not me of patience, Sir. For my part I can stay no longer. You see my condition; if you will consider, so; if not, Sir *Roger* shall know that the abuse of so innocent a person as I was, deserves better satisfaction.

Sneak. Innocent!—— 'Sbud, she was a strumpet to the whole Colledge before I knew her. Innocent, with a pox!

Snare. Sir, do not grumble, nor say your Devils *Pater Noster* to me, but give me money. Fifty pounds I demand, which I think is reasonable enough, considering the charge of my journey.

Sneak. You might have staid till I came back agen. I was not running away.

Snare. But I was, Sir, and so might you for any thing I know. Come, come, Sir, I am to be baffled no more; I am grown older now, make me thankful.

Sneak. [*Aside.*] Ay, in impudence, by *Jerico*. She has been snapt it seems formerly, but has now learnt cunning. Ah, plague o' these Sciences, I say still!—— Come, wilt thou be civil? Wilt thou take twenty pounds? Pox, use a little conscience in thy dealings; thou wilt thrive the better for't.

Snare. I'll abate not a farthing, Sir; don't tell me of conscience.

Sneak. 'Sbud, wou'd she were i' th' sea, and a millstone about her neck. I must give it; for if my uncle comes and sees her, I am undone.

Enter Betty.

Betty. O Sir, what shall we do? Sir *Roger* and my master are just coming.

Sneak. Oh unhappy minute! If he sees me I am lost for ever. No hole nor corner to hide us in, my little rogue? 'Sbud, here's a guiney for thee; do but contrive handsomly.

Betty. Well, Sir, I see you are a gentleman; therefore I'll help you. This door opens to my ladies chamber; there you may hide your selves; and at night when it begins to grow dark, I'll come and let you out.

Sneak. With all my heart! On I've an ague on me.——
(*Exeunt.*)

Enter Ranger *and* Emilia.

Ranger. Are you still resolv'd?

Emilia. Assure your self I am and shall be ever.

Ranger. Give me but hopes, and I'll forget all injuries, and ask your pardon.

Emilia. Fie, this from a man of wit, one that can plot so well? 'Tis impossible. What wou'd you have me do?

Ranger. Desert young *Rashley.* Come, I beg thee do it.

Emilia. Not for the world! Oh Heav'n! Desert him! I love him, Sir.

Ranger. Go on then, Devil, and if I don't plague thee!——

Enter Bubble, *Sir* Roger, Rashley, Fumble.

Bubble. Now for the venison, *Tom!* You'll stand to your bargain?

Rashley. Firmly, Sir; win it, and 'tis yours.—— [*Aside.*] Ha!—— What a devil makes *Ranger* here?

Sir Roger. Madam, I hope you'll excuse my last abrupt departure. My nature, Madam, is merry, and in verity careless sometimes. I have not since I came to *England* atchiev'd the polite method of courtship and address; but if blunt actions, kind behaviour, and merry songs can do it, I think I have shown an example, have I not, old Signior!

Fumble. Ifack, Sir, and 'tis right, let who will say the contrary; what does he say now? Madam, you may believe him.

Emilia. Any thing, Sir, rather than put you to the trouble of an apology.   (Emilia *frowns on* Rashley.)

Rashley. What think you now, Sir? Do you observe her angry look? Do but see what an eye of indignation she casts upon me!

Bubble. Ay, ay,—— I'll put out her eye of indignation presently; I'll fetch her down with her haughty looks in a moment; I'll make her look as I'd have her, or I'll put her head into a pudding-bag.

Ranger. [*Aside.*] 'Sdeath, how she looks! Here's another plot a hatching.

Bubble. Wife! I have brought honest *Tom* here to be reconcil'd to thee; and to take away all manner of distastes, he says he will give thee a squirril at any time; woult thou not, *Tom*?

Rashley. Sir, and my heart into the bargain, if she please to pardon me.

Bubble. Why, look ye now; he's as honest a fellow as lives, I'll say that for him.

Emilia. Sir, the affront he offer'd me was so contrary to my nature, and his behaviour so opposite to his duty and character, that to forgive him, wou'd argue my

spirit as mean as by his late deportment one might guess
his breeding. 95
 Bubble. What! Dare you be refractory?—— Hoh!——
Do it, or by the Lord *Harry* I shall be very sharp upon
you, that's in short.——
 Ranger. [*Aside.*] Now all the fiends that dwell beneath
the center, and hourly study deeds subtle and horrid, to 100
sooth and snare the souls ye mean to dam, in favour of
your commonwealth appear, and to be still more devil-
lish, coppy her.
 Bubble. Still refractory? Then thus, I break the truce,
and sally out with my full power. 105
 Ranger. Sir, do you not see her artifice? This is nothing what she intends; 'tis all feign'd, and you are
abused, by Heav'n. Sir, there's nothing of this real.
 Bubble. Ah! Wou'd it were not. But *Ned,* thou canst
talk well; prethee go and try if thou canst reconcile 'em. 110
Faith I'll do as much for thee; prethee try.——
 Ranger. Insufferable ignorance! No brains! No sence
of feeling! Sir, this is all dissimulation, and to carry on
their design of abusing you.
 Bubble. Why, peace, I say, not a word of this. 'Sbud I 115
shall lose my venison by this fools prating, if I let him
alone a little longer. Wife, I command you once more,
and instantly obey upon this summons, or I'll turn you
away like a vagabond for contempt of my government.
Sir *Roger!* Try you to perswade her. 'Sbud this *Ned* here 120
had lik'd to have spoil'd all; but what says *Scoggen?*
 Emilia. 'Tis hard to force lost friendship to the blood
when once 'tis banisht.
 Ranger. Had she been bred a witch she had lost half
her character. 125
 Sir Roger. Come, Madam! Forget and forgive; 'tis
necessary your husband should be obey'd. Mr. *Rashley,* I

am sorry to see you so deserted by the ladies you us'd to be most in favour withal.

Rashley. Not I; but you weigh my merits in your own scale, Sir *Roger.*

Sir Roger. No faith, I am old now; but about some thirty years ago I could have said something. I could have fetcht 'em about, with a horse-pox ifaith; I never flincht. I was a true knight-errant, I.

Fumble. [*Aside.*] What is the meaning of all this? Ifack I cannot guess the matter. But mum, I must not discover my failing.

Emilia. Well, Sir, rather than be thought disobedient I will submit; but Heav'n knows with what an ill will——

Bubble. Why so, now all's well, and the venison's mine.—— Ha, ha, ha,—— I thought I should have it. Faith, *Tom,* be civil, and kiss her; 'tis no confirmation else.

Ranger. Oh dam him, dam him! Was ever such a coxcomb?

Rashley. (Aside [*to* Emilia].) 'Tis now about five; at seven I will not fail ye, Madam.—— You have given me new life with this favour.

Ranger. (Aside.) At seven? (Good!) Thanks to my ear for that discovery. I shall go near to spoil your assignation.

Bubble. Go now, get you in, and begin a set at Ombre, and I'll come and make one presently. By the Lord Harry I am glad they are friends with all my heart.

(*Exit Sir* Roger, Fumble, Rashley, Emilia *smiling.*)
Enter Maria.

Ranger. So *Paris* stole the wife of *Menelaus,* and *Troy* grew bright with fire.

Bubble. Hey day!—— *Troy!* Why what hast thou to do with *Troy? Ned,* prethee let us talk of our own affairs.

Maria. And wisely too; for your reputation suspended one hour will grow nauseous. The rabble will shout at ye, and point their fingers, and by your name you will grow infamous.

Enter Betty *at door.*

Bubble. My name, Sister! What dost mean? What name?

Maria. A cuckold. Can you bear it, Sir? A cuckold-buz.

Bubble. By the Lord *Harry,* 'tis but a scurvy name for a man of honour, that's the truth on't; but what is't to me?

Ranger. Nothing, Sir, nothing; only you are the man, that's all.

Bubble. That's all, quoth-a? What a pox does he mean?

Maria. Dull man! I blush to call ye brother; that kind name, your want of sence has taken from you. Can you see the guilty love 'twixt *Rashley* and your wife, the melting touches, and the glancing eyes? The often pressings, sighs, and kind caresses, and all the signs of shame and burning lust, and yet be patient? Oh the insipid dulness of a husband! A husband.

Bubble. Rashley and my wife! Pish,—— Why, I reconcil'd 'em but just now; she has been angry with him this week for not giving her a squirril she promis'd her.

Ranger. A squirril?—— Hah! A very fine present that, if you understood all.

Betty. [*Aside.*] Happy discovery! This shall to my lady immediately. (*Exit.*)

Maria. That anger was design'd. You are abus'd; and I that have a share in all your ignominy, have now resolv'd prevention. Oh that ever I shou'd live to be a witness of this shame! (*Weeps.*) Heav'n knows how I have lov'd her, instructed her, and told her the duty of a wife was to obey and be constant; yet all would not do. Therefore I am resolv'd to right *my self* and you in the discovery; nor shall our race in future times be branded with any spurious offspring.

Ranger. I could not be believ'd; I was impertinent. But if you knew what I have seen, Sir.

Bubble. Seen! Why prethee what has thou seen, *Ned*?

Ranger. Faith, 'twill be no secret long; therefore I'll tell you. I have seen her lie in *Rashley*'s arms and kiss him; play with his nose, and clap his cheeks, and laugh till her whole frame was shook with titulation. I guess, Sir, 'twas at you, but will not swear it. She'd sing, and breathe upon him, and with her hand lockt fast in his, and eyes with rapture gazing on his face, she'd tell him wanton stories of her love, and of her easie husband. He, to requite her, wou'd display her charms, and betwixt every word imprint a kiss to prove his amorous argument.

Bubble. And you have seen this?

Ranger. More than this, Sir; I have seen (but to tell you is to be call'd impertinent!) such things, such monstrous things.

Bubble. My head begins to ake; all is not well. Prethee, *Ned,* out with 'em. Come, I am thy friend; and 'sbud, if I thought any thing were done in hugger mugger.

Maria. What would you do then?

Bubble. Do!—— Why, I'd ask him civilly whether his meaning were good or no.

Ranger. His meaning?——

Bubble. Ay.—— You know 'tis best to begin mildly, that afterwards, if occasion be, a man may cut his throat with greater assurance.

Maria. Stare on your infamy with eagle-aspect! Behold the evidence of shame writ in her eyes and actions! See every glance, each touch, each kind embrace; and when you have seen 'em in the very fact, stand coldly unconcern'd, and ask the meaning. Ah! Curse upon all dulness.——

Ranger. Let *Rashley* smile and point his fingers at ye, tell you a story of a *quondam* mistriss, (which is indeed your wife) how oft he has lain with her, and pleasantly deceived the easie cuckold;—— Yet as a president of excellent nature, I cou'd advise you still to ask his meaning,——his meaning.

Maria. Watch all his actions; and when some kind genius has, to undeceive you, made you a spectator of *Rashley,* full of hopes, and all undrest, entring your bed with a glad lovers haste, step in, and pull him back, and ask his meaning, his meaning!

Bubble. My bed! My bed is my castle; and, by the Lord Harry, he that violates it but with a look, my fist shall crush him into mummy.

Ranger. *(Aside.)* So! Now he begins to take fire.——

Bubble. He's a son of a whore, a dog, a bitch, a succubus; and if I find this true, I'll cut him piece-meal though he were sword-proof, and had a witch to his mother.

Maria. Ay, this is meaning now! Go on and prosper.

Ranger. These words display a reviv'd sence of honour, nor shall you want encouragement to forward it; and since I see your eyes and understanding are open'd, I, as your friend, will give this secret to you. 'Twas my good fortune to hear an assignation appointed between 'em this night at seven a clock. I guess 'tis now very near the hour. You have a key to the chamber; go thither at the time appointed, and then never trust your friend if you find her not the falsest of women.

Bubble. If I do, I'll make her the ugliest in Christendom, for I'll cut off her nose, and send her to the Devil for a New-Years-Gift.

Maria. Here she comes, we must not be seen, 'twill spoil all. Talk of going abroad, and carry it handsomly, for fear she mistrusts.

Bubble. But where shall we meet?

Ranger. At my lodging in the *Strand,* about half an hour hence.

(*Exeunt* [Ranger *and* Maria].)
Enter Emilia.

Emilia. What, studying, my dear? Come, come, indeed you must not be so thoughtful. Did you not promise to come and make one at Ombre?

Bubble. [*Aside.*] Now if I might be hang'd, cannot I speak an angry word, no.—— I wont play; I am busie, I am going abroad for two or three hours.—— Farewel.

(*Exit.*)

Emilia. 'Tis so; our intrigue to night is discover'd to him, I find by his actions; the infernal collegues, *Ranger* and *Maria,* have been possessing him with some strange resolutions. But since 'tis but what I expected, it gives me the less trouble, and 'tis ten to one but I have a counterplot left that shall undo their policies, tho' the Devil made one in the invention. Did you meet my husband?

Enter Rashley.

Rashley. Yes, but in a strange humour. He lookt with so dull an aspect, and return'd my salute so coldly, and so far from his usual manner, that I more than half fear——our intrigue is discover'd.

Emilia. Without doubt it is.—— They have plaid their parts to discover, and it now belongs to us to study to repel. Come, summon your wits together, and advise what's to be done in so critical a conjuncture; you had a contriving genius once.

Rashley. Ay, 'tis true, Madam, I had once; but this damn'd champaigne has so dull'd it, that Igad 'tis now worth little or nothing. Madam, you know my talent in plot is insignificant; but if a rancounter, or cutting *Ranger's* throat may do the bus'ness, I'll thrust my hand as far as any man. I'll spoil his plotting by Heav'n, say you but the word.

Emilia. No! Fighting will do in any other bus'ness better than this. For in stead of defending, it blasts my reputation.

Rashley. The Devil take me, if I had not like to have forgot that too. Well, I am a dull rogue, Madam, that's the truth on't.

Enter Betty.

Betty. Oh Madam, you are betray'd! Mr. *Ranger,* by what means Heav'n knows, has been inform'd of your assignation. I accidentally overheard him telling it to my master, and Madam *Maria* coming in, seconded his story with an extravagant fury; and in conclusion 'twas design'd that he should pretend business abroad, but privately return home and surprize ye.

Emilia. 'Tis as I imagin'd, and I am glad of this caution. Now we may take breath agen.

Rashley. Gad and so am I.—— But is there no way to keep on the plot, and deceive 'em still?

Emilia. 'Tis in my head, and will have birth presently.—— *Betty,* you have *Sneak* still fast in my chamber?

Betty. Yes, Madam, he's securely lockt in, and here's the key.

Emilia. Follow me then, and do as I directed you. In the mean time, Sir, go you to your chamber, and put on your gown and night-cap as if you had been in bed; and when you hear me stamp, come out, and wonder. Let me alone for the rest,—— I'll plague 'em with an after-plot. Away, the minute's near.——

(*Exit* Emilia *and* Betty.)

Rashley. What she intends I know not, but am certain of the success by the assurance she does it with.—— Hah! 'Tis a rare creature, and by Heav'n is mistriss of the sweetest nature, and noblest trust, and most substantial good English principles of any woman in *Europe.* Well,——if cuckolding be a crime, 'tis the sweetest crime in Christendom, and has certainly the most practisers. But let that pass; now to my gown and night-cap. *(Exit.)*

    Enter Sir Roger, Fumble, Cordelia, *and Servant.*

Sir Roger. 'Sdeath! I have had confounded luck to night;——not a good chance since I begun; nor no mirth neither, there's the plague on't.—— Had I had the liberty to have sung two or three merry catches, and have lost my money with a Trolly Lolly Lo, it had been nothing.—— Here;—— Hey;—— Where's *Cob;* call him hither quickly, and let us go.

Servant. Sir! I have not seen him these two hours; I believe he's gone home.

Sir Roger. How! What without taking leave of his mistriss? 'Tis impossible.

Fumble. Sir *Roger,* you are distrub'd me thinks; what is the matter? Hah! Your behaviour seems to publish that——

Sir Roger. No great matter, Sir. Pox o' this old fool.

Cordelia. Sir, it ill becomes a person of your gravity to be angry on so small an occasion.

Sir Roger. Small! By Heav'n, Madam,—— 'Tis a matter of moment. What, run away without taking leave? In verity 'tis barbarous, and derogates from his birth and breeding; nor can I, though his kinsman, excuse——

Fumble. What does Sir *Roger* say, Madam? Does he rally? Ha! He's a merry man, and a good fellow, and ifack I love mirth. For my part I hate your drowsie, insipid, flegmatick fellows, that sleep over a glass, and talk of nothing but state-politicks.—— But Sir *Roger* is a man for the purpose, a merry jolly-man, he.

Sir Roger. Sir, you may spare your commendations for them that delight in 'em. What an impertinent old fellow 'tis?—— Pray, Sir, no more of this, I am not pleased with it.

Fumble. Your song of Sir *Thomas Fairfax,* and the rest of the brave old fellows, was very fine, Sir *Roger.*—— Well! I'll not be positive, but there was certainly a great deal of judgment and sheer wit in some of those Rump-Songs.

Sir Roger. 'Sdeath! This is the most insufferable old fellow. Pox, tell not me of Rump Songs. Sir in verity, wou'd you had been hang'd up in stead of the Rump, that I might have been free from the noise.—— But, Madam, as I was saying, upon my honour I never knew *Cob* in such an errour.

Fumble. Then, Sir *Roger,* Chevy-Chace, and The Hunting of the Hare, is finely penn'd! Finely penn'd! Ifack it was——

Sir Roger. Oh the Devil, is there no riddance of this clack? Because he can hear nothing, he would speak all.

Fumble. Ay, so it was, Sir, so it was.—— But Ifack that Hunting was most excellently contriv'd. Ah! He makes the dogs speak notably. *Icod,* and the hare repartées agen very well for an animal of her magnitude.——

Sir Roger. 'Sbud, I shall grow as deaf as he if I stay longer. I must go seek my nephew. Come, Madam, lets go away and leave him; I am sure his eyes are so defective he cann't miss us presently.   (*Exeunt.*)

Fumble solus. And tho' some petulant, insignificant, and disaffected persons have rais'd calumnies by calling it doggrel and fustian, and such like; yet Ifack the thing is really a witty, facetious, (nay, and as some think) a moral satyr. For mark me, Sir *Roger,* and Madam pray give your attention, for the dogs were hieroglyphick-characters of Fanaticks, as the hare was of the Quakers, and ifack I have often heard the sisters sing it in stead of an hymn or an anthem, for the conversion of unbelievers; and nay, and as a greater rarity I have heard it acted to the life betwixt a Dog-Phanatick and a Conny-Quaker.—— But ifack,—— I think you mind me not.—— Ha, Sir *Roger*,—— Madam,—— Sir *Roger*, Madam,—— What, a vacuity?—— Gone? Well.——

(Pulls out spectacles.)

I'll after, and redeem all; but *Icod,* this was a little uncivil. *(Exit.)*

        Enter Ranger, Betty *with a candle, sets it on the table.*

Betty. Come, Sir, and with as little noise as you can, for fear of discovery. I swear were you not a man, to whom I am sensibly oblig'd, I should not be drawn to this infidelity.

Ranger. I will reward thy care; are they together?

Betty. Yes, Sir, in that room there.

(Pointing to the little door.)

Ranger. Take this, and begone, I have no further service for thee, and I would have her ignorant that this is thy discovery. Away.——

Betty. (Aside.) The discovery will add little to your content. But since I have the profit, I care not. *(Exit.)*

        Enter Bubble *and* Maria.

Bubble. Ned! What says she? Are they met?

Ranger. Securely, and with a great deal of content; they are in that room in the dark. (Met!) Ah, Sir! They are both better practis'd than ever to be tardy in a love-intrigue.

Maria. (Aside.) Now I think I have trapt her finely.——

Oh my joy!—— I shall not be able to contain my self.——

Bubble. A man of wit and honour thus abused! 'Tis horrible! A cuckold! 'Sbud, 'tis a worse name than a conjurer, and has more of the Devil in't.—— But I'll be so reveng'd, the world shall tremble at it. I'll first cut off her hair, to affront her family; then the want of a nose shall proclaim her bawd, and the penny-pot-poets shall make ballads on her.—— (Exit [*into* Emilia's *room*].)

Ranger. So! This thrives as I would have it, and we have snapt 'em finely in the nick! Just when the intrigue was at its best perfection! Oh revenge!——

Maria. Ha, ha, ha! Nay, and at such a time when all help is deny'd 'em; when her blushes, sighs and entreaties are all fruitless; when her exasperated husband's rage flows high, and best of all when *Rashley* is defenceless. O wit! I love thee for this stratagem!

Ranger. She dar'd us to persevere; slighted our plots, and had the confidence to make descriptions of her kind intrigue before her husbands face, then laught at us.

Maria. 'Tis now our time. Ha, ha, ha! I thought I could not fail.

Ranger. No; and this happy minute brings me more perfect pleasure, and more true delight, than pristine ages. For she's one whom Hell design'd for its chief instrument. She will out-lye a Syren, cheat the Devil, and dam more souls to further her intrigue than *Charon*'s boat has room for. (*Aside.*) Yet I own a kind of mungrel love, and must enjoy her tho' legions were her guard.

(*A shreik within.*)

Maria. Hark!—— He's as good as his word. Now I hope she'll own her sisters wit above her.—— Well!—— This was rarely plotted.——

Ranger. By Heav'n it was, and fit to be chronicled,

Madam.—— Your wit surpasses humane thought, and shou'd be spoken of with wonder. You plot with such assurance, that—

Enter Emilia [*from another door*].

Hell! Death! And confusion! Can I believe my eyes? She here!

Maria. I am confounded, and have lost my sences. Sure, Sir, we dream. Are we awake, think you?

Emilia. No! Nor shall never wake when I design to raise my wit above the poor weak creatures. I could laugh now, but I swear I pity ye. Wear out your tedious nights in dull design, and then i' th' morning hatch the abortive brood which ere night turns to nothing; slender encouragement, Heav'n knows, for wit. And you, Sir, plot and sweat, and plot agen for moon-shine in the water. Poor reward, Sir, for one so well skill'd in intrigue as you are!

Maria. Oh that I had thy heart here in my hand! How pleasant were the diet?—— Fate and death! Was ever such a devil?

Ranger. No! Never! Therefore since thou art a devil, as I now am sure thou art, have mercy on me, and do not take my soul for my first crime, and I will plot no more. (*Kneels.*)
Thou art my conquerour; I'll honour thee.—— Good Devil, do not hurt me. (*Shreiking within.*)

Enter Bubble *dragging in* Snare.

Bubble. Strumpet! Whore! Witch! I'll spoil your curls by the Lord *Harry*. O Lord! My wife—— And she that I have beaten a stranger.

Snare. Oh Heav'n! Was ever poor sinner so abused?
(*Weeps.*)

Bubble. (Bubble *looks amazedly at his wife, then at* Snare, *then at a lock of black hair in his hand.*) Madam, I beg your pardon, and am asham'd of my fault; but I'll make you amends presently.

Ranger. (*To* Emilia *kneeling.*) Well, nothing but the greatest devil could have brought this woman hither for this intrigue, and therefore once more I acknowledge thy power.

Bubble. Ay! You had need ask her pardon; 'tis you have betray'd us. Chicken! Dear Chicken,—— Don't frown so.—— I confess I was a fool;—— But forgive me but this once, and if ever I offend agen, I'll give thee leave to cuckold me indeed.

Emilia. Indeed, Sir, your jealousie is a little severe. I wonder what I have done to deserve it.

Bubble. Nothing, I know thou hast not; prethee forgive me.

Emilia. But to be disturb'd thus when I was at my devotion.

Bubble. Prethee forget it. Come, *Tom,* you may come out now; here's none but friends.

Emilia. Who do you mean, Sir? (*Stamps with her foot.*)

Bubble. Tom Rashley.— Poor fellow, I warrant now he'll be so bashful.

Ranger. So, that's something yet, and I'll fetch him out or bleed for't.—— (*Exit* [*into* Emilia's *room*].)

Enter Rashley *at the other side.*

Emilia. Look, yonder he is!

Maria. I find it now, and this is all design'd. O Devil! Devil!

Enter Sir Roger *after* Rashley.

Sir Roger. What's the matter, Mr. *Rashley?* What's the matter?

Bubble. Rashley here? Hey day! Who the devil is that yonder then?

Enter Ranger *dragging out* Sneak.

Ranger. Come, Sir, appear; I find you are now no *Hercules.* Hah!—— Death, more miracles, *Sneak!*

Sir Roger. 'Sdeath, my *Cob!*—— And taken with a wench. Why how now, Sirrah!

Emilia. [*Aside to* Rashley.] Now it works to my wish; prethee observe how they look.

Rashley. Hush.—— I do.

Sneak. O Lord, Uncle, your mercy;—— I was betray'd, seduc'd, as a man may say.—— (*To* Snare.) Go, go,—— Begone, I'll speak with you to morrow.—— I say, Uncle, I was seduc'd, chowsed, cheated.

Sir Roger. Catcht with a wench?—— Come, Sir, I'll talk with you.—— Oh disgrace to the family.—— With a wench? A lewd wench? Come along, Sir;—— I'll watch you henceforth.——   (*Exit Sir* Roger, Sneak.)

Rashley. Ha, ha! Why, here has been a great deal of intrigue to night I see, ha, Sir?—— I am sorry now I went to bed so soon.—— But I have been in the sweetest dream yonder.——   (*Gapes.*)

Bubble. Here has introth been a great deal of intrigue, as thou sayst, *Tom.* But no matter; now all's well. And since it has happen'd so well, a day of jubilee shall crown it. To morrow is my wedding-day, and in memory of that happy hour that conjoined me and my sweet Chicken there together, we'll have a feast;—— And I'll sing, and roar, and drink *cum privilegio.* Go, wait on her in, *Tom.*—— Chicken, remember we are friends. Go,—— I'll be with you presently.——

(*Exit* [Emilia *and*] Rashley *bowing scornfully to* Ranger *and* Maria.)

Ranger. Never was such a day, nor such a deed.

Bubble. Ned! Let me have no more of your doubts nor counsels. D'ee hear! 'Sbud, I say once more my wife is the

honestest woman in Christendom, and you shall hear from me. (*Exit* Bubble.)
 Maria. Was ever the like known?
 Ranger. Never since *Adam;* but she was a devil before the Creation. 575
 Maria. I'll not give over thus.
 Ranger. Nor I.
 Maria. Your hand on't.

Ranger.
 Here! And may all the demons that have pow'r 580
 In subtle plots help now, tho' never more.

Maria. I'll die but I'll perform it.——

 My slights shall with immortal wit be wrought;
 And all my sences shall convert to thought.
          (*Exit Ambo.*) 585

The Fourth Act.

[Scene 1. *A public place.*]
Enter Sir Roger *and* Sneak.

Sir Roger. Sirrah! Haunt me no more, I know thee not.

Sneak. Nay, Uncle.

Sir Roger. Go to your wench, and let her entertain you; then stock Sir *Jeremy*'s mannor-house at home with bastards, birds of night, and teach 'em all to know their father when you ha' done.

Sneak. Good Uncle, let me speak.——

Sir Roger. No place to bring your cattel to but thither, under your mistrisses nose, thou most notorious ass? Mercy o' me, what will this world come to? Who could imagine that sheeps face of thine; that mouth, whence ne'er came any thing that had sence; that person that has as oft been thought a Puritan as thou hast been a fool? Then that hanging dog-look. I'll say no more, but the Devil is subtle.

Sneak. Uncle, you know 'tis an old saying: we cannot appoint our own destinies; nor did I foresee this. Besides, Sir, if you knew her as well as I do, you'd find the

Act IV Scene 1

woman has some parts that are not contemptible.——
'Sbud, I know what's what; I am not such a fool.

Sir Roger. Not such a fool! In verity if thou wert but a grain nearer to a natural, I'd beg thee of the King, and adopt another to inherit thy estate. Not such a fool!

Sneak. No, so I say, Sir, since you go to that. Whoop! What a pox, you have forgot since you were young your self?

Sir Roger. I young! Why, Sir, I hope I got no bastards.

Sneak. No.—— But you kept whores, that you did, and that's all one, *bona fide*.

Sir Roger. [*Aside.*] This rogue has heard all; I must stop his mouth. How, Sirrah, I kept whores?

Sneak. It has been thought so, Sir, since you go to that. Nay, 'tis no such miracle now adays; there's many an old badger about town does the like; 'tis grown a custom now.

Sir Roger. But 'tis not so customary with your uncle, Sir. But come, pray express your self; what women do the infamous world lay to my charge?

Sneak. What women! 'Bud are you ignorant? Hum, *Nan, Pegg, Joan of the Dairy, Sara, Jenny, Dorothy, Mary, Bridget.*

Sir Roger. Hold! Hold, I say! 'Sdeath, he'll reckon the whole country presently. I must quiet him; the rogue has me upon the hip. Harkee, *Cob.*

Sneak. Then the parsons wife, Sir, and the old hostess at the Towns-end. You see the fool has a good memory.

Sir Roger. A waggish one I see thou hast. Ha, if thou could'st remember law-cases as well, thou wouldst be a brave fellow. Why, *Cob,* thou think'st thou hast paid me off now, dost not?

Sneak. I know not. If my wit flow too fast, Sir, I cannot help it; 'tis a good that's thrown upon me, 'tis not my seeking. 'Tis true, I have an unhappy way with me sometimes, but 'tis over presently; it never lasts long, that's one comfort.

Sir Roger. In verity I see thou hast wit, and now I'll cherish it. Why, *Cob,* my instruction is for thy good, Child. What will thy mistriss think when she hears of it?—— Come, come, in verity, *Cob,* 'twas ill done, 'twas ifaith.—— But mum, no more words on't, I'll make all well agen.

Sneak. [*Aside.*] So, so, I have brought him about finely. 'Sbud I did not think I had so much wit, but I see a man may be mistaken in his own parts.

Sir Roger. But d'ee hear, *Cob,* not a word more of these wenches, let the foolish world say what it will. Thou art a good boy in verity. I like thy wit well. Thou know'st I have no heir, and when I die, *Cob,* I will not say I'll give thee any thing, lest I should make thee proud; but expect, expect wonders may fall, who knows?——

Sneak. By *Jerico* I would not have spoke on't now, but that I had nothing else to say, and you know 'tis a disgrace to a scholar to be silent in company.

Sir Roger. 'Tis no matter, 'tis no matter. Prethee how cam'st thou to know that *Pegg* and I were so intimate?

Sneak. Ah, you'll be angry if I shou'd tell you.

Sir Roger. In verity not I.—— Angry?—— Come, come, out with it, *Cob,* out with't.

Sneak. Why, the truth is, I lay with her one night, and the quean told me all.

Sir Roger. Didst thou! God a mercy. (Dam him! What a snake have I foster'd?) Done like a cock o' th' game, in verity. Ah, when I was of thy years I cou'd have done as much my self.

Sneak. Yes, she told me you had done as much. But mum, Sir, not a word more. I know my kew.

Sir Roger. 'Sdeath, I shall be a by-word to th' town.——

Enter a Servant.

Servant. Sir *Roger,* I was just coming to your house for you; my master desires yours and Mr. *Sneak*'s company immediately.

Sir Roger. What, the solemnity holds? This is his wedding-day?

Servant. Yes, Sir.

Sir Roger. Tell him I am coming.—— (*Exit Servant.*) Come, *Cob,* let us go; and mum, d'ee hear? You understand me?

Sneak. I warrant you, Sir.—— (*Exeunt.*)

Scene 2. [Bubble's *lodging.*]

Bubble, Emilia, Maria, Rashley, Ranger, Cordelia, Fumble *sitting at a table.*

Bubble. Come, come, another bumper about; my Chickens health. Here, I am not wet through yet; *Tom,* what sayst thou?

Rashley. With all my heart, Sir! Oh here comes Sir *Roger* and his nephew.

Enter Sir Roger *and* Sneak.

Sir Roger. Mr. *Bubble* and gentlemen, your most humble servant.

Bubble. Yours, good Sir *Roger;* I am glad to see you ifaith; and you, sweet Mr. *Sneak.* Well, faith, Sir *Roger,* we have been bumping it about here; we have been dipt, as the saying is. *Tom Rashley,* send it round; come, Sir *Roger*'s a freshman, he'll drink an ocean.

Rashley. Fill every man's glass there. Mr. *Ranger,* you want it; 'tis Madam *Emilia*'s health.

Ranger. I'll do you reason, Sir;—— (*All drink.*) (*Aside.*)

And ten to one but I have a stratagem shall dash this mirth. [*To* Maria.] Are they ready?

Maria. Hush! We are observ'd; they are——

Bubble. So, so! Come, now the song and then the dance. Look ye, Gentlemen, you must know——

Fumble. Come, come, Mr. *Bubble*, let's have t'other soop, I say; ifack we loose time. Ah Sirrah, are you there? Gad I'll be with you presently; dust it about once more, I say; the wine has a pretty smack with't; it cherishes, I like it well. Come, another soop, and then do what you will.

Bubble. Fill wine there!—— Gentlemen, (as I was saying) I got this song made purposely; 'tis in praise of marriage, and there was not one ready made of 'em in town. I searcht it all over.

Ranger. Were you at the poets lodging?

Bubble. Yes, but they had none; for they told me 'twas a song would not take. Besides, they were so busie getting plays up for the next term, that I could hardly get one made.

Sir Roger. Sir, you needed not have troubled 'em; you once had a very good vein that way your self.

Bubble. Yes, I was mightily given to rapture and flame once; I writ *Tom Farthing*. I had a hand too in *Colly my Cow,* a song that took well I can assure you. But this is of another kind, in praise of marriage, Sir; and they told me the town lov'd nothing but satyrs against marriage, and the reason was because they were afraid of being cuckolded. When, alas, poor silly rogues, there's no such thing in nature.

Ranger. (*Aside.*) Well, of all stupid animals a drowsie husband is the most notorious. But I shall change your note presently, I doubt not, Sir.

Bubble. You shall hear, Gentlemen. Hey, the song there and the dance?

SONG.

Under the branches of a spreading tree,
Silvander sate, from care and danger free,
And his inconstant roving humour shows
To his dear nymph, that sung of marriage-vows;
But she with flowing graces charming air,
   Cry'd, Fie, fie, my dear, give o'er,
   Ah, tempt the gods no more!
But thy offence with penitence repair.
For though vice in a beauty seem sweet in thy arms,
An innocent virtue has always more charms.

2.

Ah Phillida! *the angry swain reply'd,*
Is not a mistriss better than a bride?
What man that universal yoke retains,
But meets an hour to sigh and curse his chains?
She smiling cry'd, Change, change that impious mind;
   Without it we could prove
   Not half the joys of love.
'Tis marriage makes the feeling joys divine.
For all our life long we from scandal remove,
And at last fall the trophies of honour and love.

Bubble. Well sung, ifaith. Look'ee, Gentlemen, is it not as I told you?
Sir Roger. In verity very well, very well, Sir.
Bubble. Come, now the dance.—— (*Dance.*)
      Enter Servant.
Servant. Sir, here's a letter for you; it was left by a porter, who said it requir'd no answer, and is gone.
Ranger. [*Aside.*] So, now for a change of countenance.—— [*To* Maria.] I think this will do.
Maria. If not, I've writ a letter that will. But let's observe.——

A DANCE.

Bubble. What the Devil has this fellow given me here? A letter? Pray Heav'n it be no challenge.—— How?—— What's here? (*Reads.*)

> Sir, *That you are blind, I have heard; that you are a fool, I know; and that you are a cuckold, I believe.*—— *However, as a friend, tho' unknown, I am bound in conscience to give you this information. Your wife is false; you are abus'd; the author of your wrong you know as well as your self, if you know your self as well as you know Rashley.*

Oh Heav'n! Was ever such fate?—— But hush, I'll smother my resentment till they are gone.—— Come, Sir *Roger* and Gentlemen, there's a tongue in the next room; pray go and eat; I'll be with you presently.

(*Exit all but* Bubble, Ranger *and* Maria.)

Ranger. So, I see by this behaviour it takes, and I'll away, lest he should suspect me.—— Now for my t'other plot. (*Exit.*)

Bubble. O Sister, here's a new discovery; the Devil is come abroad agen.

Maria. How? The Devil?

Bubble. Ay, in the likeness of a letter. Here, prethee read it; 'tis his character; I am sure it looks as if 'twere writ with a cloven hoof.—— Hah!—— What think'st thou?

Maria. Sir, he calls you fool here.

Bubble. Ay, he's a little uncivil, that's the truth on't. But what's to be done, Sister?

Maria. A cuckold too.

Bubble. Ay; was ever such an impudence?

Maria. I never heard of any. But 'tis no more, Sir, than I expected. Alas! 'Tis nothing to be a cuckold now.

Bubble. Oh unfortunate estate of marriage! By the Lord *Harry,* if this be true, I have prais'd it to fine purpose. But, Sister, thou wert wont to be kind; prethee advise me.

Maria. 'Tis to no purpose, Sir; you know I am envious; my words have double meaning. I did my sister wrong in my last story; pray let me offend no more.

Bubble. Well, I confess I was to blame; but who the Devil cou'd have mistrusted her when the plot was carried so hansomly?

Maria. Oh you will find, Sir, she has still more plots, and I find you so credulous and so wedded to your infamy, that for my part I am afraid to have any thing to do with it.

Bubble. Help me but this once, and if I fail thee agen, may I be prov'd a cuckold to the whole county, and my case try'd in *Westminster-Hall*.

Maria. Well! Once more then I'll assist you, and to confirm what that letter has inform'd, know, Sir, she is false; and tho' she frustrated our last plot by her waiting-womans means, she certainly met *Rashley* that night. I am glad you credit a strangers letter; for my part I love her so well, I should have hardly caus'd a second breach between ye else. But since 'tis out, and you desire my assistance, follow me, and ere night I doubt not but to give you sufficient proof of your misfortune.

Bubble. With all my heart, dear Sister.—— 'Sbud, a cuckold?—— 'Tis impossible, I ha' no cuckolds face;—— But I'll be resolv'd immediately.   (*Exeunt.*)

                Enter Ranger *and* Governess.

Ranger. Do this, thou shalt command me.

Governess. In truth, Sir, I am afraid 'twill be discover'd, and I would not have my lady know it for the world.

Ranger. I swear she never shall. What, dost thou doubt me? Besides, I'll be so grateful to thee, thou shalt never have cause to repent this courtesie.

Governess. Sir, you know you always might command me in any reasonable thing. Pray speak it agen, Sir; what wou'd you have me do?

Ranger. Why only plant me in or near her chamber for a design I have; she shall be ignorant why, or by what means I got thither. I'll still be careful of thy reputation. Come, take this purse, and prethee do it willingly.

Governess. Well, Sir, what you mean I know not; but Heav'n direct all for the best. I can deny you nothing, Sir; I lie in a closet that joins to her chamber, where you may both over-hear and speak to her.

Ranger. That above all things! Prethee let's go.

Governess. But for Heav'ns sake take care she knows not that I brought ye thither; I would not be seen in such a business for the world.

Ranger. Ne'er doubt, I warrant thee I'll be careful.

Governess. Follow me then, Sir.   (*Exeunt.*)

Scene 3. [*Another room in* Bubble's *house.*]

Enter Fumble *and* Spatterdash [*behind him*].

Fumble. [Spatterdash!] Sirrah!

Spatterdash. Here, Sir, here.

Fumble. Whither is this rascal gone? Well, ifack, I am too full of clemency; I must swinge this rogue, or he'll never be good for any thing; he's at nine-holes now, I'll lay my life. A damn'd villain, that spends me three-pence a day I know not how.

Spatterdash. O Lord, who I, Sir?

Fumble. Who's within there? What, will no body hear me? Am I left desolate? I have not the plague I think.—— Ha!

Spatterdash. Why, here am I, Sir; I have been here all this while.——

Fumble. Oh Sirrah, are you come? Where have you been, ha? I say, where have you been, Rogue?

Spatterdash. No where, Sir, not I.

Fumble. Sirrah! I must be left alone! Must I! And when I have a message to send, go my self.—— Hah!—— Sirrah, Mr. *Little-Pox* has a boy, that tho' he was stinted at nurse, and is not above pocket-high, can run, and frisk, and jump upon occasion, Sirrah, know a bayly by his nose, and a wench by her buttocks, ye rogue, and a good linguist, and a pretty pimp, Sirrah, and can hold the door with a steady hand, ye rogue. But thou, a rascal, a drone, art good for nothing.

Spatterdash. Any thing, Sir, I warrant you. Try me, and you shall find I can hold a door as well as he.

Fumble. Why, how now, Sirrah? What, make mouths at me? Is your master grown your mirth? Ha, this will teach you better; this will new-mold you; I'll fetch you out of your damn'd looks ifack. French grimaces, Rogue, French grimaces? *(Beats him.)*

Spatterdash. O Lord, what shall I do? Because he's deaf, and cannot hear me, he thinks I mock him.—— Hold, Sir.—— For Heav'ns sake; upon my faith I don't mock you. *(Aloud.)* 'Tis all a mistake; and, Sir, you have beaten me for nothing.

Fumble. What a noise the rogue makes! Why, Sirrah, cannot you speak temperately, but you must roar thus? I am not so deaf, but I can hear without this thunderclap. But you do it in contempt, do you, Sirrah? Bless us, to what an impudence this age is grown! But I'll fetch the Devil out, lest he should grow in ye,—— Thus.——
(Beats Him.)
I should be loth to see thee hang'd till you come to years of discretion.

Spatterdash. Mercy o' me, what a master have I? If I stay long here I shall be beaten into mummy.

Fumble. Come, Sir, now I have perform'd the part of a master and a friend in your castigation, I have now a word or two by way of instruction. Mark me, Sirrah,—— Nothing exasperates more than scorn, nor nothing pleases more than observance; a master should be strict in finding occasion to beat his servant, and a servant should be careful in avoiding the beatings of his master.

Spatterdash. So he has taught me; now I shall be careful of avoiding it hereafter, if my legs will carry me.

Fumble. What, mouths agen, Sirrah, mouths agen?

Spatterdash. Umph.——

(*Makes a low congee; says nothing.*)

Fumble. Oh this submission pacifies. Come hither, I have a message for ye, and let me see how you can behave your self; 'tis a matter of moment.

Spatterdash. I'll do my best to please ye, Sir.

Fumble. What dost thou say now?—— Look, look!—— Was ever such a rascal as this? This rogue knows well enough that I cannot hear him. Sirrah, come and lay your mouth to my ear, and then speak, if you would have me understand ye.

Spatterdash. Yes, Sir, I shall be very careful to remember it hereafter.

Fumble. Rafters?—— What rafters, Rogue?

Spatterdash. (*Aloud.*) Sir, I shall be careful to remember it hereafter.

Fumble. O shall you so, Sir? And 'twill become you ifack. For look'ee, Sirrah, 'tis my humour as long as I am healthy and jovial, to cover failings and imperfections in nature as well as I can; 'tis a wise-mans vertue, and I have paterns for't every day. Ah! Here are a sort of jolly, brisk, ingenious, old signiors about town, that with false calves, false bellies, false teeth, false noses, and a false fleering face, upon the matter fill up society as well as ere a masquerading fop of 'em all.—— But to the matter. Sirrah, you must carry this ring to *Cordelia*, and possess her with my love in an elegant manner. Stand there, and let me see how you can carry your self in such a business.

Spatterdash. Thus, Sir. I had my honours from the dancing-school.

Fumble. O damn'd Rogue! What a bow's there? 'Tis worse than a country counsellors to a client that has no money. Sirrah, pull me your hat off thus,——with a grace.—— Ah! I cou'd have done it rarely twenty years ago; but ifack time and gravity defaces all things. Come, Sirrah.

Spatterdash. Madam! My master too well knowing the charms of your wit and beauty are too sharp at all times to be opposed, has by me sent this ring, and humbly desires——

Fumble. Well, that last honour was pretty well.—— But come now, let's hear what you can say?

Spatterdash. 'Sdeath! He has not heard me all this while.—— What shall I do? (*Knocking.*) Oh some-body knocks; this was happy. Sir, there's some-body at door to speak with you.   (*Aloud.*)

Fumble. Go see who 'tis; I'll follow.——

[*Exit* Spatterdash.]

This is a plaguy dull rogue, but I must have patience, and take pains with him.—— Nor shou'd he do any thing in this business had I not a design in't; and ifack I like the woman well.—— She's young, and plump, free in her nature, and of a sanguine complexion, and *bona fide*, I never see her but some secret motions in my blood seem to imply that she is the cause.—— What? I am not bedrid.—— I can dance yet, ay, and run and jump too if occasion be, and why not the t'other thing?—— Come, come,—— It must, it must.—— Mine was ever a stirring family.—— It must, I say, and she shall know it suddenly. (*Exit* Fumble.)

Scene 4. [*A corridor in* Bubble's *house.*]

Enter Maria *and* Bubble.

Maria. Come softly, Sir, and plant your self here at this back-door; I have already made a discovery.

Bubble. Are they together?

Maria. I believe so; they seldom miss such an opportunity, especially when they think you absent.

Bubble. No; they are politick with a pox to 'em. Sister, what revenge, ha? I am resolv'd to be a tyrant. 'Sbud I'll pinch her to death with a pair of tongs.

Maria. O fie, that will be too cruel.

Bubble. Cruel! By the Lord *Harry* 'tis justice, palpable justice! Why, shou'd she live, she'd cuckold the whole nation.

Maria. Consider better on't; 'tis but a venial crime, and deserves not such rigour.—— But come, meditate of no revenge till you are certain of the fault. Keep close at that door; be sure you discover not your self till I come to you; I'll go and observe.

Bubble. I'll try my patience; but 'tis a damn'd cause.

(*Exeunt.*)

Enter Rashley *and* Emilia; *scene a bed-chamber.*

Emilia. Our intrigue as yet goes well.

Rashley. I swear to admiration; and had I not seen each passage, I shou'd have thought 't had been impossible. Oh my dearest! How shall I gratifie thee? My love's too poor, and my desert too mean ever to equal it.—— (*Kisses her hand.*)

Enter Ranger [*from* Governess' *closet.*]

Ranger. [*Apart.*] I am glad I've got air agen; this damn'd old gib-cat has mew'd me this half hour into such a hole, that had I staid a minute longer I had certainly been smother'd. It stinks worse than a pothecaries shop, and is furnisht with nothing but gally-pots full of nasty oyl, into which groping about I often thrust my fingers.—— Fough!—— Assafoetida, as I live!—— A most intolerable stink!—— Ah! The Devil grind her old chops.—— Stay!—— This is sure *Emilia*'s chamber, and if I am not mistaken, I heard a whispering here; it may be they're together. I'll be still and listen.

Rashley. Our love shall last whole ages, and each kiss add new and fierce desires. Death shall want power to separate us, and Envy droop and pine it self away to see its stratagem succeed no better.

Ranger. By Heav'n, 'tis so; they are here.—— Blest minute! Now I shall make a rare discovery.

Emilia. I am confirm'd, and will proceed in loving. A husband is a dull insipid thing, pall'd and grown stale within a week. But a lover appears still new and gay, and is to perpetuity the same he was at first——all mirth, all pleasure.

Ranger. A most excellent theme. Oh that that property, that fool her husband, stood now to hear this devil of a wife make out this free confession!——

Rashley. He, dull creature, Heav'n knows, is blind to all your charms. Marriage acts only the decrees of duty; love has the least share in't. In this age a husband with a wife is like a bully in a church; the only pleasure he takes is to sleep away the hours shou'd be employ'd in conjugal duty.

Emilia. Well! I am very glad our plots succeed so well.

I swear I was half frighted t'other day when my sister-in-law *Maria* discover'd us. Was it not done subt'ly? Did I not fetch all off agen with an excellent invention?

Ranger. Good! Rarely good! This devil cannot sure have so much impudence to deny this agen.

Rashley. Ha, ha, ha! By Heav'n I'm ready to die with laughing when I think what asses we made of 'em. *Ranger* too, that busie coxcomb—— What a fretting, and plotting, and sweating did he make for nothing!—— Alas, poor fool!—— Ha, ha, ha!

Emilia. Ha, ha, ha!

Ranger. O the Devil fleer you.—— 'Sdeath, am I still their property? I shall have a slice at your nose ere long. I doubt not, my young gallant, I shall dash your mummery.

Rashley. Come, we lose time.—— Let talk be our diversion when we are old and can reap nothing else; our minutes now should all be spent in rapture.—— Thus, thus, my sweet!—— Oh that we cou'd live thus ever!—— How now, what noise is that?

Bubble. (Within.) Bawds! Strumpets! Whores! Witches! Break open the door there, break open the door.——

Maria. [*Within.*] Fetch a leaver, or call the smith over the way presently.

Emilia. Oh Heav'n, my husband and *Maria!* We are undone.

Ranger. 'Tis *Bubble's* voice sure! This compleats my joy. Now let *Belzebub*, if he owes her any kindness, fetch her from hence; I'll guard this passage.

Rashley. What! What shall I do, Madam?

Emilia. Here quickly, run into this closset, Sir, and jump out of the window into the garden; if you were gone, let me alone for the rest.

Ranger. Who steps a foot this way, steps on his death; his soul shall not be his a minute.

Emilia. Ha! *Ranger* here? I am lost in my amazement.

Rashley. Death! And Hell! And I defenceless too! O cursed minute!

Ranger. No, Madam, I'll secure you from this stratagem. This window shall be no bawd to th' intrigue now; that I'll be sure on.—— *(Exit into the closset.)*

Bubble. (Within.) Quickly, quickly! A leaver, a leaver!

Rashley. No way t' escape? Can I not climb the chimney? Any thing to get free this once.—— Oh fate, taken i' th' midst of our security, when we least thought of it! What shall we do?

Emilia. I have it. Come hither, get ye under this table, and diligently listen to what I say. 'Tis ten to one he never searches here. Come, in, in, quickly, and pray the rest may prosper.

Rashley. I never had more need of pray'rs.—— I'll try.—— *(Goes under table.)*

Enter Ranger *from the closset.*

Ranger. So! That conveyance is fast enough. Now, Madam, what think'ee of a fleering jest upon the fool *Ranger,* the coxcomb, the ass *Ranger,* and your jolly spleen to laugh, ha, ha? I think the dice are mine now. Now, Devil, I have trapt ye.—— *(Knock within.)*

Emilia. [Aside.] This key may add to my design.—— *(Takes out the key o' th' door.)*

Bubble. (Within.) Down, down with it, break it open there.

Ranger. What think you of that, Madam? Does your husbands voice refresh you extreamly?

Emilia. Now help me, Wit, or I am lost. *(She goes and puts the key into his coat-pocket, and then lays hold of him, and cries out.)* Help, help there, for Heav'ns sake. I am undone, ruin'd for ever. A rape, a rape!—— Help, help!——

Ranger. Hell and the Devil, what does she mean?

Emilia. Ah, cruel man, cannot these tears prevail? Will nothing stop barbarity? What have I done that cou'd deserve this usage? O most unfortunate of women.

Ranger. Dam her, I shall be finely catcht if this hold; I must get away.—— *(Struggles; she holds him.)*

Emilia. A rape, a rape! Help there, for Heav'ns sake, help.——

Enter Bubble *and* Maria *with a light.*
They stand amaz'd.

Ranger. By Heav'n, I am snapt agen, catcht in my own snare.

Emilia. Has my husband been so much thy friend, and wouldst abuse him thus, (thou base man?) But Heav'n forgive thee.

Bubble. 'Sbud, what's this I see? *Ranger?*

Maria. Ranger here, and *Rashley* absent. I have plotted finely. 'Tis plain now that traytor loves her, and has only made me an engine to work his design with more facility.

Ranger. Rashley gone too? Now has the Devil to spite me convey'd him away in a mist. Here's like to be fine work towards; but I must stand the brunt now I am enter'd.

Bubble. Now, Sir, what a pox make you here with my wife? Hah?——

Ranger. So, it begins rarely! O this subtle devil! Why, Sir, as I am a gentleman, and upon my honour.

Emilia. O my dear, a thousand thanks for this deliverance; and by all our love I charge thee, by our marriage-vows, by all our pleasures since, and joys to come, I charge you revenge me upon that traytor there.—— He would have ravisht me!—— Oh Heav'n, that ever I should live to be so put to't!——

Bubble. 'Sbud! Ravish my Chicken? *Ranger,* you are the son of a whore, and I shall presume to cut your throat.

Ranger. Sir, do but hear me; upon my honour all this is false.

Maria. (Aside.) It must be true! What should he come hither for, but upon some ill intent? I am resolv'd I'll be reveng'd on him however.

Ranger. 'Sdeath! She against me too? This is worse and worse.

Bubble. Discover the matter, that I may do justice on both sides.

Emilia. Sir, know then, *Ranger* long has lov'd me; often sollicited me unlawfully. But finding something in my vertue that shook his designs, his recourse was to make you jealous of me and *Rashley,* who, poor man, has often told me with sighs how deeply he has resented your unkind suspitions.

Bubble. Alas, poor fellow!

Ranger. O confusion! He begins to believe her agen.

Emilia. At last, Sir, finding his suit to be too troublesom for me to bear, and being loth to vex you with such fooleries, I told *Rashley,* who promised all assistance imaginable. I desir'd him also to be careful, and watch lest I should be surpriz'd; as to night (Heav'n knows) I was.

Ranger. Dam her, what a lye is this! Pray, Sir, let me speak.

Bubble. Not in my house, Sir, you have talkt too much already; and by the Lord *Harry* I'll talk with you anon. But let that pass, go on, Chicken.

Emilia. At last, Sir, this unhappy night coming hither as I used to do to my devotions, he it seems having corrupted some of my servants, got into the closset, and thence came and surpriz'd me, first locking the door, and putting the key into his pocket.

Ranger. I a key? Sir, as I live I saw none. This is the most notorious lye——

Emilia. Oh wretched man! Was it not crime enough to make such an attempt, but you must persist in falshood? Sir, he has it now about him there in that pocket; I saw him put it in.

Ranger. This pocket?—— Why, thou devil! Hah!——
(*Puts his hand in's pocket; pulls out a key.*)
'Sdeath, how came it here? Magick, witchcraft—— The Devil and all combine against me! Wou'd I were well out—— If ever I plot agen——

Maria. 'Tis evident now he would have ravisht her! Lockt her in for the purpose. Perfidious traytor, see me no more.

Ranger. A very fine bus'ness this!

Bubble. Is it so, Sir? I'll do your business for you.
(*Goes to run at* Ranger, *and overthrows the table.*)

Emilia. Discover'd? I am lost agen.

Bubble. 'Sbud, *Rashley!*

Rashley. 'Sdeath and Hell, what will become of me now?

Ranger. How! *Rashley* under the table? Then fate is mine agen. Now, Sir, do you perceive any thing yet?

Maria. Stranger and stranger! What can this mean? Or what could they both do here?

Bubble. (*To* Emilia.) 'Sdeath! How came he here?—— Hoh!——

Ranger. Ay, examine that point closely; sure this will make for me.

Bubble. As Gad jidge me, and so I will. Speak, I say, how came he here?

Emilia. Nay, Heav'n knows, not I; I believe for the same design with *Ranger.*

Rashley. 'Sdeath, she'll betray me too.

Emilia. Tell him, tell him, Sir.—— (*Softly.*) Speak for your self; say any thing.

Rashley. Speak? Why,—— 'Sbud, Madam, have I not done as you commanded me? Have I not watcht here this two hours to frustrate *Ranger's* design? What, d'ee think to make an ass of me?

Ranger. How, Sir, my design? Dam me this must not pass upon me, Sir.

Rashley. Nor you shall not pass upon my friend here neither, Sir; I heard you this evening when you corrupted one of the women to get you into that closset, that you might accomplish with more ease, Sir. But, Madam, this is a little unnatural, to make me suspected as his collegue, when my design was so far different.

Bubble. 'Sbud I cannot find the meaning of this.

Rashley. The meaning! Why, Sir, she hid me under the table as a defence against *Ranger's* insolence. But when she heard you at the door, and knew you were coming in, she conjur'd me by all the love I bore her to sit still, and not discover my self; and all her excuse was your jealousie; (Jealousie with a pox!) A very fine slight for the abuse she intended to me. 'Sdeath, Madam, my service deserv'd a better reward if you consider it.—— (Pray Heav'n this lye prosper.)

Emilia. Ha, ha, ha!—— I knew I should vex him; but I confess 'tis all true. For (my poor dear rogue!) I am so hourly tormented with fear of thy naughty jealousie, that I dare not tell thee any thing. Prethee desert it, do, my dear Sweet; Ifads thou wouldst be the best husband in the world if thou wouldst but leave it. (*Kisses him.*)

Bubble. Well! It must be so; this cannot be feign'd. Come hither to me—— I will forsake it.—— By the Lord *Harry* thou art the best wife in Christendom, and I the most ungrateful husband; but forgive, my dear, forgive.——   (*Kisses her.*)
We have all failings thou knowest; prethee forgive me.

Ranger. So! Now may I hang my self. 'Sdeath! All the fiends are asses to her.—— I'll begone for shame, lest worse befall me.—— *Succubus,* farewel;
   There is not such a sorceress in Hell. *(Exit.)*
Bubble. Come! Hast thou seal'd my pardon?
Emilia. You know the softness of my temper; but your unkind jealousie will kill me one day.
Bubble. Igad I'll kill my self first. Come, prethee no more. *Tom,* thy hand too; come, I know thou canst bear with my frailty.
Rashley. I Sir, I can bear well enough! But me thought 'twas a little strange to tax me.
Bubble. Come, come, all shall be well;—— Faith, we'll go in and frolick. Oh my dear, suspect thee!—— Well, I am a fool, that's the truth on't.——

(Exit Bubble *and* Emilia.*)*
Maria. The Devil helps her sure; for this was certainly an assignation. I'll after *Ranger* and know the truth on't. *(Exit.)*
Rashley. Ha, ha, ha!—— Was ever plot carried thus? Sure never! Her wit has more supplies than I have thoughts, and happily they end still; and Gad for my own part I shall love lying the better as long as I live for the success of this.—— Once more all is well, and he the cuckold still. Ha, ha, ha! I must go in and laugh with her.

   Intrigue's her masterpiece; and all may see,
   A woman's wit's best in extremity.

(Exit.)

The Fifth Act.

[Scene 1. *A room in* Bubble's *house.*]
Enter Cordelia.

Cordelia. Well, of all creatures that vex mortality, a superannuated lover is certainly the most troublesom, especially to one of my years. Our inequality is so preposterous, and his address so unnatural, that I always entertain rather hate for his person, than compliance for his love. From fourscore and five, Heav'n deliver me; 'tis an age of doting.—— Here he comes; I knew I could not be quiet one hour.

Enter Fumble.

Fumble. Sirrah, Sirrah! Rogue, Rogue! And how and how! Hah! Art thou jolly, blithe, like a bird in a tree? Ifack I was impatient till I came to see thee. Well, and how fits the ring? Does it shine? Does it glitter? Hah, little black rogue!—— Ifack I bought it of the best goldsmith in *Cheapside,* a man of good reputation; a cuckold too, and they are always the honestest fellows.

Cordelia. From henceforth let me desire you, Sir, to bestow your presents on some body else. I sent your ring back by your man; he can best give you an account of it.

Fumble. Hah!—— What sayst thou? Counterfeit? Ifack thou art mistaken, Bird; thou art, *bona fide.* They are as well cut as any in Christendom, and of the right blackwater. What, dost thou think I'll put any false stones upon thee ifack? I am more civil, *Icod.* [*Aside.*] There I was waggish; but she's a witty rogue, she'll apprehend the jest.

Cordelia. Was ever such an insipid piece of antiquity? Pray, Sir, forbear these impertinences, and assure your self I hate an old fellow for a husband, as much as an old gown, or an old piece of wit, that after forty years oblivion, with a new name, is publisht for a new *Lenten* play.

Fumble. What does she say now? But no matter, I'll go on. Well said, Bird, well said. *Bona fide,* thou hast wit in abundance; that colour, and such a sort of nose, never fail. But come, we lose time, I know 'tis ordain'd I must marry thee. I am the man that must gather the rosebuds.—— Ah Rogue!—— I'll warrant thou'rt a swinger, and Ifack that black a top there fires me strangely. I am all flame, and *bona fide,* me thinks as youthful and mercurial as any spark of 'em all.

SONG.
And he took her by the middle small,
And laid her on the plain;
With a hey down derry down, come diddle,
With a ho down derry, &c.

What think you, Madam? Am I old?

Cordelia. So old, that your presence is more terrible than a deaths-head at supper. For my part I tremble all over. There's a kind of horrour in all your antick gestures; 'specially those that you think become you, that fright worse than the Devil; (*Aloud.*) than the Devil, Sir.

Act V Scene 1

Fumble. The Devil! What of him, Bird? Pish, the Devil's an Ass, I ha' seen't in a play; and ifack we lose time in talking about so worthless a matter. Lovers shou'd ne'er be slow in their affairs. For, as my good friend *Randolph* tells me, nothing is like opportunity taken in the nick; in the nick, Sweet-heart!—— *Icod,* I was waggish again, I was waggish agen ifack.—— Come, Bird, come.

Cordelia. What will you do, Sir? Heav'n, how he tortures me!

Fumble. Come along then.—— I have got a priest ready, and paid for the licence and all.—— Prethee let me kiss thee; I long to practise something that might please thee. Never was man so alter'd! Never! Come, prethee Bird.—— Come; ifack I have not patience.

Enter Governess *and Sir* Roger.

Governess. Here's Sir *Roger Petulant,* my dear mouse, desires to speak a word or two with you.

Cordelia. Oh here's some hope of deliverance! Sir *Roger,* your humble servant. Come hither, *Lettice,* and stand just in my place. I am so tortur'd with this old fellow—— Prethee be kind to him, and follow him whither he'd have thee; it may be a husband in thy way, and a good estate.

Governess. A husband! Marry that's fine! I warrant you, sweet mouse, I'll be very punctual.

Cordelia. So, now let us slip aside and observe; 'twould be an excellent revenge if he shou'd marry her.—— He's coming to her already, and his eyes are so old and dim that he perceives not his mistake.   *(They step aside.)*

Fumble. Delays, Sweet-heart, are dang'rous ifack; I have consider'd it. The time I have liv'd in the world has given me the benefit of knowing more than another of fewer minutes.—— Along, along—— I say, thou shalt be my queen, my paramour, my *Cleopatra,* and I will live another age in love, and then farewel old *Simon* ifack. Come, come along.

Governess. Oh sadness! What happy fortune's this? Well, I'll go with him; pray Heav'n he be blind enough, that's all I fear.

Fumble. She seems kinder than usual; ifack I have wrought her finely. Come, poor Rogue, come.——

Governess.
   I am ready, Sir;—— This was a happy hour;
   And if it hit but right, I'm made for ever.

(*Exeunt.*)

Sir Roger *and* Cordelia *re-enter.*

Cordelia. Ha, ha, I am glad I am rid of him any way. But now, Sir *Roger,* to your bus'ness.—— I hear your nephew is sick.

Sir Roger. In verity, Madam, most dangerously sick, and the cause of my giving you this trouble was in verity to give you information of it; for by his melancholy I find love is the cause. Ah, Madam, your last indifference was very prejudicial to him. 'Tis true, he denies it; but I am old enough to judge of the contrary, and therefore have found out 'tis passion, nay passion for you has laid him thus low, and nothing but your smiles can raise him, 'tis gone so far in verity.——

Cordelia. I am sorry, Sir, I have the misfortune to be th' occasion of such a disaster. But is there any remedy? What would you have me do?

Sir Roger. Madam, my suit to you is, that you would be pleas'd to go with me and give him a visit; the surprize of your presence I am confident will dissipate his melancholy, and perhaps totally banish his distemper.

Act V Scene 2

Enter Maria.

But I see we are interrupted; let's retire, Madam, and if you please now will be a very good time to visit him.

Cordelia. Softly, Sir, I would not have my cozen *Maria* know any thing of it; but if that can do him any good, I'll not be so cruel to deny it.—— 'Tis an act of charity.—— Come, Sir, I'll go with you.

Sir Roger. Madam, you oblige us both—

(*Exeunt* [Cordelia *and Sir* Roger].)

Maria. Still baffled! Sure this cannot last long; the Devil will be weary of obliging her in a little time. I have been yonder sifting *Ranger* about the last plot, and by all circumstances find what he said was true; and shall I leave off thus poorly? Pish, I cannot for shame. I have truth and honesty on my side; she's only cunning, and 'tis impossible that shou'd last ever. Once more then have at 'em.—— I have by several false messages buz'd it again into my brothers ears; he believes, and will once more follow my counsel. Besides, I have here a false key to her chamber, and can surprize 'em when they least suspect. This, if *Ranger* be at all diligent, must needs effect it; for I am resolv'd not to rest till 'tis done, for the satisfaction of my revenge on that false man.(*Exit* Maria.)

[Scene 2. *Sir* Roger's *lodging.*]

Enter Apothecary *and* Sneak *in a night-gown.*

Sneak. Uh! Uh!

Apothecary. Nay, Sir, if you would have the effects answer your expectation, you must suffer, Sir, and be patient.

Sneak. 'Ounds! I cannot have patience. Sure a civil clap might be cured without all this stir. 'Tis not a miracle in this age.—— Oh Lord!

Enter Sir Roger *and* Cordelia.

Sir Roger. O horrible! What's this I see?

Sneak. My uncle! Oh I am undone, lost for ever.

Apothecary. But, Sir, your civil clap might ha' been an uncivil pox in time.

Cordelia. How, Sir *Roger?* Was it fit to make me spectator of this object?

Sir Roger. (Aside.) The pox? In verity I have brought his mistriss to fine purpose. Ah damn'd rascal! The pox? What shall I do? I am disgrac'd for ever.

Cordelia. Hark ye, Sir, pray what is that there?
(*Pointing to a sweating-chair within.*)

Sir Roger. What shall I say? (Death, she has found out his sweating-chair!) Why, Madam, 'tis——umph——'tis a mathematical engine they use at *Cambridge.*—— *Cob* was always addicted to study.

Cordelia. 'Twere a fault to hinder him then, Sir, being so well employ'd.—— Farewel.—— (*Exit* Cordelia.)

Sir Roger. She has found it out.—— Sirrah, see my face no more. From this hour I abhor thee, a damn'd rascal!

Sneak. Good Uncle!——

Sir Roger. The pox! A sneaking, sniveling rogue! Heav'ns, was ever the like seen?—— But 'tis now a general maxim, and your sandy, sheeps-face, unthinking villain, is always the greatest whoremaster.

Sneak. Why, by *Jerico,* it was by chance, Uncle; hab-nab as a man may say. As I hope to be sav'd 'twas against my will.

Apothecary. Sir, your anger makes an addition to his distemper.

Sir Roger. What, you are his Pandar, Sir, are you? But I think you may be the Devil for your honesty;—— So may ye all;—— Such as you sooth 'em in vices;—— I warrant you are tired with such customers,—— Ha, Sir,—— Are you not?

Apothecary. In troth, Sir, my rotten patients are so loath to die, and my sound ones, which for my arts improvement I would make rotten, so hasty to recover, that I confess I am often weary, but not tir'd, Sir.

Sir Roger. So, Sir, in verity you are all a company of rascals; and as for his part, I'll instantly write to his father to disinherit him, that I may revenge my disgrace, and punish his folly.—— The pox! A son of a whore! The pox! *(Exit.)*

Apothecary. A mad old fellow, but your penitence will recover all.

Sneak. Wou'd you were hang'd, by *Jerico,* for leaving the door open.—— Oh what shall I do? This comes of learning the Sciences in the Devil's name.——

Apothecary. Patience, Sir, have patience.——

(Scene shuts. Exeunt.)

[Scene 3. Emilia's *chamber.*]

Enter Rashley, Emilia *and* Betty.

Rashley. A trap-door, say you, Madam?

Emilia. Yes, we happily discover'd it yesterday looking for a ring accidentally dropt; it opens upon the stairs the backside of the kitchin; I am sure 'twill be very necessary in our intrigue.—— Here, take the candle you, and go and watch; and when I give the sign, be sure be ready.

Betty. I'll not fail, Madam. [*Exit* Betty.]

Emilia. 'Tis good to be secure, for I know *Maria* has still an eye over us, and my husbands new jealousie gives me fresh cause of doubt.

Rashley. Igad, 'tis unnecessary.—— This trap-door must needs be very useful; I see Fortune is ours still, and will not leave us. Let us doubt when we see danger; there is none now, nor can be whilst our love continues.

Emilia. Which I fear will be but a short time. For what is indirect is seldom permanent; therefore let us consider on't.

Rashley. Dam consideration; 'tis a worse enemy to mankind than malice. Let impotent age consider, that is fit for nothing but dull tame thoughts of what he has been formerly. Let the lawyer and physitian consider, what quibbles, and what potions are most necessary. And let the slie Phanatick think his time out, and consider how to be securely factious. But let the lover love on, still transported, whilst all his thoughts and sences are employ'd in the dear joys of rapture, endless passion, without a grain of dull consideration.

Emilia. I swear the softness of our tempers abuses half our sex; we shou'd not else be won so easily.—— But we are such kind fools!

Rashley. Ay, we are all fools, Madam, that's the truth on't; but how shall we help it?

Emilia. Resolve upon a remedy; love no more.

Rashley. Resolve upon the contrary; love for ever. Gad the world would be at a fine pass if all were of your mind. How now? *(Noise of a lock.)*

Enter Maria *with a light.*

Maria. Stand there till I fetch you in; I'm sure they're here.

Emilia. My sister as I live! Malicious accident!

Rashley. Ha, with a light too! How the Devil got she in?

Emilia. Heav'n knows, unless with a false key.

Maria. Nay, y'are caught, and finely too; I'm cozen'd else. What plot now, Madam, to convey you hence? Now show your mighty skill; and if there is a devil at your service employ him now; you never had more cause. Me thinks you are melancholy; why d'ee not laugh? Smile at your wit and great security? You, I know, have a thousand ways to get off still; or if you want, that gentleman can supply you.

Rashley. I supply! A plague o' your damn'd jest!

Emilia. Hush,——and leave me to her.—— Nay, Sister, this is barb'rous to triumph o'er our misfortunes. You know your self what love is, and what inconveniences it brings poor women too.

Maria. You can confess now; and here's a gentleman not far off,—— your husband, Madam. I know this cannot chuse but be grateful to him; I'll call him to hear it.

Emilia. Ah, be not so cruel to undo me quite! I'll confess all to thee, and from this minute be converted. Ah, had I taken thy counsel before, I had been happy.

Maria. Ay; but you would persist, and now see what comes on't.

Emilia. Oh! I am miserable! Forgive me, dear Maria! *(Weeps.)*

Maria. Nay, Heav'n forgive you. But come, will you confess? *(Aside.)* I have her at a rare advantage.——

Emilia. Most faithfully; but let me do't i' th' dark; let no light see my guilty blushes; it is enough my tongue dares utter it. Dear Sister, let me not be too much asham'd.—— Oh misery! Misery!—— *(Weeps.)*

Maria. Well, here is a light not far off, and thus much I'll comply with you.——— Now begin.——

(Puts out the light.)

Rashley. [*Aside.*] By Heav'n I grow cheerful; we shall 'scape, I am sure, we shall.—— Oh this dear devil!——

Emilia. My grief ties up my tongue.

Maria 'Tis time to grieve. But come, when d'ee begin?

Emilia. This cruel man seduc'd me: cruel *Rashley.*— *(Aside.)* Where are you, Sir?

Rashley. (Softly.) Here, Sweet, here!——

Emilia. First won upon me with his comely presence, hansom demeanour. Every several grace my soul admir'd.—— (*To* Rashley.) Give me your hand.—— But when he came to speak, his tongue, his charming tongue, Oh Heav'n, that I shall live to utter it! so ensnar'd me, that I no longer knew my liberty, but as his victim gloried in my passion.

Maria. With shame you live to speak it.

Rashley. 'Twas my misfortune too.—— But Heav'n forgive me. [*Aside.*] I shall laugh out; I am not able to hold.——

Emilia. Down, quickly down.—— (*Both sink in the trap.*)

Maria. Now could I laugh till my heart ak'd agen to think how I have caught 'em.—— I knew 'twas impossible she shou'd 'scape always, and I will tyrannize more than a Turk over his slave.—— For my part I am sorry for your infamy, and were it not that by the laws of nature I have a great concern in any of my brothers injuries, you might love on for me; but since my blood runs in his veins, I dare not see his infamy and let it pass unquestion'd. Therefore either swear from this hour to desert *Rashley,* and never see him more; or your disgrace I will this instant publish, or call your husband to be spectator of his shame and yours.—— What, are ye dumb? Not answer me! It seems you dislike this proposal; but do not provoke me.—— Not yet? Nay then—— Within there?—— Brother—— Here they are; a light, a light, quickly.

Enter Bubble *with a light and long sword.*

Bubble. Where? Where is this traytor? This strumpet? By *Scanderbeg,* I am ready for a charge; I'll push him with a vengeance.—— Where is he?

Maria. Here, here! How now? What, are you got

under the table agen? Or into a corner?—— Give me
the candle, Brother; I am sure I have em fast.——
                                        (*Looks about.*)
  Bubble. Here's nothing; another mistake, as Gad jidge
me.
  Maria. She is a devil, and I lose my labour. Gone!
What, both gone? Oh I could tear my self. Which
way?—— How! By what means could they escape?
  Bubble. 'Scape?—— 'Sbud! 'Tis impossible they shou'd
escape if they were here.—— Pish, this is only one of
your maggots, Sister; you do but fancy you saw 'em.
  Maria. Fancy? Eternal light forsake me, if I did not
both see and speak to 'em two minutes since; heard her
confess the crime, and vow repentance; here, in this
very place. But by what means they 'scapt, I only can
admire, not imagine.
  Bubble. Prethee hold thy peace; I say once more 'tis
only a maggot. Sleep, Fool, and purge thy head from
fancies. How now, *Ned?*
         Enter Ranger *and* Betty *behind*.
  Ranger. Sir, I know not whether the news I bring may
please you; but I have made a strange discovery yonder.
  Bubble. Discovery! Of what prethee?
  Ranger. Sir, I saw *Rashley* and your wife, going laughing arm in arm through the entry——the backside of
the kitchin into the parlour——where, if you please to
give your self the trouble, you may find 'em.
  Betty. [*Aside.*] This is as my mistriss suspected, and I'll
inform her immediately.   [*Exit* Betty.]
  Bubble. Hey day! My wife and *Rashley?* Art sure on't,
Ned?
  Ranger. As sure, Sir, as I live, I saw 'em there. Nay,
what's more, my curiosity inducing me to peep through

the key-hole, I saw his head lie in her lap, whilst she with a fond passion strok'd his cheeks, and dalli'd with his hair. Faith, Sir, I could not see this and be silent; but you I fear will think the worse of me for it.

Bubble. In the parlour, sayst thou? 'Sbud, was ever such a confusion? Why, my sister says that within these two minutes she saw and spoke to 'em here in this chamber. They are here, and there, and every where, and yet I can find 'em no where; what a pox shou'd a man think of this?

Ranger. They are there this instant, Sir, upon my honour.

Maria. Sure, I have not dreamt all this while! Did I not see her? By Heav'n I saw the Devil in her likeness then.

Bubble. Why, peace, I say; if you are mad, offend no one but your self with it. What a pox, shall I not believe my eyes? The house is not haunted that I know of, unless it be with fools.—— There's a bob for you by way of conclusion.

Maria. Yes, cuckolds too! There's a bob for you by way of repartée.

Bubble. Cuckold? I'd have you to know I scorn your words; and were you not my sister, I'd fetch you out with your repartées. What, because you are a fool, you guess all persons are alike? Do you but conceive me, Mrs. *Juniper?* I am a Turk at matter of fact when I see occasion.

Ranger. Good Sir, no more of this, but go down and satisfie your self in the truth of my story. If I tell you a lye, call me fool, horse, any thing; do but go and see.

Bubble. 'Sbud, I know not what to do. One brings me up, another carries me down; one jilts me, another abuses me; a third laughs at me; and yet I find nothing, nor see nothing, nor know nothing,——and you are nothing but fools to make all this stir about nothing. But come, I'll go with thee, *Ned*.

Maria. And I, that I may say once in my life I saw a miracle.

Ranger. I have her once more in the noose of the slip; now the Devil hold her fast in th' other world.—— 'Tis above mortal power! Come, Sir.   (*Exeunt.*)

Scene 4. [*The parlor.*]
Enter Rashley *and* Emilia *in night-gowns,*
Betty, Jeremy.

Emilia. Here, here, quickly take my night-gown, and put it on; you are sure they are coming.

Betty. Very sure, Madam; I stood at the door and heard all.

Rashley. What must I do, Sweet? Prethee do not let us be surpriz'd agen.

Emilia. Uncase, uncase, Sir; and let your man represent you as *Betty* does me. *Jeremy,* be sure you play your part well, and court her to the life.

([Betty *and* Jeremy] *put on the gowns.*)

Rashley. D'ee hear, Sirrah!

Jeremy. I'll warrant you, Sir. Come, Mrs. *Betty*.

Emilia. Stay, a word more in thy ear.—— [*Aside.*] I see this fellow is but a blockhead, and therefore am afraid of trusting him too far.—— Keep him as ignorant of our intrigue as thou canst; and if my husband ask where I am, tell him I am gone to visit my Lady *Courtly*. I'll be in my chamber; and when they are all gone, bring me word what *Ranger* and *Maria* are doing.

Betty. Yes, Madam, I'll be very careful.

Rashley. I will reward thy care, my pretty little——

(*Noise.*)

Emilia. Hark! I hear 'em coming; now to your postures.　　　　　　　　　　　　(*Exit* Rashley *and* Emilia.)

Jeremy. Now, Mrs. *Betty,* we having so fit an occasion, let us make love in some heroick vein.

Betty. No, I am for the plain-dealing way.

Jeremy. Pish! T'others a great deal better, as thus:

> Your eyes with so bright charms are deckt about,
> That I could kiss 'em till I kist 'em out.

Betty. Oh I hate that; I vow 'tis very silly.
　　　　　　Enter Ranger, Bubble *and* Maria.

Ranger. There, there, Sir; d'ee see 'em now? Will you believe next time?

Bubble. O dismal object! I am a cuckold then.

Maria. This is miraculous; how was it possible they cou'd get hither? But I am glad they are here however.

Bubble. Now for a good full blow at his head before he sees me. 'Tis a cuckolds way of revenge I'm sure; have at him!——　　　　　　　　　(*Offers to strike.*)

Jeremy. Oh Lord, what mean you, Sir, what mean you?

Bubble. Traytor! Rogue! Rascal! I'll—— Hah, *Jeremy*?

Jeremy. Ay, Sir, 'tis I, poor *Jeremy,* Sir.

Maria. And *Betty* in her mistrisses night-gown.
　　　　　　　　　　　　　　(Ranger's *amaz'd.*)

Ranger. Their old friend the Devil has fetch 'em away agen.

Bubble. What make you here in their night-gowns?

Betty. Only, Sir, through an ambition to make love as gentilely as we cou'd.

Bubble. Go, go, and find your mistriss out, and tell her, her humble servant and husband desires to speak with her.——　　　　　　　[*Exit* Betty *and* Jeremy.]
Look ye, *Ned,* you are a fool, I see.

Ranger. I am so, Sir, I acknowledge it.

Bubble. And you, Madam, are a little leaning that way, are ye not?

Maria. I can say nothing for my self, Sir.

Bubble. Then I can say y'are a couple of fools. Did I not tell you what all this wou'd come to? Ha, ha, ha! It makes me laugh to think how busie you two asses have been about nothing; and I am no better than a third fool for believing you. But from henceforth, he that speaks against my Chickens vertue, is the son of a whore; for 'Uds Bood she's the honestest woman in Christendom, and he that denies it, I will immediately invade him with battle-ax, poinard and pistol.

Ranger. She is a very saint, Sir.

Maria. A very devil, Sir! O Death, is there no remedy?

Bubble. I'll go instantly and reconcile my self to her, with a strict vow never to doubt her more.—— Oh Sir *Roger!* Welcome.

Enter Sir Roger *and* Cordelia.

Faith! I was wishing for some good company to be witness of my reconcilement to my dear Chicken. You are melancholy, Sir—— I heard your nephew was sick; I suppose that's the cause.

Sir Roger. If he has heard of what, I am disgrac'd for ever.

Bubble. Come, Sir, cheer up, cheer up, he will be well agen, doubt not.

Sir Roger. I hope so, Sir. [*Aside to* Cordelia.] Madam, this generous act of concealing the infamy of our family, has so wrought upon me, that if I cou'd requite——

Cordelia. No more, Sir. Your nephews forbearance is all I desire. You are sensible now that I have some reason to request that.

Sir Roger. I am, Madam, and am extreamly bound to

your generosity; and Gad I have another nephew whom I'll make better by 200 £. a year to make you amends.—— Well, Mr. *Bubble,* I am glad to come at so good a time, when mirth is going forward; you are a merry man, Sir, and in verity I like your company.

Bubble. And I yours, Sir *Roger;* for I am very merry for some private reason best known to my self. We'll toss a bumper about by and by, faith!

Enter Fumble *pushing in* Governess.

Fumble. An old cronee, a sorceress.—— What ifack, and in the Devils name, am I to be popt in the mouth with fourscore and twelve? A beldame, a witch, that expects next winter to be turn'd into a gib-cat, thought fit to be yok'd with me! No, no, some wiser than some; and I'll have her know within this week that I am as fit for two and twenty, as two and twenty is for me.—— In the mean time avaunt *Jezabel*; I like thee not, *Icod*; thou hast no black o' top, ifack; thou art not for my turn.

Bubble. What, old Signior *Fumble*? What's the matter, man?

Fumble. Yes marry am I, Sir, and chows'd damnably too, and some shall know't when I can find 'em.

Cordelia. He's groping for his spectacles; now I expect to be rated.

Fumble. Ah, are you there, Rogue, are you there! Why, you very wag, wou'd you offer to serve me so? But hang thee, thou'rt a rogue, and come ifack tho' 'twas a knavish trick, I am pleas'd with the wit on't.—— Give me thy hand, and come and kiss me, and all shall be well agen.

Cordelia. Upon condition you never trouble me more, there 'tis.

Fumble. Icod, she has a pretty touch with her, she has ifack; I forgive thee with all my heart.—— Well, old woman, depart in peace; old woman, I say, depart, and trouble me no more. I am busie, and cann't dispence with the fopperies of age now.

Governess. Well, this comes of eating sweet-meets when I was young. He had never found out the trick, if my want of teeth had not discover'd me.

Bubble. Ha, ha!—— Here had like to have been fine sport ifaith.—— But wou'd I knew where my wife is, that we might all go and address, now I am in this good humour.

Governess. Sir, just as I came in, I saw her go up into her chamber.

Bubble. Didst thou? I am glad on't ifaith. Come, let's all go.

Enter Betty.

Betty. Sir, I cannot find her; but I heard her say about an hour since, she intended to go and visit my Lady *Courtly.*

Bubble. No no; I know where she is now.—— Poor creature! I warrant she sits so melancholy above now.—— Well, I dare proudly say I have the best wife in Christendom. For ifaith I have been very jealous of her, but I was wrought upon, when o' my conscience the innocent wretch wou'd not hurt a worm.—— But come, we'll all go to her, and be sure, Sir *Roger,* you plead for me; in troth my heart akes to think how I have us'd her.

Betty. [*Aside.*] I must prevent their going up, or we are undone.   (*Is running;* Maria *stops her.*)

Maria. Whither are you running? I have some bus'ness with you.

Betty. Good Madam, I'll wait on you immediately.

Maria. Ye shall not stir till I have spoke to you.—— [*Aside.*] Here must be something in this I find by her eagerness to be gone.

Sir Roger. Well, Mr. *Bubble,* in verity I'll do my best in your behalf; my tongue is at your service at any time.

Bubble. Sir *Roger,* you will oblige me in't. She is the most innocent, sweetest, and most vertuous person in the whole world, and I shall never be able to make her amends.—— Come, let us go.

Ranger. Now will I see how she behaves her self, and wonder at the prosperous impudence Hell has endow'd her with, tho' it lies not in my power to repel it.

Maria. Now I think better on't, I'll defer my bus'ness till another time. You may go where you please. (*Exeunt.*)

Betty. This cunning devil has undone 'em; nor lies it now in my power to hinder it.—— Oh I cou'd curse——

(*Exit.*)

Scena ultima. [Emilia's *chamber.*]

Enter Rashley *and* Emilia.

Emilia. The plague of living with such a husband you must imagine is very disagreeable to my temper; and were it not for the happy hours I have the good fortune to enjoy in thy society, my life wou'd be wholly uncomfortable. But, my dear, thou wilt forget me; one day I shall grow cheap to thee, shall I not?

Rashley. No, never; never, my sweet!—— Thou hast more charms each hour added to thee, rather than one diminisht.—— Forget thee! I sooner shall forget to feed my self, or that the sun ere shone in midst of summer, than thy more precious favours. Thou bring'st each hour new sweets, and every minute a thousand thousand graces throng about thee. My dear,—— Dear, charming, sweet,—— Precious!—— (*Kisses her.*)

Enter Bubble, *Sir* Roger, Fumble, Ranger, Maria, Cordelia.

Bubble. (*Entring.*) Softly, softly, Sir *Roger.*—— Poor soul, I warrant she's at prayers.—— Hah! What's this I see?—— Gad jidge me——

Ranger. By Heav'n, they're here a kissing!—— Oh happy minute!

Emilia. Ah, who could have the heart to leave thy blisses for such a fool, such a beast, such a dull, sordid, filthy, insipid creature as my husband?

Bubble. How's that? Oh devil!

Rashley. I am smother'd with thy charms; oh for some air! Hah!—— Oh horrour, curs'd minute! Taken thus? *(Stares.)*

Emilia. My husband! Nay then I am lost for ever.

Bubble. Ah cursed creature! Is this thy vertue?—— But I'll—— *(Goes to wound her.)*

Sir Roger. Hold, Sir, in verity that must not be; no swords against women in my company.

Bubble. [*To* Rashley.] Then here let my vengeance light. Traytor! Have I oblig'd thee so often for this?—— Have at thee!

Ranger. Your pardon, Sir, I must hinder dishonourable proceedings; in the field you may do what you please.

Bubble. Speak, Witch, speak! What reason hadst thou to use me thus? Thou limb of the Devil, speak, I say.

Emilia. Use you thus?—— Why,—— Sir, your rage makes you suggest strange thoughts without cause. My kindness to Mr. *Rashley* was only because——he promis'd to be my friend in urging my reconcilement with you;—— And because I knew he was your friend, I therefore—— I say, because I knew you lov'd him, I desir'd him to——to—— I was very urgent with him——about——about—— No I mistake! 'Twas he was urgent with me to intreat you to do me the favour——no——to do him the favour. I mean, hum——to——to——

Bubble. Pox! What a story's here? Oh strumpet! Witch!

Maria. To cuckold him, was that it, Sister?

Ranger. Madam, me thinks your speech fails you exceedingly.

Emilia. All will not do. O spiteful minute! Taken thus at last? Shame ties my tongue, and absence is most necessary. *(Exit.)*

Bubble. Oh farewel in the Devils name! Oh horns! Horns! Found a cuckold at last! I have spun a fair thread, by the Lord *Harry*; a cuckold at last!

Rashley. A cuckold! Why, Sir, have I done any thing but by your directions? Why do you suggest such things to your self? Well, Sir, if I have injur'd you, I wear a sword, Sir,—— And so—— Farewel.—— *(Exit* Rashley.)

Sir Roger. In verity this was a strange discovery; but such things will happen——sometimes.

Cordelia. So it seems; yet this me thinks is wonderful.

Bubble. Oh unfortunate husband! Well, I'll go instantly and get a divorce, and spend the remainder of my life in penning a satyr against women. I'll call it, A CAUTION FOR CUCKOLDS; where I will deplorably set down my own case, and as a warning-piece for rash young men, and for the benefit of my country.

Felix quem faciunt aliena cornua cautum.

(Exit.)

Fumble. Something is the matter now, if I cou'd guess. But mum! I must not yet discover my failing.

Ranger. Now the mighty sophistress is o'erthrown!

Maria. Thank chance for that; but no wit of our own.

Ranger. Right, Madam; and by this a man may see how unnecessary a thing it is, to strive to turn the current of a womans fancy, when it is bent to another. 'Tis a damn'd thing this wenching, if a man considers seriously on it; and yet 'tis such a damnable age we live in, that, Gad, he that does not follow it is either accounted sordidly unnatural, or ridiculously impotent.—— Well, for my part henceforward this shall be my resolution:

> I'll love for interest, court for recreation;
> Change still a mistriss to be still in fashion.
> I'll aid all women in an amorous league;
> But from this hour ne'er baulk a love-intrigue. 95

(Exit omnes.)

Epilogue spoken by Fumble.

Well, Gentlemen, how d'ee?— Icod *you sit,*
As if you had no souls, no brains, no wit.
What, not a word now in the poets praise?
Hah!— *Faith, I was a spark in my young days.* 5
I clapt, and clapt;—nay, sometimes to my cost.
I clapt so long,— *Gad, I (was) clapt at last.*
There I was waggish;— *You know what I mean;*—
The Devil was in't, a plaguy Yorkshire *quean.*—
But 'tis no matter,—'twas but thought a jest, 10
And, Gad, I was as brisk then as the best.
So I am now; for Ifack I'd have you know,
Your old man, though he only serve for show,
Yet give him a young wench with black o' top,—
And you shall see him frisk, and jump, and hop;— 15
Icod, *and wriggle!*— *Hah!*— *Th' old bell will sound,*
Though there is ne'er a clapper to be found.
But let that pass. Now your applause disburse;
Why,—*what the Devil makes you silent thus?*—
What say ye,— *The play does not deserve it?*— *Hah!*— 20
Icod, *you are mistaken.*— *For I'll tell ye,*
I once could write and judge,—*and 'fack did do*
Very strange things;—*but I've forgot 'um now.*—
But I remember what a wag—*I was.*—
I had so many smutty jests those days, 25
I could get none but women to my plays.
But that's all one;— Icod, *the youth that writ,*
Does well— *And who knows,*—*may do better yet.*
Therefore you should incourage him, d'ee hear?
And he that fails, I wish this curse may bear, 30

That he be really my character,—
Lascivious, deaf, and impotent as I;
And Gad that's plague enough,—and so God bu'y.

FINIS.

NOTES TO
A FOND HUSBAND

Epistle dedicatory.
    2. Duke of Ormond: James Butler, twelfth Earl and first Duke of Ormonde (1610-1688), one of D'Urfey's early patrons. Both *Madam Fickle* and *A Fond Husband* are dedicated to him.
    17. indifferently: impartially, without bias.
    28. departure from England: In August, 1677, Charles II sent Ormonde to Ireland to preserve peace and reorganize the Irish government.
    36. resent: appreciate.
    42. my last: i.e., the dedication of *Madam Fickle.*
    44. doubt: suspect or believe.

Dramatis Personae.
    1. The actors' names in the 1711 and 1735 editions are different from those in the first three quartos, being the names of the cast of the Theatre Royal (Drury Lane) company. That cast is given as: Rashley—Powel, Ranger—Mills, Bubble—Dogget, Fumble—Johnson, Sir Roger—Estcourt, Sneak—Penkethman, Spatterdash and Jeremy—Richards, Apothecary—Percival, Emilia—Mrs. Knight, Maria—Mrs. Rogers, Cordelia—Mrs. Sherborne, Betty—Mrs. Baker, and Governess—Mrs. Powell. Mrs. Snare is again omitted.
    5. Bubble: The name means "gull" or "dupe."
    10. black women: *i.e.,* dark-complexioned.
    21. raw: possibly should read "law."

Prologue.
    13. mock-song: satiric song.
    36. cabal: clique, coterie.

Act I. Scene 1.

5. Scene 1: *sic*, though the act is in a single scene.

7-8. Shuttle-Cock and Battle-Dor's: a parlor game in which the shuttle-cock is hit with the battle-dor between two players; similar to parlor badminton.

10-22. The song is by D'Urfey and in another version begins: "No more, cruel nymph, my passion despise." It was also printed in D'Urfey's *New Collection of Songs and Poems* (1683), p. 47.

20. my scepter: with an obvious phallic allusion.

32-33. resentment: appreciation, acknowledgment.

60. propriety: property.

70. carrest: caressed; shown favor or affection.

87. Let . . . him: Leave him to me.

88. turn thee loose to: match you with.

89. Lapland: fabled home of witches and magicians.

103. Mrs. Jilt: harlot, strumpet.

129. insipid: dull, foolish.

147. busie: prying, meddlesome.

161-62. The beginning of a song by D'Urfey.

167. perspective: an optical device. "Through the right end of the perspective" means "in proper proportion."

176. Tom: Rashley was called Jack at line 104 above.

177. in the mumps: out of sorts / pop: a meaningless interjection, used frequently by foolish D'Urfey characters.

197. Turk: fierce or savage person.

206. flearing'st: most contemptuous / quean: used here in an affectionate sense, but usually "harlot."

209. tropes and figures: figurative language.

209-10. when her hands in: when she gets going.

213. non parelio: nonpareil, one without equal.

218-20. I can . . . love-affairs: The sense is obscure. Possibly, "I can be affectionate with my friend (Bubble) as usual, without his discouraging me in my affair with his wife." Or possibly "friend" refers to Emilia, in the sense of "lover."

248. property: butt, victim.

261. represents: Exact meaning is unclear. Possibly "makes visible or manifest," with a gesture toward Emilia.

263. quirks and quiddits: verbal tricks and evasions.

263-64. Cambridge . . . quibbles: referring to the rhetorical tricks of both Cantabrigians and the lawyers of Westminster-Hall.

273. gold watch: referred to at line 133 above as a necklace.

309. bubbl'd: cheated, fooled.

325. huff: show contempt for.

339. powdering-tub: literally, in which the flesh of animals was salted. But also a cant expression for the hospital at Kingland where syphilis was treated and, thus, a *double entendre*.

359. the man: *i.e.*, Sneak, not Sir Roger.

381. Cob: Sir Roger's nickname for Sneak denotes a huge, lumpish person. Also a possible pun on "testicle."

387. parts: talents, abilities.

Notes to *A Fond Husband*

394. salute: kiss by way of salutation.
401. Ifack: In faith.
407. Aloud: i.e., shouting.
440-41. *Sawny Broome*: Alexander Brome (1620-1666), a Royalist songwriter and playwright, noted for his bacchanalian lyrics. He strongly influenced D'Urfey's own songs. Brome appears as a character in *The Royalist* (1682).
442. Miter under the Rose: possibly the same tavern referred to in *Wit for Money* (p. 9) as the Rose, D'Urfey's favorite haunt. / leveller: unclear. Possibly the drink, which "levelled" all men by making them equals; also possibly a play on the Levellers, a reform party of the Commonwealth years that was the frequent subject of Brome's satiric songs.
448. Betty *sings*: She has evidently remained on stage since line 163 above.
449. Though D'Urfey states in the epistle dedicatory that the song is not entirely his, no collaborator is known. *Wit for Money* (p. 5) ridicules D'Urfey's ineptitude in all his Scotch songs, noting the spurious vocabulary and dialect. The present example is no exception. It is found also in *Choice Ayres and Songs* (London, 1679), p. 46, and in *Wit and Mirth*, 1:306, both with music.
450. Munnonday: Monday.
452. leaked: looked / *knough*: knoll.
453. *Yen glenting*: one (yin) moving / *brent*: smooth.
456. *Bekt lew*: curtseyed low / *sine*: then, thereupon.
457. speard: asked.
458. brough: bridge.
460. sike: such.
461. gate: way.
462. Dow: Dear.
463. light: lift. An alternate reading is *dight* (*put in order, tidy*), that of the *Choice Ayres* and *Wit and Mirth* printings.
468. [ma]: All editions read *your*. Emendation is from the *Choice Ayres* and *Wit and Mirth* printings.
472. rew: rue, show scorn (?).
475. leath: loath.
476. eaght: aught.
477. boo: bow.
489. bumper: a toast. Cf. *Madam Fickle*, I, i, 275., and V, i, 81.

Act II. Scene 1.

15. discover: reveal.
17. still: even.
21. politick: cunning, crafty.
25. insult: exult, triumph scornfully. Cf. *Madam Fickle,* II, ii, 131.
35. masculine person: unclear; possibly Maria refers to her "active soul" as making her masculine.
40. hand-granado: References to explosive missiles thrown by hand occur as early as 1661.
45. obscure: dark.

Act II. Scene 2.

9. provided: prepared.

10. remember . . . tardy: take care to be alert.
12. nearly: privately, intimately.
32. all-a-mort: struck dumb, confounded.
37. jest: The intent of the word-play is unclear. Possibly, Bubble uses *gammon of bacon* to describe Rashley's lifeless expression, then realizes his pun on *gammon* (foolish talk or nonsense). Rashley then takes *gammon* for a third meaning: to distract a person's attention while robbing him. *Bacon* is also slang for the body.
51. then: used frequently for *than* in the period. See 1. 78 below.
61. mumpt: overreached, outguessed.
66. Leviathan: literally, a whale; but possibly suggesting Thomas Hobbes's *Leviathan* (1651), a political treatise affirming the supreme authority of the sovereign.
76. pinch: reproach, reprove.
90. convenient: suitable, proper.
104. squirril: exact meaning of the pun is unclear, though the obscene intent is clear.
118-19. tory-rory: uproariously.
120. spell: trick, stratagem.

Act II. Scene 3.

47-48. Plato's Great Year: literally, a theoretical year (*c.* 25,800) when all the planets will return to their original relative positions; figuratively, the impossibly distant future.
55. take . . . away: excepting the Court wits.
63. period: point.
77. Round Cap: a Cambridge undergraduate.
86. daggled gown: a mark of the law student; daggled means mud-splashed.
87. rotten mutton: with a pun on pox-rotten (syphilitic) and mutton (prostitutes).
101. slie: possibly should read "shie" (shy).
123. bona fide: truly, absolutely.
126. patch: a small piece of silk or court-plaster worn on the face as a fashion accessory. "Further" is the verb in this sentence, and "generation" is its object.
126-27. tissues: gauzy fabrics, woven with gold or silver.
129-30. rotten: syphilitic.
132. swinge: beat, thrash.
141. wag: rogue, rascal.
143. knows . . . handsaw: knows what's what. "Handsaw" is a corruption of "hernshaw" (heron). See *Hamlet*, II, ii, 397.
161. pottle: two quarts.
163. turn her back: retreat. The entire passage is suggestive of sexual allusions.
195. swinger: rogue, rascal. Much like contemporary usage.

Act II. Scene 4.

14-15. indifferently: impartially.

Notes to *A Fond Husband*

28. fitted: answered, retaliated.
30. cautious . . . confession: careful not to make a scrupulous confession.
55. took . . . way: been more candid.
99. dam: be damned.

Act III.

7. stay: wait.
22. snapt: caught, taken at a disadvantage; with a possible pun on "snap" as sexual intercourse.
77. put out her eye: with an obscene suggestion.
80. pudding-bag: literally, for boiling pudding; possibly with a pun on "pudding" as "penis."
99-103. This speech is set as verse in all editions. Such arbitrary composition occurs frequently in the printings of D'Urfey's plays. The present editions retain them only where they scan as verse. Cf. *Madam Fickle*: II, ii, 239-53; V, i, 4-17, 143-48; *et al.*
116-17. let him alone: leave it to him.
121. Scoggen: clown, buffoon; from John Skogan, court jester to Edward IV; probably addressed to Emilia by way of reprimand.
124-25. Had . . . character: possibly, "Even had she been a witch before, she just damaged her reputation."
130-31. weigh . . . scale: "You attribute to me your own accomplishments in courtship," a back-handed compliment, since Sir Roger has long been deserted by the ladies.
153. Ombre: a popular three-handed card game.
169. cuckold-buz: rumored cuckold; subject of gossip.
204. titulation: obsolete form of "titillation."
209. display: describe, expound.
216. head . . .ake: He feels his cuckold's horns sprouting.
218. hugger mugger: secrecy, concealment.
235-36. president . . . nature: possibly, "precedent (sign, indication) of your excellent disposition."
245. mummy: dead flesh.
253. want: lack.
262. cut . . . nose: a punishment frequently referred to by D'Urfey. Cf. lines 442-43 below.
263. New-Years-Gift: Gifts were customarily given at New Year's.
285. made one: participated.
292-93. plaid . . . discover: determined to expose us.
300. rancounter: also rencounter; a duel.
313-17. Betty could not have overheard the plot to feign Bubble's departure, because she exited at line 188, before it was formulated. Such carelessness is not uncommon in D'Urfey's plays.
347. Trolly Lolly Lo: like Tra La La.
374. Song of Sir *Thomas Fairfax*: One of a number of songs by Alexander Brome (See note I, i, 440, above.) ridiculing the Rump Parliament of the Commonwealth. The subject is Thomas, third Lord Fairfax (1612-1671), who led the Parliamentary Army against Charles I.
378. Rump-Songs: popular ballads ridiculing the Rump Parliament of the Commonwealth.

385. Chevy-Chace: a popular ballad, much admired by such writers as Jonson, Sydney, and Addison, chronicling the Battle of Otterburn (1388). Addison called it "the favorite ballad of the common people of England." (See *The Spectator*, 70 and 74.)

385-86. Hunting of the Hare: title for a number of popular hunting songs. (See Minnie Earl Sears, ed., *Song Index* [New York, 1926], p. 247.)

389. clack: chatterbox.

403-4. hieroglyphick-characters: symbols.

404. Fanaticks: Puritans.

408. Conny: rabbit, hare.

439-40. conjurer: cant term for confidence men, such as astrologers, physiognomists, etc.

443. penny-pot-poets: cheap ballad makers.

446. snapt . . . nick: caught them at the right moment; also, punning on "snap" and "nick," sexual slang.

454. kind: in the sense of loving or intimate.

459-60. pristine ages: former times.

463-64. mungrel love: animal love, lust.

484-85. moon-shine in the water: mere illusion, naught.

556. Gapes: yawns.

563. cum privilegio: with impunity.

583. slights: artifices, stratagems.

Act IV. Scene 1.

9. birds of night: prostitutes.

12. cattel: cant term for prostitutes.

14-18. The sense is obscure. Perhaps, "Who could imagine your face, mouth, and person belonging to a fool?"

26. natural: half-wit. / beg . . . King: petition the Court of Wards for custody (of an idiot, etc.).

48. upon the hip: at a disadvantage.

98. solemnity: any celebration of special importance.

Act IV. Scene 2.

14. bumping it about: drinking bumpers, toasting.

15. dipt: made drunk.

16. freshman: new arrival.

18. want it: lack a drink.

26. soop: drink. Cf. the Irish "supeen." / Sirrah: probably the servant pouring the wine.

27. dust it about: drink around quickly.

29. cherishes: cheers, gladdens.

43. Tom Farthing: unidentified; probably a folk song.

43-44. Colly my Cow: a folk song. (See Sears, *Song Index*, p. 103.)

50. drowsie: dull, witless.

55. SONG: The song is by D'Urfey and was set to music by "Mr. [William (?)] Turner." It is also printed in D'Urfey's *New Collection of Songs and Poems* (1683), p. 31.

80. *Dance*: possibly a prompter's warning cue, as the dance is again indicated at line 88 below.
100. resentment: sense of injury.
137. *Westminster-Hall*: law court.

Act IV. Scene 3.

7. nine-holes: a game similar to billiards.
8. spends: costs.
24. bayly: bailiff.
30. make mouths: grimace.
34. French grimaces: a popular term for affected facial expressions.
62. *congee*: the deep French bow or *reverence*.
83. false calves: Fashionable gentlemen wore padded hose if their legs were not shapely.
90. had my honours: learned to make bows.
114. sanguine complexion: and thus, according to the *humours* theory, brisk, bold, and probably amorous.
121. suddenly: immediately.

Act IV. Scene 4.

22. *scene a bed-chamber*: The stage direction indicates that the previous scene was played before scenic panels, or shutters, which are now drawn apart to reveal the bedroom scene.
31. gib-cat: literally a tom cat, but used derogatorily of old women/ / mew'd: confined or concealed, with a pun on the mew of a cat.
34. gally-pots: apothecaries' ointment jars.
75-76. dash your mummery: ruin your pretense.
115. conveyance is fast: exit is secure, blocked.
117-18. jolly spleen to laugh: impulse or eagerness to mock.
152-53. Here's . . . towards: roughly, "This is going to develop into a fine situation," spoken with irony.
254-55. A very . . . to me: unclear; possibly, "A fine stratagem, considering how she now intends to abuse me (by denying knowledge of my presence)."
271. to her: compared to her.
276. unkind: unnatural.
291. happily they end still: they continue to result in good fortune.

Act V. Scene 1.

11. quiet: *i.e.*, left in quiet, alone.
30. the jest: the jest is a pun on "stones," slang for "testicles."
34-36. old piece . . . play: a derisive allusion, probably to Mrs. Behn's *Debauchee; Or, The Credulous Cuckold*, an adaptation of Richard Brome's *Mad Couple Well Matched* (1636), which played at Dorset Garden shortly before *A Fond Husband*. Nicoll dates its performance *c*. February, 1676/7 (*A History of English Drama*, 1: 390).
46. SONG: unidentified; probably a popular ribald ballad.
53. deaths-head at supper: referring to the ancient Egyptian custom of placing a skull on the dining table, as a remembrance of mortality. According

258   *A Fond Husband; or, The Plotting Sisters*

to Herodotus (Book II, Chapter 78), it was not a skull, however, but a small carved mummy, which was carried about by a slave. Another allusion to the custom occurs in Wycherley's *Plain Dealer* (II, i), which had been acted in January of 1677 and from which D'Urfey may have taken the idea. In that comedy Olivia ridicules a fashionable hostess who "revives the old Grecian [*sic*] custom, of serving in a death's head with their banquets." D'Urfey alludes to it once again in his preface to *The Royalist*: ". . . the Moral Antients, in the midst of all their Feasts and Luxurious Entertainments plac't a dead Man's Scull upon the Table to qualify their Joy, and give a Contemplative Reflection of their Mortality."

54. antick: antique.

58. the Devil's an Ass: the title of a play by Ben Jonson (1616), though there is no evidence of its having been recently performed.

61. Randolph: possibly Thomas Randolph (1605–1635), poet and dramatist. The quotation has not been identified and may be spurious.

63. waggish again: Fumble congratulates himself on his pun on "nick," with an obscene meaning. Cf. D'Urfey's *Richmond Heiress*, Act I: the only cure for young girls' fevers is "to get them Husbands just in the Nick."

79. in thy way: for you.

82. punctual: attentive.

92. another age: a second lifetime / farewel old *Simon*: possibly a current expression; perhaps intended as Fumble's given name.

103. re-enter: i.e., come forward; they have been on stage all along.

111. prejudicial: damaging.

134. sifting: questioning, trying.

137. she's: she has.

139. buz'd: rumored, whispered.

141. false key: pass key.

Act V. Scene 2.

13-14. civil . . . pox: The clap (gonorrhea) is so common as to be civil (popular), but not the pox (syphilis), which is more serious.

21. sweating-chair: a device to induce the sweating thought to be a cure for the pox.

34. sandy: shifty, unreliable.

47. sound: free from venereal disease.

49. tir'd: possibly a play on "retired."

Act V. Scene 3.

32. kind: natural.

39. with a light: a convention indicating to the audience that the stage is to be supposed in darkness.

54. jest: The pun is on "supply," meaning both "aid or assist" and "satisfy sexually."

104. for me: for all I care.

115. Scanderbeg: an oath used frequently in the period; from Iskender Bey (1403-1467), the popular Albanian hero who defeated the Ottoman Turks. Cf. *Madam Fickle*, III, i, 152.

128. maggots: whimsical ideas, perverse fancies.
169. bob: a jeering rebuke.
177. Mrs. *Juniper*: a contemptuous epithet, especially for a prostitute. Cf. *Madam Fickle*, V, ii, 159.
190. noose of the slip: hangman's noose.

Act V. Scene 4.
2. night-gowns: dressing gowns.
103. beldame: beldam; loathsome old woman, hag.
108. Jezabel: popularly used for a shrew or termagant.
115. rated: chided, scolded.
127-28. dispence with: frequently, as here, used with the exact opposite of contemporary meaning; "put up with."
165. Possibly Bubble and Sir Roger should exit at this point, since Betty despairs of saving her mistress at line 171.

Act V. Scena ultima.
63-64. spun a fair thread: made a mess of things.
71. wonderful: astonishing.
78. Felix . . . cautum: Happy is the man who is made cautious by another's horns.

Epilogue.
7. clapt at last: with an obvious play on "clap."
17. clapper: a triple *entendre*; "applauder," bell clapper, and a phallic allusion.

Textual Notes

MADAM FICKLE;
OR, THE
WITTY FALSE ONE

Madam Fickle went through three printings: one each in 1676, 1682, and 1691. D'Urfey was notoriously careless about the printings of his plays and there is no evidence for believing that he had any influence over any of the editions of *Madam Fickle*. The first quarto (Q) was probably set from a playhouse copy, since there are two prompter's cues included; these are recorded in the Notes. The second quarto (Q2) is set from Q, though it does correct some obvious errors such as reassigning mistaken speech tags and eliminating the prompter's cues. The third quarto (Q3), though the most careless of the three, attempts to regularize punctuation and spelling of Q2, but in no case does it show evidence of any influence from Q. The transmission of the text, then, is not complicated, and the first quarto of 1676 has been used as the copy-text for the present edition.

The copy-text has been collated with Q2 and Q3, and all variants have been recorded. Line numbers have been assigned to the text by scenes. The spelling and use of italics of the copy-text have been preserved, but in the interest of readability punctuation and capitalization have been brought more closely into accordance with modern practice. Where variants in either punctuation or capitalization affect the sense, they have been noted. Where readings from Q2 and Q3 have been used, the reading of Q is always noted; brackets denote editorial emendations.

All speech tags have been regularized and spelled out, as in the Dramatis Personae, and each tag has been italicized, capitalized, and followed by a period. Stage directions have been uniformly enclosed in parentheses, capitalized, and followed by a period. Asides have been moved to precede the speeches to which they refer. Obvious errors, such as transposition or inversion of a single letter, have been silently corrected.

MADAM FICKLE

Emendations of Copy-text

Dramatis Personae.
   2 *Bellamore*] Q2 Q3; *Bellamour* Q
  12 *Jevon*] *Jevan* all eds.
  14 *Norris*] Q3; *Norrice* Q Q2
  18 *Barry*] *Barrer* all eds.

Act I. Scene 1.
  140 Don't] Do'nt all eds.
  173 I'th'] Q2 Q3; Ith' Q
  291 o're] Q2 Q3; ore' Q
  301 *dementia*] *dementio* all eds.
  305 *Zechiel.*] Q2 Q3; omit. Q
  327 *Zechiel.*] Q2 Q3; *Flail.* Q
  335 Mall] Q2 Q3; Mail Q
  407 I'th'] Q2 Q3; Ith' Q
  427 Seventeen] 17 all eds.

Act II. Scene 1.

1 *Mall*] *Mail* all eds.
21 presently. Jack,] presently, Jack! Q Q2; presently. Jack! Q3
27 fiddles] Q3; fidles Q Q2
35 opportunity to perform it. I'le] Q3; opportunity. To perform it, I'le Q Q2
65 haste] Q2 Q3; hast Q
68 flesh] Q3; Flash Q Q2
88 Good-bye] good Boy Q; good-Boy Q2; good Buoy Q3
103-4 pleasure of my] Q2 Q3; pleasure my Q
155 *Mall*] *Mail* all eds.
172 *Mall*] *Mail* all eds.

Act II. Scene 2.

21 descent] Q2 Q3; discent Q
48 *What*] *with* all eds. (See Note, 1. 41.)
256 *Exit.*] *Exeunt.* all eds.

Act III. Scene 1.

59 Q adds *Call Servant* (probably a prompter's notation)
130 fecundity] Q2 Q3; facundity Q
173 This . . . of] This certainly the Lady Hurry told me of. all eds.; *Hurry* Q2 Q3
226 age, yet] age. That all eds.
269 Well] *Will* all eds.
318 *Constantia*] Constance all eds.

Act III. Scene 2.

22 I'le] Q3; I'l Q Q2
36 than] then all eds.
42-43 obliging . . . shou'd] obliging, when I am with her I shou'd Q; obliging when I am with her, shou'd Q2 Q3
176 one] Q3; our Q Q2
190 *Bellamore.*] omit. Q / *Manley*] *Manly* all eds.
192 *Bellamore.*] Manley, all eds.
216 carrest] Q2 Q3; carest Q
301 Q adds [*Call* Bellmore *Footman* (a prompter's notation)

Act IV. Scene 1.

96 my body] Q2 Q3; by body Q
110 run] Q2 Q3; runs Q
141 man . . . you] Q2 Q3; man from him, you Q

Act IV. Scene 2.

130 Manley] *him* all eds.

146 D'ee not] Q2 Q3; Dee yee not Q
183 gifts] Q2 Q3; guifts Q
244 Has] Q2 Q3; Ha's Q
260 there . . . he] there, unknown; To be he Q there, unknown To be, he Q2 Q3
285 blue] Q2 Q3; blew Q
308 than] Q2 Q3; then Q
349 is] Q2 Q3; as Q
355 it. Visit] Q2 Q3; to visit Q
378 I am] Q2 Q3; Im Q
379 far] Q2 Q3; farr Q

Act V. Scene 1.

31 *Bandog*] Q2 Q3; *Bimdog* Q
35 alas / cannot] Q2 Q3; alass / canno Q
69 we'll] Q2 Q3; Wee'l Q
101 Q repeats speech tag *Tob.* before Nay

Act V. Scene 2.

58 him a wreath] Q2 Q3; him wreath Q
91 *slain*] conjectural emendation; space blank in all eds.
111 I'gad] Q3; 'igad Q Q2

Act V. Scene 3.

85 *Cleio's*] Q2 Q3; *Chio's* Q
178 how now, Neece] Q2 Q3; how, Neece Q
236 am] Q2 Q3; 'em Q
236 we'll] Q2 Q3; wee'll Q
254 fiddle] Q2 Q3; fidle Q
259 disasters] Q2 Q3; distasters Q

Collation of Texts

Epistle Dedicatory.

6 Majesties] Majeisties Q2
14 *piece*] *peice* Q2
24 *clemency*] *clememcy* Q3
24-25 *extremely*] *extreamly* Q2 Q3
44 *though*] *tho'* Q3
48 *bosome*] *bosme* Q2; *bosom* Q3
52 *quarelling*] *quarrelling* Q2 Q3
58 *blessing*] *blessings* Q2 Q3

Dramatis Personae.

19 Mrs. *Gibbs*] Mr. *Gibbs* Q2 Q3

Textual Notes

Prologue.
- 3   *t'imbellish*] *t'imbelish* Q2 Q3
- 26 *playes*] *plays* Q3 / *th'*] *the* Q2 Q3
- 30 *off then*] *off, then* Q2 Q3
- 34 *you*] *your* Q3
- 35 *playes*] *plays* Q3

Act I. Scene 1.
- 6   *Sirrah*] variously *Sirra* throughout all eds.
- 9   *melancholly*] regularly *melancholy* throughout Q2 and Q3
- 14 20] twenty Q3
- 19 money] mony Q2
- 20 lye] lie Q3
- 28 shou'd] should Q2 Q3
- 60 wer't] wert Q3
- 66 *spirits*] *spirts* Q3
- 69 *trouble*] *troubles* Q3
- 97 he'l] he'll Q2 Q3
- 106-7 squeezing] sqeezing Q2; squezing Q3
- 119 ith'] i'th' Q2 Q3
- 123 hear] here Q3
- 125 another-ghess] another-guess Q3
- 130 wellcome] welcome Q2 Q3
- 208 rascall] rascal Q2 Q3
- 209 you'r] you're Q3
- 224 There's] There is Q2 Q3
- 234 they'r] they're Q3
- 246 peale] peal Q3
- 249 Wellcome] Welcome Q2 Q3
- 259 accedental] accidental Q2 Q3
- 277 countrey] country Q2 Q3
- 305 money] mony Q2 Q3
- 310 sence] sense Q2 Q3
- 317 ne'r] ne're Q2 Q3
- 330 frends] friends Q2 Q3
- 331 Manley] variously Manly throughout all eds.
- 335 Footmen] Footman Q2 Q3
- 364 bred] breed Q3
- 375 partredges / jowl] partridges / joul Q2 Q3
- 377 sawce] sauce Q2 Q3
- 379 sawce] sauce Q2 Q3
- 380-81 Christendome] Christendom Q2 Q3
- 386 Therefore] Therfore Q2
- 397 Maior] Major Q2 Q3
- 414 hear] here Q3
- 418 we'l] we'll Q2 Q3
- 419 we'l] we'll Q2 Q3
- 420 *Filloflorido*] *Fillostorido* Q3 *Rounsivell / Rounsivell*] *Rounsivel* Q3

428 puncks] punks Q3
431 *AEgypt*] *Egypt* Q2 Q3 grashopper] grashoper Q3
435 we'll] we'l Q2
440 *Finis . . . Primi.*] omit. Q3

Act II. Scene 1.
41 wearst] wear'st Q2 Q3 clothes] cloaths Q3
42 mene] meen Q3
52 conquerors] conquerours Q3
56 oth] o'th' Q2 Q3
61 *Poltron*] *Paltron* Q3
70 plays] playes Q2
74 bawdy] baudy Q2
85 speak] speaks Q3
94-95 maxime] maxim Q3
113 accomplish'd] acomplish'd Q3
140 ancient] antient Q3
141 Christendome] Christendom Q3
143 steakes] stakes Q3
152 folly] follies Q2 Q3
166 the] omit. Q3
183 mushrumes] mushroms Q3
190-91 He'l / he'l] He'll / he'll Q2 Q3
195 have I] I have Q3
198 What] Why Q3

Act II. Scene 2.
4 parler] parlor Q3
33 and] nad Q2; nay Q3
99 mis] miss Q3
121 vertue] virtue Q3
144 faught] fought Q2 Q3
150 wooes] woes Q2 Q3
156 handkerchief] handkerchife Q3
170 mones] moans Q3
200 be always] be alwayes Q2
232 pitty] pity Q2 Q3
234 pitty] pity Q2 Q3
244 Councellor] Counsellor Q2 Q3
248 countrey] country Q3
251 they'r] they're Q3
253 pitty] pity Q2 Q3

Act III. Scene 1.
3 Dorrel] variously Dorel and Dorell throughout all eds.
50 an] omit. Q2 Q3
62 implement] impliment Q3
92 'Sbodikins] 'Sbodikens Q3

93 order'd] ordered Q3
 132 acquir'd] acquired Q3
 136 ere] e're Q3
 152 *Scanderberg*] *Scanderburg* Q3
 155 *Pompey / Pompey*] *Pomphey / Pomphey* Q3
 174 Udsbores / I'll] Odsbores / I'le Q2 Q3
 186 dastard] distard Q3
 189 bear-bating] bear-beating Q2 Q3
 196 Heav'n] Heaven Q2 Q3
 199 relique] relick Q2 Q3
 204 I'll] I'le Q3
 218 Onely] Only Q3
 230 *Fleetstreet*] *Fleestreet* Q2 Q3
 241 onely] only Q3
 244 entreat] intreat Q2 Q3
 262 I'le] I'l Q3
 266 repertee] repartee Q2 Q3
 267 Ounds] Ouns Q3
 270 not I be now] I not now be Q2 Q3
 271 onely] only Q3
 285 viniger] vineger Q2; vinegar Q3
 286 pacify] pacifie Q2 Q3
 308 then] when Q2
 311 disingage] disengage Q2 Q3
 316 bear] beare Q2

Act III. Scene 2.

   6 sayes] says Q3
   7 sayes] says Q3
  14 aire] air Q2 Q3
  17 seldome] seldom Q2 Q3
  19 knowes] knows Q2 Q3
  22 malitious] malicious Q2 Q3
  32 *mistriss*] *mistress* Q3
  41 mistriss] mistress Q3 / that omit. Q2 Q3
  42 extremely] extreamly Q3
  43 come] came Q3
  49 dores] doors Q2 Q3
  54 ere] e're Q3
  59 gracefull] graceful Q2 Q3
  70 leasure] leisure Q2 Q3
  71 unckle] uncle Q2 Q3
  76 she's] she is Q2 Q3
  86 hear] here Q3
  93 extremest] extreamest Q3
  97 rellish] relish Q2 Q3
 101 Hark'ee] Hark ye Q2 Q3
 104 moneths] months Q3
 106 mistriss] mistress Q3

113 I'll] I'le Q3
   118 onely] only Q3 shou'd] should Q2 Q3
   121 *claimes*] *claims* Q2 Q3
   141 onely] only Q2 Q3
   143 onely] only Q3 an] and Q2 Q3
   159 I'll] I'le Q3
   162 I'll] I'le Q3
   168 Here] rere Q2; There Q3
   170 I'll] I'le Q3
   171 I'll] I'le Q3
   173 perform'd] performed Q2 Q3
   176 arm'd] armed Q2 Q3
   188 imagin'd] imagined Q2 Q3
   198 sence / grand] sense / great Q3
   205 tyranize] tyrannize Q2 Q3
   214 *Jollyman*] *Jolliman* Q2 Q3
   227 So!] O! Q2 Q3
   228 onely] only Q3
   244 orator] orators Q3
   258 Perfidious] Perfideous Q3
   259 crocodills] crocodils Q2 Q3
   261 startle? Yea,] startle? ye Q2; startle ye? Q3
   267 rowle] roll Q2 Q3
   275 compos'd] comps'd Q2 Q3
   277 footman / houres] footmen / hours Q2 Q3
   283 dye] die Q2 Q3
   287 Heav'n] Heaven Q3
   296 *Jollyman*] *Jolliman* Q2 Q3
   299 serenader] serenador Q2 Q3
   304 I'll] I'le Q3
   314 He'll] He'l Q3
   318 *Exit.*] omit. Q2
   323 drencht] drench'd Q2 Q3
   327 entreaties] intreaties Q2 Q3
   338 *joyes*] *joys* Q2 Q3

Act IV. Scene 1.
     2 Jollyman] Jolliman Q3
     8 spilt] split Q2
    10 unparalleld] unparallell'd Q2 Q3
    18 proposition] proportion Q3
    23 despis'd] dispis'd Q2
    28 off] of Q2
    32 Sir—countrey] Sir—country Q2
    33 countrey / countrey] country / country Q2 Q3
    37 than] then Q2
    42 neece] niece Q2 Q3
    50 I'le] I'll Q2
    52 persuade] perswade Q3

Textual Notes

    56 employ'd] imploy'd Q2 Q3
    91 vail] vale Q2 Q3
    93 believ'd] believed Q2 Q3
   111 shrowd] shroud Q2 Q3
   113 knowledge] knowledg Q2
   134 knowledge] knowledg Q2
   145 prepar'd] prepared Q2 Q3
   153 thee] the Q2
   159 mistriss] mistress Q3
   160 unconstant] inconstant Q3
   173 sware] swear Q2 Q3
   177 fretting] freeting Q3 feaver] fever Q2 Q3
   185 than] then Q2 Q3
   197 ocular] occular Q3
   199 joins] joyns Q2 Q3

Act IV. Scene 2.

    14 I'll] I'le Q3
    19 I'll] I'le Q3
    24 *Arthur's*] *Arthur* Q2 Q3
    49 Humm] Hum Q2 Q3
    61 I'll fit] I'le fit Q3
    62 repertee] repartee Q2 Q3
    68 been] bin Q2 Q3
    69 employ'd] imploy'd Q2
    74 dayes] daies Q2; days Q3
    83 I'll] I'le Q3
    86 protest! Methinks] protest methinks Q2 Q3
    88 cloath'd] cloathed Q3
    89 you'r] you're Q2 Q3
   106 bread] breed Q3
   107 fopp] fop Q2 Q3
   110 lustre] lusture Q3 foiles] foils Q2 Q3
   116 catch'd] caught Q2 Q3
   119 number] numberd Q2; nmbred Q3
   120 themes] theams Q3
   138 swear] sweare Q2
   141 there] their Q3
   146 stare] start Q3
   147 know not] know you not Q2 Q3
   157 been] bin Q2 Q3
   160 been] bin Q2 Q3
   167 been] bin Q2 Q3
   180 been] bin Q2 Q3 dreamt] dream'd Q2 Q3
   182 shun'd / presents] shunn'd / presence Q2 Q3
   189 I'll] I'le Q3
   191 ere] 'e're Q3
   196 armes] arms Q3
   209 onely] only Q3

216 dore] door Q2 Q3
217 Was] Were Q2 Q3
225 *Drawes] Draws* Q2 Q3
264-65 unseasonable] unreasonable Q3
266 knowes] knows Q2 Q3
272 dore] door Q2 Q3
275 dullness] dulness Q2 Q3
282 eare] ear Q2 Q3 burnes] burns Q3
285 eates onions] eats onyons Q2 Q3 veines] veins Q2 Q3
291 incredible] credible Q3
304 pollicy's] policy's Q3
305 extreamly] extremely Q2
313 by] omit. Q3
321 Heav'n] Heaven Q2 Q3
324 tryal] trial Q2 Q3
327 ordain'd] ordained Q3
333 *Phosporus] Phosphorus* Q2; *Phosphorous* Q3
353 carry'd] carri'd Q2
363 employ] imploy Q2 Q3
364 dy] die Q3
368 knowledge] knowledg Q2
369 talkes / laughes] talks / laughs Q2 Q3
374 might] may Q3
376 drawes] draws Q2 Q3
378 deceipts] deceits Q2 Q3
380 mistery] mystery Q2
384 storme] storm Q3

Act V. Scene 1.
2 Flaile] variously Flail throughout all eds. *Linkboyes] Linkboys* Q2 Q3
3 *Musicians] Musitians* Q2 Q3
4 boyes / boyes] boys / boys Q2 Q3
5 honor] honour Q2 Q3
6 frollick] frolick Q3
10 the] omit. Q3
13 with't] with ye Q3
14 rascal] rascall Q3
19 yield] yeild Q2
25 I'll] I'le Q3
35 ne'r] ne're Q3
39 cannot whistle] cannot wistle Q3
42 *Assafoetida] Assafetida* Q2; *Assafedita* Q3
43 custome] custom Q2 Q3 wee'll] we'll Q3
45 drowsy] drowzy Q2 Q3
48 Petticoates] Petticotes Q2; Petticoats Q3
59 shall] should Q2 Q3
64 you'r] you're Q2 Q3
77 *the sences] his senses* Q2 Q3
82 *rore] roar* Q3

Textual Notes 273

   87 *Heav'n*] *Heaven* Q2 Q3
   89 *joyes*] *joys* Q2 Q3
   90 *charmes*] *charms* Q3
   91 *lye*] *lies* Q3
   93 *Whil'st*] *Whilst* Q2 Q3
  100 performe] perform Q3
  110-111 mystery] mistery Q3 cloaths] clothes Q2
  114 than] then Q2
  116 unravel'd] unravell'd Q2 Q3
  134 as] or Q3
  143 Heav'ns] Heavens Q2 Q3
  144 shou'd] should Q3
  147 shou'd] should Q3

Act V. Scene 2.

    4 valor] valour Q3
    5 Heav'n] Heaven Q2 Q3
  14 I'm] I am Q2 Q3
  19 Whoo] Who Q3
  42 cou'd] could Q2 Q3
  45 butt] but throughout Q2 and Q3
  46 frolicks] frollicks Q2 Q3
  48 *Burgundy*] *Burgandy* Q3 you'll] you'l Q3
  53 devottees] devotees Q2 Q3
  77 *sprightly*] *spritely* Q2; *sprightley* Q3
  80 *rejoyce*] *rejoice* Q2
  81 *voyce*] *voice* Q2 Q3
  86 *vigor*] *vigour* Q3
  89 *Whil'st*] *Whilst* Q3
  91 *extreme*] *extream* Q3
  104 sayes] says Q3
  114 unmorgag'd] unmortgag'd Q3
  118 countrey] country Q2 Q3
  124 queen] quean Q2 Q3
  127 line omit. Q2 Q3
  132 Howl!] How! Q3
  137 beggars] beggers Q3
  159 *Juniper*] *Jupiter* Q3
  167 *follow, follow*] *fellow, fellow* Q3
  175 than] then Q2 Q3
  181 o'] of Q3
  188 remember'd] remembr'd Q3
  197 Neighbors] Neighbours Q2 Q3
  199 dog'd] dogg'd Q2 Q3
  228 gives] give's Q2 Q3
  233 *peals*] *peels* Q2 Q3
  235 popinjayes] popinjay's Q2 Q3
  274 pray'd] prayed Q3
  301 escap'd] escaped Q2 Q3

303 rifl'd] rifled Q2 Q3
306 reproches] reproaches Q2 Q3

Act V. Scene 3.

5 could] cou'd Q2 Q3
8 should] shall Q2 Q3
9 Heav'n] Heaven Q2 Q3
12 But bring] Bring bring Q3
14 renown'd] renoun'd Q2 Q3
16 neece] niece Q2 Q3
19 alwayes] always Q3
26 *Augustines*] *Augustin's* Q2 Q3
67 interest'd] interess'd Q2 Q3
73 insufferable] unsufferable Q3
75 virtue] vertue Q2 Q3
77-78 virtue] vertue Q3
86 neece] niece Q2 Q3
107 Heav'n] Heaven Q2 Q3
110 unsensible] insensible Q3
113 mein] meen Q2 Q3
114 pity] pitty Q2
116 Mourn'd] Mourned Q2 Q3
119 Heav'n] Heaven Q2 Q3
124 interest'd] interess'd Q3
134 troublesom] troublesome Q3
139 shou'd] should Q2 Q3
141 impudentst] impudent'st Q2 Q3
147 gyant] giant Q2 Q3
151 atoms] attoms Q2 Q3
152 through] throw Q2 Q3
153 bathe] bath Q2 Q3
157 timorous] timerous Q2 Q3
160 my] omit. Q2 Q3
166 Heav'n] Heaven Q3
170 your] a Q3
177 *Pharoah*] *Pharaoh* Q2 Q3
178 Neece] Niece Q2 Q3
189 favor] favour Q3
190 too / to] to / too Q2
193 us'd you thus] us'd thus Q2
208 metamorphiz'd] metamorphos'd Q2 Q3
211 finely well!] finely! well, Q3
212 horns] hornes Q2
214 been cruel / virtue] been very cruel / vertue Q3
226 thoughts now] thoughts are now Q2 Q3
236 *Pharoah*] *Pharaoh* Q3
244 catcht um] catch'd 'em Q2 Q3
246 I'll] I'le Q3
249 frollicks] frolicks Q2 Q3

```
253  I'll] I'le Q3
256  unmarry'd] unmarri'd Q2
260  yee] ye Q2 Q3
262  repugne] repugn Q2 Q3
263  debauchee] debauch Q2 Q3
264  nightrap] night-trap Q3  guilded] gilded Q2 Q3
265  Armes] Arms Q2 Q3
273  gentile] gentle Q2 Q3
277  rellish] relish Q2 Q3  stockado's] stockadoe's Q2 Q3
278  gentile] gentle Q2 Q3
279  terme] term Q2 Q3
287  sayes] says Q2 Q3
288  loose] lose Q2 Q3
290  wayes] ways Q3
```

Epilogue.
```
  5  sayes] says Q3  knowes] knows Q2 Q3
  6  caball] cabal Q2 Q3
```

A FOND HUSBAND; OR, THE PLOTTING SISTERS

A Fond Husband went through five printings: one each in 1677, 1678, 1685, 1711, and 1735. Some previous sources have cited a 1676 printing and a second 1677 edition, but both citations have been proven erroneous. [See the editor's "A D'Urfey Play Dated," *Modern Philology* 64 (May 1967): 322-23.] The transmission of texts is not complicated, and there is little reason for believing that D'Urfey influenced either the printing of the first quarto or emendations in later editions.

The first quarto (Q) was most likely set from D'Urfey's manuscript, there being no evidence to support a conjecture that a playhouse copy was used. Unfortunately, the manuscript is not extant. [The Bodleian Library MS of *The Fond Husband* is not this play. (See Day, "Dates and Performances," p. 3.)] The second quarto (Q2) was set from Q, as it duplicates format almost exactly and perpetuates many of the obvious errors of Q. The third quarto (Q3) is in turn set from Q2, as is obvious in the identical pagination and catchwords, as well as in the perpetuation of a missing line on leaf F3a, the wrong catchword on F4a, and other errors. The fourth quarto

(Q4) shows evidence of reliance on all three previous printings, Acts I, II, and IV closely imitating Q, Act III showing influences from Q3, and Act V evidencing transmission from all three sources. The duodecimo edition of 1735 (D) is a case of simple transmission from Q4 with some changes in punctuation and capitalization.

The copy-text for the present edition is the first quarto, and emendations are made on the basis of Q2, Q3, and Q4. The copy-text has been collated with all other editions and variants have been recorded.

Line numbers have been assigned to the text by scenes. The spelling and use of italics of the copy-text have been preserved, but in the interest of readability punctuation and capitalization have been brought more closely into accordance with modern practice. Where variants in either punctuation or capitalization affect the sense, they have been noted. Where readings from Q2, Q3, or Q4 have been used, the reading of Q is always noted; brackets denote editorial emendations.

All speech tags have been regularized and spelled out, as in the Dramatic Personae, and each tag has been italicized, capitalized, and followed by a period. Stage directions have been uniformly enclosed in parentheses, capitalized, and followed by a period. Asides have been moved to precede the speeches to which they refer. Obvious errors, such as transposition or inversion of a single letter, have been silently corrected.

A FOND HUSBAND

Emendations of Copy-text

Dramatis Personae.
   3 *Emilia*] Q2 Q3 Q4 D; *Emillia* Q

        5 *Peregrine*] Q2 Q3 D; *Perrgrine* Q; *Perrigrine* Q4
        7 *Emilia*] Q2 Q3 D; *Emillia* Q Q4
       20 *Jevon*] *Jevan* Q Q2 Q3
       26 *Emilia*] Q2 Q3 D; *Emillia* Q Q4 Mrs. *Barry*] Mr. *Barrer* Q Q2 Q3
       27 *Marshall*] Q2; *Marshal* Q Q3
       29 Mrs. *Snare*] omit. all eds.
       30 *Emilia*] Q2 Q3 D; *Emillia* Q Q4
       31 *Norris*] *Norrice* Q Q2 Q3

Head Title.
        1 A] The all eds.

Act I. Scene 1.
       71-72 have I feign'd] Q3; have feign'd Q Q2 Q4 D
       343 must I do] must do all eds.
       393 mistress] Mrs. all eds.
       468 *ma*] *your* all eds.

Act II. Scene 2.
       35 thee Q3 Q4 D; the Q Q2
       85 *Tom*] Q2 Q3 D; *Dom* Q Q4
      108 ne'er] D; near Q Q2 Q4; nee'r Q3

Act III. Scene 1.
      104 refractory] Q2 Q3 D; refrectory Q4
      176 sence has taken] Q3 Q4 D; sence taken Q Q2
      474 She] Q2 Q4; Shee Q Q3 D
      498 She] Q2 Q4; Shee Q Q3 D

Act IV. Scene 2.
       47 afraid] Q3 Q4 D; affraid Q Q2

Act IV. Scene 3.
        3 *Spatterdash!*] *Spat!* all eds.

Act IV. Scene 4.
       98 *Rashley.*] Q2 Q3 Q4 D; *Rang.* Q
      151 *Rashley*] Q2 Q3 Q4 D; *Rashly* Q

Act V. Scene 1.
       73 *Petulant*, my dear mouse,] Q3; *Petulant!* my dear mouse Q Q2 Q4 D

Act V. Scene 3.
      119 sure I have] Q2 Q3 Q4 D; sure have Q
      164 see her] Q2 Q3 Q4 D; see here Q

Act V. Scena ultima.
   69 this] Q2 Q3 Q4 D; his Q

Collation of Texts

Epistle Dedicatory.
   3 Majesties] Majesty's D
   5 MAJESTIES] MAJESTY'S D
   13 character] charactar Q4
   14-15 hinderance] hindrance Q3 D
   21 who ever] whoever Q4
   47 prolixity] proxility Q4
   49 stiling] styling Q3 D
   51 GRACES] Grace's D

Dramatis Personae.
   1 *Drammatis*] Dramatis D
   2 *Rashley*] *Rashly* Q4 D
   8-9 superannuated] superanuated Q2
   17 *Sandford*] *Sanford* Q3

Prologue.
   6 *cry it*] *cry, It* Q3
   11 *chattle*] *chattel* Q3 Q4 D
   19 *bare*] *bear* Q4
   23 o'er] o're Q4 D
   29 *priviledges*] *privileges* D
   36 *judge*] *judg* Q2 Q3

Act I. Scene 1.
   8 *Battle-Dor's*] *Battledor's* Q3
   12 *titles*] *title* Q4 D
   18 Elizium] Elyzium Q3
   29 absence] abcence Q4
   35 sences / sence] senses / sense Q3
   39 sometimes] sometime Q3
   40 melancholy] melancholly Q4 D
   41 Melancholy] Melancholly Q4 D
   42-43 melancholy] melancholly Q4 D
   46 melancholy] melancholly Q4 D
   57-58 inconveniences] conveniencies Q3
   59 malicious] malitious Q2
   60 propriety] property Q2 Q3
   62 tho'] though Q4 D
   69 heav'n] heaven Q4 D
   70 carrest] carest Q3; caress'd D

72 mistriss] mistress Q4 D
 73 him all] him of all Q3
 75 wisht] wish't Q4 D
 77 Heav'n] Heaven Q4 D
 79 profest] profess'd Q4 D
 83 dang'rous] dangerous Q4 D
 88 loose] lose Q3
155 unparallell'd] unparrallel'd Q3
158 little ill I] little I Q2 Q3
171 Battle-dor] Battledor Q3 D
208 ne'er] nee'r Q3
215 goes] go D
227 prethee] prithee Q4 D
236 *High-Gate*] *Highgate* Q3
244 pity] pitty Q4
245 ifaith] regularly i'faith throughout Q3
249 insufferable] insufferably Q4
271 oblig'd] obliged Q4
274 *amaz'dly*] *amazedly* Q2 Q3
279 are you] you are Q4 D
328 craggy-brancht] craggy, brancht D
342 join] joyn Q4 D
401 Ifack] regularly I'fack throughout Q3
428 troublesom] troublesome D
442 Miter] Mitre Q4 D
450 Munnonday] Monday D
451 *corne*] *corn* Q2 Q3
460 *weel*] *weell* Q3
463 *light*] *lift* D
466 *light*] *lift* D
468 *light*] *lift* D
473 *light*] *lift* D
476 *eaght*] *aught* D
491 mistriss] mistress Q3 Q4 D
498 melancholy] melancholly Q3 Q4

Act II. Scene 1.
 20 raillery] railery Q3
 35 bestow'd] bestowed Q4 D
 48 flow] fly Q4 D
 66 then] they Q4
 68 she] he Q2 Q3
 73 Divil] Devil Q2 Q3 Q4 D
 74 'm] 'em Q2 Q3 Q4 D
 77 strait] straight Q3

Act II. Scene 2.
 20 strait] streight Q3
 37 afaith] ifaith Q4 D

38　simile] smile Q3
　　41　melancholy] melancholly Q4
　　45　ne'er] n'ere Q2; ne're Q3　tho'] though Q4 D
　　51　then] than Q2 Q3 D
　　52　ne'er] ne're Q3
　　60　ha, ha, ha] ha, ha Q2 Q3
　　65　us? But] us But? Q4
　　74　thee] the Q3
　　79　waspish-cross] waspish cross Q2 Q3 Q4 D
　　82　civilly] civily Q3
　　97　you must] must you Q3
　　98　examining] axamining Q2

Act II. Scene 3.
　　 5　handsom] handsome Q3 D
　　18　prethee] prithee Q3 D
　　19　Colledge] College Q4 D
　　29　lye] ly Q2 Q3
　　47　hoord] hoard Q3 D
　　87　rotten] rotton Q4
　 117　sick, Sir.] sick. Q2 Q3
　 143　hawk] hauk Q4
　 152　chatt'ring] chattering Q3 D
　 158　extreamly] extremely Q2 Q3; extreamely Q4
　 163　ne'er] n'ere Q4
　 179　I'll] I Q3
　 196　*Exeunt*] omit. Q3 Q4 D

Act II. Scene 4.
　　 3　women] woman Q3 Q4 D
　　10　sence] sense Q3 Q4 D
　　13　lowdly] loudly Q4 D
　　19　eccho] ecchoe Q4; echo D
　　33　withal] withall Q3 D
　　64　o'er] o're Q3 Q4
　　68　indure] endure Q4 D
　　69　that I might] that might Q3
　　85　mystery] mistery Q3 Q4
　　92　thee] the Q2
　　98　that] the Q4 D
　　99　fail thee] fail there Q2 Q3

Act III.
　　 6　Sir] omit. Q4 D
　　11　Colledge] College Q4 D
　　16　came] come Q4 D
　　27　don't] do'nt Q3
　　30　uncle] unckle Q3

    38 handsomly] handsomely Q2
    65 address] addresses Q2 Q3
    85 squirril] squirrill Q2
   100 subltle] subtil Q3 Q4 D
   101 ye] you Q3
   121 lik'd] like Q3
   167 dost] do'st Q3 Q4 D
   176 sence] sense Q3 Q4 D
   191 shou'd] should Q3 Q4 D
   205 it] omit. Q2 Q3 Q4 D
   206 breathe] breath Q2 Q3 Q4 D
   209 wou'd] would Q4 D
   214-15 monstrous] monstruous Q2
   216 head] hand D
   216 Prethee] Prithee Q3 Q4 D
   220 civilly] civily Q2
   233 mistriss] mistress Q3 Q4 D
   248 him piece-meal] him in piece-meal Q4 D
   249 though] tho Q4; tho' D
   251 is meaning] is the meaning Q4 D
   252 sence] sense Q2 Q3 Q4 D
   280 collegues] colleagues Q3 Q4
   293 it now] now it Q4 D
   296 contriving] contriuing Q3
   297 once] one Q4
   298 Igad] I'gad Q3 Q4 D
   313 overheard] overhear'd Q3; over-heard D
   325 lockt] lock't Q3 Q4; lock'd D
   335 by] from Q4 D
   336 mistriss] mistress Q3 Q4 D
   340 practisers] practicers Q3
   350 these] this Q4
   352-53 mistriss] mistress Q3 Q4 D
   363 though] tho Q4; tho' D
   370 commendations] comendations Q2
   383 knew] new Q4 D
   384 errour] error Q3 Q4 D
   395 lets] let's Q2 Q3 Q4 D
   397 cann't] can't Q4 D
   407 and nay] nay Q3 Q4 D
   408 Dog-Phanatick] Dog-Fanatick Q3 Q4 D
   419 sensibly] sensible Q4
   447 its] his Q4
   449-50 entreaties] intreaties Q4 D
   455 laught] laugh Q3 Q4 D
   460 she's] she is Q4 D
   465 *shreik*] *shriek* Q2 Q3 Q4 D
   476 sences] senses Q3 Q4 D
   482 ere] e're Q3 Q4 D

495 *Shreiking*] *Shrieking* Q3 Q4 D
497 curls] curles Q4
513 ever I] I ever Q4 D
517 prethee] prithee Q3 Q4 D
521 Prethee] Prithee Q3 Q4 D
539 Hah] Ha Q3 Q4 D
549 Catcht] Catch'd Q3 D
550 Oh] O Q3
551 lewd] lewed Q4 D
558 sayst] say'st Q4 D
561 conjoined] conjoyned Q2 Q3
572 *Exit* Bubble] omit. Q4 D
583 slights] slight Q3
584 sences] senses Q3 Q4 D

Act IV. Scene 1.

12 cattel] cattle Q2 Q3 Q4 D
13 mistrisses] mistresses Q3 Q4 D
14 world] word Q4
15 mouth] month Q4
16 sence] sense Q3 Q4 D
20 Uncle] Unckle Q3
41 women] woman Q4 D
43 women] woman Q4 D
44 *Sara*] *Sarah* Q2 Q3
62 mistriss] mistress Q2 Q3 Q4 D

Act IV. Scene 2.

26 loose] lose Q4 D
34 searcht] search Q3; search'd D
40 needed] need Q4 D; troubled] troubl'd Q4
48 cuckolded] cuckoled Q4
50 drowsie] drousie Q4 D
53 shall hear] shall not hear Q4 D
59 *nymph*] *nimph* Q4
61 o'er] o're Q3
65 *virtue*] *vertue* Q4 D
68 *mistress*] *mistris* Q3; *mistress* Q4
94 tho'] though Q4 D
130 hansomly] handsomly Q2 Q3 Q4 D
145 ere] e're Q4 D
157 courtesie] courtisie Q2
168 closset] closet Q3 Q4 D; joins] joyns Q2 Q3

Act IV. Scene 3.

24 bayly] baily Q3; bailiff D
33 ifack] i'fac Q3
65 'tis a matter] 'tis matter Q4 D

81 paterns] patterns Q3 Q4 D
 85 ere] e're Q3; e'er Q4 D
 111 shou'd] should Q4 D
 118-19 occasion . . . come,—] line omit. Q2 Q3

Act IV. Scene 4.

 3 self here at] self at Q4 D
 25 't] it Q2 Q3
 35 thrust] trust Q4
 72 line omit. Q4 D
 92 closset] closet Q2 Q3 Q4 D
 102 *closset] closet* Q3 Q4 D
 114 *closset] closet* Q2 Q3 Q4 D
 121 *Takes] Take* Q4
 181 suspitions] suspicions Q3 D
 190 lye] lie Q3
 192 talkt] talk't Q3; talk'd D
 197 closset] closet Q3 Q4 D
 201 lye] lie Q3
 202 Oh] O Q4 D
 211 would] wou'd Q4 D
 224 could] cou'd Q4 D
 244 closset] closet Q2 Q3 Q4 D
 247 collegue] colleague Q3
 257 lye] lie Q3
 260 naughty] naugty Q4
 262 Ifads] I'fads Q3
 272 worse / farewel] worst / farewell Q2 Q3
 277 Igad] I'gad Q3
 291 they] the Q4

Act V. Scene 1.

 18-19 cuckold] cockold Q4
 27 any false stones] any stones Q4 D
 32 impertinences] impertinencies Q4 D
 39 colour] color Q3
 42 thou'rt] thou art Q3
 68 Prethee] Prithee D
 69 practise] practice Q2 Q3
 92 farewel] farewell Q3
 109 melancholy] melancholly Q3
 121-22 melancholy] melancholly Q3
 139 buz'd] buzz'd Q3
 141 counsel] councel Q2

Act V. Scene 2.

 18 mistriss] mistress Q2 Q3 Q4 D
 24 mathematical] mathematical Q3

Textual Notes

   27 Farewel] Farewell Q2 Q3
   47 loath] loth Q3

Act V. Scene 3.
   13 Igad] I'gad Q3 Q4 D
   20 Dam] Damn D
   23 physitian] physician Q3 D
   25 slie Phanatick] Fanatick Q3
   27 sences] senses Q3 D
   56 o'er] o're Q3
   58 too] to Q3 D
   86 hansom] handsom Q3 Q4 D
   99 shou'd 'scape] should escape Q4 D
   145 mistriss] mistress Q2 Q3 Q4 D
   152 dalli'd] dallied Q4 D
   169 bob] bod Q4 D
   171 bob] bod Q4 D

Act V. Scene 4.
   40 cou'd] could Q4 D
   47 mistrisses] mistresses Q2 Q3 Q4 D
   49 fetcht] fech't Q3; fetch't Q4; fetch'd D
   52 through] thro' Q4 D
   60 ye] you Q4 D
   62 y'are] ye'are Q3; ye're Q4 D
   64 busie] busy Q4 D
   68 Bood] Bud Q3 Q4 D
   70 poinard] poniard Q3 Q4 D
   81 what] that Q4 D
   91 extreamly] extremely Q3
   93 200 *l*.] 2000 *l*. Q4 D
   103 beldame] beldam Q2 Q3 Q4 D
   109 ifack] i'fac Q3
   129 sweet-meets] sweet-meats Q2 Q3; sweetmeats Q4 D
   143 *Courtly*] *Courtley* Q3 Q4 D
   151 I have us'd] I us'd Q4 D
   152 we are] we're Q4 D
   168 repel] repell Q3

Act V. Scena ultima.
   12 ere] e're Q3 Q4 D
   82 o'erthrown] o'rethrown Q3; o'rthrown Q4
   93 *mistriss*] *mistress* Q3 Q4 D

Epilogue.
   7 *I (was) clapt*] *I was clapt* Q3 Q4 D

APPENDIX A

BIBLIOGRAPHICAL DESCRIPTION OF TEXTS

Following is a description of each of the three editions of *Madam Fickle* and the five editions of *A Fond Husband,* which served as the basis of the present texts. Facsimile transcription is employed in the recording of the title, imprimatur, and imprint only; the use of italics in the recording of the Contents indicates direct quotation. No attempt has been made to record swash italics, small capitals, or unusual type faces.

MADAM FICKLE, by Thomas D'Urfey, 1677.
MADAM FICKLE: / OR THE / Witty False One. / A / COMEDY. / As it is Acted at his Royal Highness the / DUKE's THEATRE. / [rule] / Written by *Tho: Durfey* Gent. / [rule] / HORAT. / *Non cuivis homini contingit adire Corinthum.* / [rule] / [to the left] Licensed *November* 20. 1676. / [to the right] *ROGER L'ESTRANGE.* / [rule] / LONDON, / Printed by *T.N.* for *James Magnes* and *Rich. Bentley* / in *Russel-street* in *Covent-garden* near the *Piazza's.* / [short rule] / M.DC.LXXVII.
   HT] MADAM FICKLE, / OR THE / Witty False One. / [rule] / ACT. I. / Scene I. / [rule] / text
   RT] *MADAM FICKLE*; Or, / *The Witty False One.* [Or. B4ᵦ C4 ᵦ D2 ᵦ; *FICKLE: Or E1 ᵦ E3 ᵦ F1 ᵦ F3 ᵦ G1 ᵦ G3 ᵦ H1 ᵦ H3 ᵦ I1 ᵦ I3 ᵦ K1 ᵦ*]

Coll; 4°: A–K⁴ (–D3, D4, J, K3, K4) [$1+2 (–A1, D2, K2) signed], 36 leaves, pp. [*8*] 1 – 66 (omitting 21 – 24, misnumbering 6 as 9, 14 as 12, 15 as 13) [*67–68*].

Contents: A1ₐ: title page (verso blank). A2ₐ: epistle dedicatory: [heavy rule] / [light rule] / *TO HIS GRACE / THE / Duke of Ormond, / Lord High Steward of His Majesties / Houshold, Knight of the Noble Order of / the Garter, and one of His Majesties most / Honourable Privy Council.* A4ₐ: *DRAMATIS PERSONAE.* A4ᵦ: *Prologue by Mr. Smith.* B1ₐ: HT and text. C1ᵦ: *ACT. II.* E1ₐ: *ACT. III.* F3ᵦ: *ACT. IV.* H1ᵦ: *ACT. V.* K2ₐ: *Epilogue.* (verso blank).

CW] A2ₐ *cherish'd* B2ᵦ *Tob,* [*Tob.*] C4ₐ *Bella.* D2ₐ Far E2ᵦ *St Jerom,* [St. *Jerom*;] F1ᵦ *Fick.* [*Fic.*] G4ₐ *Bell.* H4ₐ *The* I2ᵦ *Arbella.* [*Arb.*] K1ₐ that

Notes: This is Wing *STC* entry D2743. It includes the following errors: omission of the speech tag *Zechiel* at the fifth speech on B4ₐ; misassignment of the eleventh speech on B4ₐ from *Zechiel* to *Flaile;* inclusion of two prompter's warning cues at the tenth line of E1ᵦ and the fifth line of F3ₐ; misassignment of the final speech on F1ᵦ from *Bellamore* to *Manley*; and repetition of *Toby's* speech tag before "Nay," in the second from the last speech on H2ᵦ. A word is omitted in the *Bacchus* song, fourth line of H4ᵦ, and the omission is perpetuated in Q2 and Q3.

MADAM FICKLE, by Thomas D'Urfey, 1682.
MADAM FICKLE: / OR, THE / Witty False One. / A / COMEDY. / As it is Acted at His Royal Highness the / DUKE's THEATRE. / [rule] / Written by *Tho. Durfey* Gent. / [rule] / HORAT. / *Non cuivis homini contingit adire Corinthum.* / [rule] / [to the left] Licensed *November* 20. 1676. / [to the right] *ROGER L'ESTRANGE.* / [rule] / LONDON, / Printed for *R. Bentley,* in *Russel-street* in / *Covent-Garden,* near the *Piazza.* / [short rule] / M.DC. LXXXII.

HT] MADAM FICKLE, / OR, THE / Witty False One. / [rule] / ACT. I. / Scene I. / [rule] / text

RT] *MADAM FICKLE*; Or, / *The Witty False One.* [*FICKLE*,; Or F3ᵦ]

Coll: 4°: A–I⁴ (–I3, I4) [$1+2 (–A1, I2) signed], 34 leaves, pp. [*8*] 1–59 (misnumbering 32 as 30, 39 as 31) [*60*].

Contents: A1ₐ: title page (verso blank). A2ₐ: epistle dedicat-

Appendix A 289

ory: *TO HIS GRACE / THE / Duke of Ormond, / Lord High Steward of His Majesties / Houshold, Knight of the Nobel Or- / der of the Garter, and one of His / Majeisties most Honourable Privy / Council.* A4a: *DRAMATIS PERSONAE.* A4b: *Prologue, by Mr. Smith.* B1a: HT and text. C1b: *ACT. II.* D2b: *ACT III.* F1a: *ACT. IV.* G3a: *ACT. V.* I2b: *Epilogue.*
CW] A2a *the* B4a *Zech.* C4a *BLEEA.* [*Bella.*] D4a *St.* [*St*] D4b warrant. [warrant] E3a [none] E4a of [an] F4a *L. Fick.* G4a Thou H3a [none] I2a Epilogue.
Notes: This is Wing *STC* entry D2744. The *Dramatis Personae* gives Mr. *Gibbs* for Mrs. *Gibbs* (A4a). The last speech on E3a repeats Q's mistaken assignment of *Bellamore's* speech to *Manley*; the missing word in the *Bacchus* song occurs at the eighth line of H1b; and Flaile's entrance is omitted before the second from the last speech on H1b.

MADAM FICKLE, by Thomas D'Urfey, 1691.
MADAM FICKLE: / OR, THE / Witty False One. / A / COMEDY. / As it is Acted at His Royal Highness the / DUKE's THEATRE. / [rule] / Written by *Tho. Durfey,* Gent. / [rule] / HORAT. / *Non cuivis homini contingit adire Corinthum.* / [rule] / [to the left] Licensed *November 20. 1676.* / [to the right] *ROGER L'ESTRANGE.* / [rule] / *LONDON,* / Printed for *R. Bentley,* in *Russel-Street* in *Covent- / Garden,* near the *Piazza.* M.DC.XCI.
HT] MADAM FICKLE; / OR, THE / Witty False One. / [rule] / ACT I. SCENE I. / [rule] / text
RT] *MADAM FICKLE*; Or, / *The Witty False One.*
Coll: 4°: A–H⁴ [$1+2 (–A1) signed], 32 leaves, pp. [6] 1–55 [56–58].
Contents: A1a: title page (verso blank). A2a: epistle dedicatory: [double rule] / *TO HIS GRACE / THE / Duke of Ormond, / Lord High Steward of His Majesties / Houshold, Knight of the Noble Or- / der of the Garter, and one of His / Majesties most Honourable Privy / Council.* A3a: *DRAMATIS PERSONAE.* A3b: *Prologue, by Mr. Smith.* A4a: HT and text. B4a: *ACT II.* D1a: *ACT III. SCENE I.* E3a: *ACT. IV. SCENE I.* F4b: *ACT V. Scene. The Street.* H3b: *Epilogue.* H4a: *A Catalogue of some Plays Printed for / R. Bently.* H4b: *A Catalogue of Plays.*
CW] A4a *Harr.* B3a *Bella* [*Bella.*] C4a Quintessence D2b *Zech.*

290   *Two Comedies by Thomas D'Urfey*

[*Zech*,] E4b 'cause, F2a *L.Fick*. [*L. Eick*.] G4a that H4a 58.*Mythridates*

Notes: This is Wing *STC* entry D2745. The *Dramatis Personae* repeats Q2's reading of *Mr. Gibbs* on A3a; *Finis Actus Primi* is omitted from B4a; E1b perpetuates the mistaken assignment of the sixth speech to *Manley; Flaile's* entrance is omitted from before the tenth speech on G3a; and the missing word in the *Bacchus* song occurs in the eighth line from the bottom of G2b.

A FOND HUSBAND, by Thomas D'Urfey, 1677.
A / Fond Husband: / OR, / The Plotting Sisters. / A / COMEDY: / As it is Acted at His *Royal Highness* / THE / DUKE's Theatre. / [rule] / *Haec, dum incipias, gravia sunt, dumque ignores, ubi cognôris, facilia,* Terent. / [rule] / Written by THO. DURFEY Gent. / [rule] / [to the left] Licensed *June* 15. 1676. / [to the right] *ROGER L'ESTRANGE*. / [rule] / LONDON: / Printed by *T.N.* for *James Magnes* and *Rich. Bentley,* in *Russel- / street* in *Covent-Garden,* near the Piazza's. 1677.

HT] THE / FOND-HUSBAND: / OR, / The *PLOTTING SISTERS*. / [rule] / ACT I. Scene I. / [rule] / Text

RT] *The FOND-HUSBAND:* or, / *The PLOTTING SISTERS*.

Coll: 4°: A−I⁴ [$1+2 (−A1) signed], 36 leaves, pp. [*8*] 1−61 [*62-64*].

Contents: A1a: title page (verso blank). A2a: epistle dedicatory: *To His GRACE, The / Duke of Ormond, / Lord Steward of His Majesties Houshold, / Knight of the Noble Order of the Garter, / One of His MAJESTIES most Honourable / Privy Council, &c.* A3b: *Drammatis Personae.* A4a: advertisements: [rule] / *Some Books Printed for James Magnes / and Richard Bentley.* A4b: *Prologue.* B1a: HT and text. C2b: *The Second ACT.* D3b: *The Third ACT.* F1a: *The Fourth ACT.* G4b: *The Fifth ACT.* I3b: *EPILOGUE spoken by FUMBLE.* I4a-b: blank.

CW] A4b THE B4b *Sneak.* C4b *Sir Rog.* D4b *Bubb.* E4b *Sir Rog.* F4b *Spat.* G4b SONG. H2b wou'd [would] I3a EPILOGUE

Notes: Dramatis Personae (A3b) contains several errors: *Emillia* for *Emilia; Jevan* for *Jevon,* the actor; *Mr. Barrer* for *Mrs.*

Appendix A 291

Barry, the actress; *Mrs. Snare* omitted entirely. G2b erroneously assigns *Rashley*'s first speech to *Ranger*. HT and RT throughout read *The Fond*, not *A Fond*. This text was previously thought to be the second edition of the play, occasioning an erroneous entry in the Wing *STC*. This text is Wing entry D2724, and entry D2725 does not exist. See the editor's "D'Urfey Play Dated," *Modern Philology* 64 (May 1967): 322-23.

A FOND HUSBAND, by Thomas D'Urfey, 1678.
A / Fond Husband: / OR, / *The Plotting Sisters*. / A / COMEDY: / As it is Acted at His *Royal Highness* / THE / DUKE's Theatre. / [rule] / *Haec, dum incipias, gravia sunt, dumque ignores, ubi cognoris, facilia,* Terent. / [rule] / Written by *THO. DURFEY* Gent. / [to the left] Licensed *June* 15. 1676. / [to the right] *ROGER L'ESTRANGE*. / [rule] / *LONDON*: / Printed by *R.E.* for *James Magnes* and *Rich. Bentley*, in *Russel- / street* in *Covent-Garden*, near the Piazza's. 1678.

HT] THE / FOND-HUSBAND: / OR, / The *PLOTTING SISTERS*. / [rule] / ACT I. SCENE I. / [rule] / text

RT] *The FOND-HUSBAND:* or, / *The PLOTTING SISTERS*.
*) *Variant:HUSBDAN*: D2b [See notes.]

Coll: 4°: A–H^4 [$1+2 (−A1) signed], 32 leaves, pp. [6] 1-57 (misnumbering 2 as 8) [*58*].

Contents: A1a: title page (verso blank). A2a: epistle dedicatory: To His *GRACE, The / Duke of Ormond, / Lord Steward of His Majesties Houshold, / Knight of the Noble Order of the Garter, / One of His MAJESTIES most Honourable / Privy Council, &c.* A3a: *Drammatis Personae*. A3b: *Prologue*. A4a: HT and text. C1a: *The Second ACT*. D2a: *The Third ACT*. E3b: *The Fourth ACT*. G2a: *The Fifth ACT*. H4b: *EPILOGUE spoken by FUMBLE*.

CW] A2b [none] A4b *Rashley,* [*Rashley*.] B4b The C3b [im-]pudent, [pudent] C4b Scene [SCENE] D1b THE [The] D4b *Emil*. E4b *Tom* F2a cl enemy [*) *Variant*: clemeny] [clemency;] F4a *Rang*. [*Rash*.] G4b *Emil*. H1b Scene [SCENE] H2b *Bub*. [*Bubb*.]

Notes: This edition, Wing *STC* entry D2726, exists in varying states, evidently the result of press corrections. An entire line is missing from F3ₐ (See Textual Notes, IV, iii. 118-119.).

A FOND HUSBAND, by Thomas D'Urfey, 1685.
A / Fond Husband: / OR, / *The Plotting Sisters,* / A / COMEDY: / As it is Acted at his *Royal Highness* / THE / DUKE's Theatre. / [rule] / *Haec, dum incipias, gravia sunt, dumque ignores, ubi cognoris, facilia,* Terent. / [rule] / Written by *THO. DURFEY* Gent. / [rule] / [to the left] Licensed *June* 15. 1676. / [to the right]*ROGER L'ESTRANGE.* / [rule] / *LONDON.* / Printed by *R.E.* for *Rich. Bentley,* and *S. Magnes,* in *Russel-* / street in *Covent-Garden,* near the Piazza's. 1685.

HT] THE / FOND-HUSBAND: / OR / The *PLOTTING SISTERS* / [rule] / ACT I. SCENE I. / [rule] / text.

RT] *The FOND-HUSBAND:* or, / *The PLOTTING SISTERS.* [HUBAND: A4ᵦ]

Coll: 4°: A-H⁴ [$1 + 2 (— A1) signed], 32 leaves, pp. [6] 1-57 (misnumbering 2 as 8, 51 as 59) [58].

Contents: A1ₐ: title page (verso blank). A2ₐ: epistle dedicatory: *To His GRACE, The / Duke of Ormond, / Lord Steward of His Majesties Houshold, / Knight of the Noble Order of the Garter, One of / His MAJESTIES most Honourable Privy / Council, &c.* A3ₐ: *Drammatis Personae.* A3ᵦ: *Prologue.* A4ₐ: HT and text. C1ₐ: *The Second ACT.* D2ₐ: *The Third ACT.* E3ᵦ: *The Fourth ACT.* G2ₐ: *The Fifth ACT.* H4ᵦ: *EPILOGUE spoken by FUMBLE.*

CW] A2ᵦ [none] A4ᵦ *Rashley.* B3ₐ [Hus-]band; [band:] B4ₐ 3. *Fair* [3 *Fair*] C3ᵦ [im-]pudent, [pudent] C4ᵦ Scene [SCENE] D1ᵦ THE [The] D4ᵦ *Emil.* E1ₐ man [a man] E4ᵦ *Tom* F2ₐ clemency [clemency;] F4ₐ *Rang.* [*Rash.*] G1ᵦ Prithee [Prethee] G4ᵦ *Emil.* H1ᵦ Scene H2ᵦ *Bubb.*

Notes: This edition, Wing *STC* entry D2727, is directly transmitted from the 1678 quarto, as is evidenced by the identical catchwords, though the entire work is reset. Lineation within a single forme often varies, and punctuation and capitalization differ widely. The missing line is still absent from F3ₐ. Notable is the use of VV for all W's on A3ₐ.

Appendix A 293

A FOND HUSBAND, by Thomas D'Urfey, 1711

A / Fond Husband: / OR, / *The Plotting Sisters.* / A / COMEDY. / As it is Acted at the / Theatre Royal / In *DRURY-LANE*. / [rule] / *Haec, dum incipas, gravia sunt, dumq; ignores, ubi cognoris, facilia,* Terent. / [rule] / Written by *THO. DURFEY*, Gent. / [rule] / *LONDON*, / Printed for *R. Wellington,* at the *Dolphin* and *Crown* at the West / End of St. *Paul's Church-Yard;* and Sold by *O. Lloyd,* near / the *Temple* Church, and *W. Lewis,* in *Covent-Garden,* near / the Piazza's. 1711. / [rule] / [advertisements]

- HT] THE / FOND-HUSBAND: / OR, / The *PLOTTING SISTERS.* / [rule] / ACT I. SCENE I. / [rule] / text
- RT] *The FOND-HUSBAND:* or, / *The PLOTTING SISTERS.* [*The PLOTTING SISTERS.* E3b F4b G1b; *SISTRS.* F4a G3a H4a]
- *Coll*: 4°: A-H⁴ [$1+2 (−A1) signed], 32 leaves, pp. [6] 1-57 [*58*].
- *Contents:* A1a: title page (verso blank). A2a: epistle dedicatory: *To his GRACE, / The Duke of ORMOND, / Lord Steward of His Majesties Houshold, / Knight of the Noble Order of the Garter. / One of His MAJESTIES Most Honourable / Privy Council, &c.* A3a: Drammatis Personae. A3b: PRO- LOGUE. A4a: HT and text. C1b: *The Second ACT.* D2b: *The Third ACT.* E4a: *The Fourth ACT.* G2b: *The Fifth ACT.* H4b: *EPILOGUE spoken by FUMBLE.*
- CW] A3a PRO- [PROLOGUE.] B2a *Bubb. A* [*Bub.* A] B2b *Bubb.* [*Bub.*] C3b *Sir Rog.* [*Sir. Rog.*] D4b [Uu-]derstanding E3a [*En.* [*Enter*] E3b [none] F2b thing [thing;] G1b com- [combine] G3a *En-* [*Enter*] H2b *Sir*
- *Notes:* The edition exists in at least two states; the title pages of the British Museum and CLC copies show *DRUYY* for *DRURY*. Principal copy-text was the first quarto (1677) since catchwords are identical through D2b; after that point, some readings evidence the use of the 1685 text as well. The line missing from Q2 and Q3 is restored on F4a. Act V is unique in beginning some speeches in the

middle of the line on which the previous speech ended.

A FOND HUSBAND, by Thomas D'Urfey, 1735.
THE / [in red] Fond Husband: / OR, THE / PLOTTING SIS-TERS. / A / [in red] COMEDY. / As it is ACTED at the / THEATRE-ROYAL / In DRURY-LANE. / [rule] / *Haec, dum incipias gravia sunt, dumq; ignores; ubi* / *cognoris, facilia.* Terent. / [rule] / [in red] Written by *THO. DURFEY*, Gent. / [rule] / [in red] *LONDON*, / Printed for W. FEALES, at *Rowe's Head*, the Corner of / *Essex-Street* in the *Strand*; A. BETTESWORTH, in / *Pater-Noster Row*; F. CLAY, at the *Bible*, R. WEL- / LINGTON, at the *Dolphin* and *Crown*, and C. COR- / BETT, at *Addison's Head*, all without *Temple-Barr*; and / J. BRINDLEY, at the *King's Arms* in *New Bond-Street*. / [short rule] / [in red] MDCCXXXV.
   HT] [rect. device: two cupids flanking a lyre] / THE / Fond Husband: / OR, The / PLOTTING SISTERS. / [rule] / ACT I. SCENE I. / [rule] / text
   RT] *The* FOND HUSBAND: *Or,* / *The* PLOTTING SISTERS. [*The* PLOTTING FOOLS. A9a; *The*: C4a]
   Coll: 12°: A-D¹² E⁶ [$1-6 (-A1, A2, E4, E5, E6) signed], 54 leaves pp. [*11*] 12-107 [*108*].
   Contents: A1a: blank (verso: engraved frontispiece). A2a: title page (verso blank). A3a: epistle dedicatory: [rect. device: foliage with mask in center] / *To his* GRACE / THE / *Duke of* ORMOND, / *Lord Steward of His Majesty's* / *Houshold, Knight of the No-* / *ble Order of the Garter. One* / *of His* MAJESTY'S *Most Ho-* / *nourable Privy Council, &c.* A4b: [rect. device: stylized foliage with two squirrels] / *PROLOGUE*. A5b: *Dramatis Personae*. A6a: HT and text. B2a: [rect. device: stylized foliage and two lions] / *ACT II*. B9b: [rect. device; stylized foliage and gryphon] / *ACT III*. C7a: [rect. device: stylized foliage and three birds] / *ACT IV*. D6a: [rect. device: same as B2a] / *ACT V*. E5b: [rect. device: same as A4b] / *EPILOGUE spoken by* FUMBLE. E6a: last seven lines of epilogue / *FINIS*. / [ornament] (verso blank).
   CW] A4a PRO- [PROLOGUE.] A5a Drama- [Dramatis] B6b *Sneak*. B12b *Bub*. C6b ACT C11a Repu- [Reputation:] D6b hast D10a Cause [Cause.] E5a EPILOGUE
   Notes: The edition is bound with five other plays by different authors. It has little authoritative significance, since it is a

simple transmission from the fourth quarto (1711). All the errors, capitalization, and punctuation of that quarto are perpetuated.

APPENDIX B

CHRONOLOGICAL LISTING OF D'URFEY'S DRAMATIC WORKS

Each entry in the following list includes the name of the theater at which the play first appeared, the date of the first performance, and publication data for the first edition. The abbreviation D.L. indicates the Theatre Royal in Drury Lane, D.G. is the Duke's Theatre in Dorset Garden, L.I.F. is the theater in Lincoln's Inn Fields, and H. is the Haymarket Threatre.

The Siege of Memphis; Or, The Ambitious Queen. Tragedy. (D.L. *c.* September 1676.) London: W. Cademan, 1676.

Madam Fickle; Or, The Witty False One. Comedy. (D.G. November 4, 1676.) London: J. Magnes and Rich. Bentley, 1677.

The Fool Turned Critick. Comedy. (D.L. November 18, 1676.) London: James Magnes and Richard Bentley, 1678.

A Fond Husband; Or, The Plotting Sisters. Comedy. (D.G. May 31, 1677.) London: James Magnes and Rich. Bentley, 1677.

Trick for Trick; Or, The Debauch'd Hypocrite. Comedy. Adapted from Fletcher. (D.L. *c.* March 1678.) London: Langley Curtiss, 1678.

Squire Oldsapp; Or, The Night-Adventurers. Comedy. (D.G. *c.*

June 1678.) London: James Magnes and Richard Bentley, 1679.

The Virtuous Wife; Or, Good Luck at Last. Comedy. (D.G. *c.* September 1679.) London: R. Bentley and M. Magnes, 1680.

Sir Barnaby Whigg; Or, No Wit Like a Woman's. Comedy. (D.L. *c.* September 1681.) London: Joseph Hindmarsh, 1681.

The Royalist. Comedy. (D.G. *c.* January 24, 1682.) London: Jos. Hindmarsh, 1682.

The Injured Princess; Or, The Fatal Wager. Tragicomedy. Adapted from Shakespeare. (D.L. *c.* March 1682.) London: R. Bentley and M. Magnes, 1682.

A Commonwealth of Women. Comedy. Adapted from Fletcher. (D.L. *c.* August 1685.) London: R. Bentley and J. Hindmarsh, 1686.

The Banditti; Or, A Ladies Distress. Comedy. (D.L. *c.* February 1686.) London: R. Bentley, 1686.

A Fool's Preferment; Or, The Three Dukes of Dunstable. Comedy. Adapted from Fletcher. (D.G. *c.* April 1688.) London: Jos. Knight and Fra. Saunders, 1688.

Love for Money; Or, The Boarding School. Comedy. (D.L. *c.* January 1691.) London: Abel Roper, 1691.

Bussy D'Ambois; Or, The Husbands Revenge. Tragedy. Adapted from Chapman. (D.L. *c.* March 1691.) London: R. Bentley and Jo. Hindmarsh, 1691.

The Marriage-Hater Matched. Comedy. (D.L. *c.* January 1692.) London: Richard Parker and Sam. Briscoe, 1692.

The Richmond Heiress; Or, A Woman Once in the Right. Comedy. (D.L. *c.* April 1693.) London: Samuel Briscoe, 1693.

The Comical History of Don Quixote. Comedy. Adapted from Cervantes. First Part. (D.G. May 1694.) London: Samuel Briscoe, 1694.

The Comical History of Don Quixote. Second Part. (D.G. *c.* May or June 1694.) London: S. Briscoe and H. Newman, 1694.

The Comical History of Don Quixote. Third Part. (D. G. *c.* November 1695.) London: Samuel Briscoe, 1696.

A Wife for Any Man. Comedy. (1695-96?) Lost.

A New Opera, Called Cinthia and Endimion. Opera. (D.L. *c.* December 1696.) London: Samuel Briscoe and R. Wellington, 1697.

The Intrigues at Versailles; Or, A Jilt in All Humours. Comedy.

(L.I.F. *c.* May 1697.) London: F. Saunders *et al.*, 1697.

The Campaigners; Or, The Pleasant Adventures at Brussels. Comedy. (D.L. *c.* June 1698.) London: A. Baldwin, 1698.

The Famous History of the Rise and Fall of Massaniello. Tragedy. First Part. (D.L. *c.* May 1699.) London: John Nutt, 1700.

The Famous History and Fall of Massainello [sic]; *Or, A Fisherman a Prince.* Second Part. (D.L. *c.* May 1699.) London: John Nutt, 1699.

The Bath; Or, The Western Lass. Comedy. (D.L. May 31, 1701.) London: Peter Buck, 1701.

The Old Mode and the New; Or, Country Miss With Her Furbeloe. Comedy. (D.L. March 11, 1703.) London: Bernard Lincott, [1703].

Wonders in the Sun; Or, The Kingdom of the Birds. Opera. (H. April 5, 1706.) London: Jacob Tonson, 1706.

The Modern Prophets; Or, New Wit for a Husband. Comedy. (D.L. May 3, 1709.) London: Bernard Lincott, [1709].

The Two Queens of Brentford; Or, Bayes No Poetaster. Opera. (Unacted.) London: William Chetwood, 1721.*

The Grecian Heroine; Or, The Fate of Tyranny. Tragedy. (Unacted.) London: William Chetwood, 1721.*

Ariadne; Or, The Triumph of Bacchus. Opera. (Unacted.) London: William Chetwood, 1721.*

---

*Published in a volume entitled *New Opera's, with Comical Stories, and Poems, on Several Occasions, Never before Printed*.

BIBLIOGRAPHY

Addison, Joseph. *The Guardian,* no. 67 (May 28, 1713).
Anthony, Sr. Rose. *The Jeremy Collier Stage Controversy: 1698-1726.* New York, 1966.
Arber, Edward, ed. *The Term Catalogues, 1668-1709.* 3 vols. London, 1903.
Baker, David Erskine. *Biographia Dramatica.* 2 vols. London, 1782.
Banister, John. *New Ayres and Dialogues.* London, 1678.
Biswanger, Raymond A. "*The Richmond Heiress*: an edition." Dissertation, University of Pennsylvania, 1951.
Catch That Catch Can. London, 1685.
Choice Ayres and Songs. London, 1679.
Collier, Jeremy. *A Short View of the Immorality and Profaneness of the English Stage.* London, 1698.
Day, Cyrus Lawrence. "Dates and Performances of Thomas D'Urfey's Plays." Charlottesville, Va., 1950. (Mimeographed.)
———. "The Life and Non-dramatic Works of Thomas D'Urfey." Dissertation, Harvard University, 1930. 2 vols.
———. "A Lost Play by D'Urfey." *Modern Language Notes* 49 (May 1934): 332-34.
———. *The Songs of Thomas D'Urfey.* Cambridge, Mass., 1933.
———. and Murrie, Eleanore Boswell. *English Song Books: 1651-1702.* London, 1940.
Dickens, Charles. "Tom D'Urfey." *Household Words* 11 (March 24, 1855): 186-88.

D'Urfey, Thomas. *A New Collection of Songs and Poems.* London, 1683.
———. *New Opera's, with Comical Stories, and Poems, on Several Occasions.* London, 1721.
———. Preface to *The Campaigners.* Facsimile reprint. Augustan Reprint Society (Los Angeles), no. 12 (1948).
———. *Wit and Mirth; Or, Pills to Purge Melancholy.* London, 1719-20. 6 vols.
———. *Wonders in the Sun.* Facsimile reprint. Augustan Reprint Society (Los Angeles), no. 104 (1964).
Forsythe, Robert Stanley. *A Study of the Plays of Thomas D'Urfey.* Vol. 1, no. 2 of *Western Reserve Studies.* Cleveland, Ohio, 1916.
Genest, The Reverend John. *Some Account of the English Stage.* 10 vols. Bath, 1832.
Graham, C. B. "The Jonsonian Tradition in the Comedies of Thomas D'Urfey." *Modern Language Quarterly* 8 (1947): 47-52.
Jordan, Thomas. *The Walks of Islington and Hogsdon.* London, 1657.
Langbaine, Gerard. *An Account of the English Dramatick Poets.* Oxford, 1691.
Lynch, Kathleen M. "Thomas D'Urfey's Contribution to Sentimental Comedy." *Philological Quarterly* 9 (1930): 249-59.
Marmion, Shackerly. *The Antiquary.* London, 1641.
Marston, John. *Parasitaster; Or, The Fawne.* London, 1606.
A New Theatrical Dictionary. London, 1792.
Nicoll, Allardyce. *A History of the English Drama.* 6 vols. Cambridge, 1952.
Rowley, William. *A Match at Midnight.* London, 1633.
Sanville, Donald W. "Thomas D'Urfey's *Love for Money:* an edition." Dissertation, University of Pennsylvania, 1950.
Sears, Minnie Earl, ed. *Song Index.* New York, 1926.
Sherburn, George, ed. *The Correspondence of Alexander Pope.* 2 vols. Oxford, 1956.
Steele, Sir Richard. *The Guardian,* no. 82 (June 15, 1713).
———. *The Tatler,* no. 1 (April 12, 1709).
———. *The Tatler,* no. 11 (May 5, 1709).
Summers, Montague, ed. *Roscius Anglicanus.* London, 1928.
———. "Thomas D'Urfey." *Bookman* 63 (1923): 272-74.

Vaughn, Jack A. "A D'Urfey Play Dated." *Modern Philology* 64 (May 1967): 322-23.

———. "'Persevering, Unexhausted Bard': Tom D'Urfey." *Quarterly Journal of Speech* 53 (December 1967): 342-48.

Ward, Adolphus William, ed. *The Poetical Works of Alexander Pope*. London, 1924.

Wit for Money; Or, Poet Stutter. London, 1691.